EUROPE'S HIGH POINTS

About the Authors

Carl McKeating has a lifetime's habit of hopping from one 'stupid hearthside idea' to another: climbing Europe's high points has been his most recent and enduring obsession. A self-professed career-phobic, Carl has managed to eke out an existence in occupations as diverse as London bus driving, acting, turkey plucking, milk delivery, teaching and being a clinical trial participant. Managing to sit still for more than five minutes, he received a first class English degree from Lancaster University: his mother deemed this no mean feat for someone who did not learn to read at all until the age of eight. His first loves are tea drinking, climbing, writing, skiing, cycling and playing guitar and football very badly. He has travelled extensively throughout Europe, Asia and North America.

Rachel Crolla (seen here with Carl on the summit of Mont Blanc) was the first woman to reach the highest point in every country in Europe. She has also travelled extensively in Asia, Central and North America. With a background in local newspaper journalism, the opportunity to make a book about her mountaineering experiences was a dream come true. Having lived in Yorkshire most of her life, she began walking in the British countryside, completing challenges such as the Coast-to-Coast walk and Dales Way. She enjoys climbing, cycling and skiing in the Alps, where she has spent an eventful season working in a chalet.

Acknowledgements

Thanks are due to David Crolla, who loaned us mountaineering equipment for our trips. Special thanks also go to Scott Barnett, who accompanied us on the epic drive to Galdhøpiggen and was an entertaining companion on our first visits to Ben Nevis and Scafell Pike. Many other individuals have helped us along the way, including Commander A Koste at Mavrovi Hanovi Police Station, and President Ljubomir and his counterpart Goran (Gilly) of Skopje Climbing Club. Also thanks to Aarvin Strand, who provided much-needed assistance after our car broke down in the Arctic Circle.

EUROPE'S HIGH POINTS

by
Carl McKeating and Rachel Crolla

2 POLICE SQUARE, MILNTHORPE, CUMBRIA LA7 7PY
www.cicerone.co.uk

Photographs by the authors unless otherwise acknowledged (in brackets at the end of photo caption).

A catalogue record for this book is available from the British Library

This book is dedicated to
Marie McKeating (1948–2006)
who was very positive and supportive about our plans to write it.

ADVICE TO READERS

Readers are advised that, while every effort is made by our authors to ensure the accuracy of guidebooks as they go to print, changes can occur during the lifetime of an edition. Please check the Cicerone website (www.cicerone.co.uk) for any updates before planning your trip. It is also advisable to check information on such things as transport, accommodation and shops locally. Even rights of way can be altered over time. We are always grateful for information about any discrepancies between a guidebook and the facts on the ground, sent by email to info@cicerone.co.uk or by post to Cicerone, 2 Police Square, Milnthorpe LA7 7PY.

WARNING

Mountain walking and mountaineering can be a dangerous activity carrying a risk of personal injury or death. It should be undertaken only by those with a full understanding of the risks and with the training and/or experience to evaluate them. While every care and effort has been taken in the preparation of this guide, the user should be aware that conditions can be highly variable and can change quickly, thus materially affecting the seriousness of a mountain walk.

Therefore, except for any liability which cannot be excluded by law, neither Cicerone nor the authors accept any liability for damage of any nature (including damage to property, personal injury or death) arising directly or indirectly from the information in this book.

To call out the Mountain Rescue, phone 999 or the international emergency number 112: this will connect you via any available network. Once connected to the emergency operator, ask for the police.

Front cover: The highest points of (top) Slovakia (Gerlachovsky), (clockwise from centre) The Netherlands (Vaalserberg), Vatican City, Poland (Rysy), Russia (Mount Elbrus) and disputed high point of Montenegro (Bobotov kuk). Back cover: Grauspitz, Liechtenstein.

CONTENTS

Map Key

B9078 road		summit of high point
track or unpaved road		other peak
primary route	2748m	spot height
alternative route	)(	col or pass
other path		water
railway/station		glacier
chair or ski lift		crevasses
cable car		wood or forest
fence		crag or cliff
via ferrata VF		boulderfield
boundary wall		town or city
river		refuge
ridge		other building(s)
sea		campsite
national border		chapel
		radar
	SP	signpost
	P	parking
		bus stop

Map of Europe

ICELAND

N

NORWEGIAN SEA

WHITE SEA

ATLANTIC OCEAN

FINLAND

NORWAY   SWEDEN

BALTIC SEA

ESTONIA

RUSSIA

LATVIA

NORTH SEA

LITHUANIA

NORTHERN IRELAND

DENMARK

IRELAND

BELARUS

UK   THE NETHERLANDS

POLAND

GERMANY

BELGIUM

CZECH REPUBLIC

UKRAINE

LUXEMBOURG

SLOVAKIA

LIECHTENSTEIN

AUSTRIA

HUNGARY

MOLDOVA

SWITZERLAND

BAY OF BISCAY

FRANCE

SLOVENIA

SAN MARINO

CROATIA

ROMANIA

BOSNIA   SERBIA

MONACO

BLACK SEA

BULGARIA

ANDORRA

PORTUGAL

SPAIN

VATICAN CITY

MONTENEGRO

ITALY   KOSOVO

ALBANIA

MACEDONIA

TURKEY

GREECE

MALTA

CYPRUS

MEDITERRANEAN SEA

Major Mountain Ranges

N

ICELAND

NORWEGIAN SEA

WHITE SEA

ATLANTIC OCEAN

SCANDINAVIAN MOUNTAINS

BALTIC SEA

CALEDONIAN CHAIN

NORTH SEA

MASSIF CENTRAL

CARPATHIANS

CAUCASUS

BAY OF BISCAY

A L P S

DINARIC ALPS

BALKANS

BLACK SEA

PYRENEES

APENNINES

SIERRA NEVADA

MEDITERRANEAN SEA

Switzerland's highest mountain Monte Rosa/Dufourspitze (4634m) from Weissmies (4023m)

INTRODUCTION

Rysy (left), Gerlachovsky stit (centre) and Vysoka (right) (Route 34) (Dariusz Bogumil)

A EUROVISION FOR MOUNTAINS

This guide to climbing the high points in every European country serves as a celebration of the wide variety of national identities in Europe – a 'Eurovision for mountains', if you like. The European mainland is on our doorstep and may feel like familiar territory, but there is a wealth of adventure waiting in every one of its countries.

Heading to the highest point of any European country – a high altitude mountain or a comparative molehill – is an experience we wholeheartedly recommend. The sheer variety of Europe's national high points, collected here in a book for the first time, offers a wealth of fantastic experiences. In short, you are holding in your hand the key to a treasure trove of discovery, adventure and fun. Some of Europe's greater mountains and ranges may already be well known and celebrated, but many remain untrampled by international hiking boots. The vast majority of Europe's countries take great national pride in their highest points and most have their own version of a treasure like Ben Nevis, be it gargantuan or diminutive.

Attempting to climb all Europe's high points is a challenge like no other. You can experience the majesty of Mont Blanc and the Alps, confront Zeus on Mount Olympus, and feel quite baffled in the former Yugoslav nations. Lose yourself body and soul deep on Finland

and Sweden's highest mountains while the aurora borealis shimmers across the night sky. Race uphill and plod down dale. Head east, west, north and south, springing from peak to peak like a mountain gazelle. Leap crevasses, dodge marmots, watch eagles soar from beneath your feet. Climb above rolling blankets of white clouds. Shake hands with shepherds and wayward travellers. Share drinks (and even foods you may wish you had never been offered) with Bulgarians, Albanians, Norwegians, Italians and Bosnians as each makes a pilgrimage to their national high point.

Inevitably we have found that a country's highest point tends to be in one of its most beautiful areas. From the splendid 100m waterfalls of Iceland's Skaftafell in the west to Russia's awe-inspiring Caucasus Mountains in the east, and from the arid red rock of Spain's Sierra Nevada in the south to the Arctic tundra of Finland's

Grauspitz from the Schroarzhorn (Route 22) (David Alexander)

The Stefani fore summit on Mount Olympus (Route 16) (Wade Schwartzkopf)

Halti in the north, this book will take walkers and climbers to some of the best scenery in Europe.

There is no governing body or infallible source for the designation of European state high points, and readers may be surprised to discover that disputes (or maybe debates) over national high points exist in many countries including Italy, Denmark and Montenegro. This is not a phenomenon unique to Europe; even the summit of Everest is claimed in its entirety by both China and Nepal. We have aimed to sift out the chaff to give the high-pointer a clearer picture, and disputes are all discussed in the relevant chapters. As well as disputed high points, there are also some common misconceptions about certain peaks. For example, some people mistakenly assume that Mont Blanc is Europe's highest mountain, when in fact that award goes to Russia's Mount Elbrus by a considerable margin.

Motivation

The start of our own quest to climb Europe's highest points can be traced back more than ten years. Just after Christmas in 1996 we drove up to Scotland with three friends to climb Ben Nevis. Five teenagers piled into a Ford Fiesta, badly equipped and utterly naïve as to what lay in store. We drove through the night. In the morning we were fed to the brim at a B&B and eventually followed the icy tourist path to the summit of the Ben. We arrived at the top just as the sun set over the highlands. There was just enough time for us to stand on the highest ground and say, 'Look at me, there is no one higher in Britain right now,' before a storm and impending night engulfed us. It was our first national high point and an adventure to boot. At the heart of that day there was the elation of a personal and spiritual fulfilment.

Climbers talk a lot about the clarity and personal enlightenment brought about by mountaineering and for the outsider it is all too easy to scoff; but such emotions are voiced time and time again, even by the most down-to-earth Yorkshireman. A common theme keeps arising: man and woman's search for an understanding of themselves and their place in the world. It is this philosophical search which inspired the ancient Greeks to make their highest mountain the home of the gods; that caused Babel-like towers to be built on the highest ground in Portugal, Belgium, Denmark, Estonia and Latvia; which triggers Tibetans to utter prayers as soon as Chomolangma (Mount Everest) comes into view.

We all like to have a hobby and a challenge. Climbing the European national high points is, in our view, one step (or maybe two) above stamp collecting.

WHY THIS GUIDE?

Never before have all the national high points of Europe been gathered together in one place. While information and route descriptions for some of the high points exist elsewhere, collating them can be exceedingly time-consuming and troublesome and, even then, knowing which routes to choose might not prove easy. For some national high points there are no route descriptions beyond the pages of this book. Additionally, complicated geographical disputes have arisen over the designation of certain national high points and this book aims to resolve them. We have outlined any such disagreements and explained the reasoning behind our own choices. (Readers may be surprised to find Italy amongst these and perhaps the most complicated. Italy surprisingly has four different claims for its high

point, but at the centre of the dispute is a virtual tug-of-war for the summit of Mont Blanc/Monte Bianco (see the France/Italy chapter).)

The beauty of the European high points in walking and mountaineering terms is that they range from ludicrously easy ascents (Denmark, Estonia, the Netherlands and so on) to ones that will prove challenging to most people (France, Switzerland, Russia). There are also plenty in between. Someone who enjoys a good Lakeland hike will, by acquiring a few mountaineering and climbing skills along the way, be easily capable of working up to ascents of the more demanding national high points. None of the mountains require you to be the next Chris Bonnington or Julie Tullis, but a competent approach to mountaineering will prove invaluable (the foolhardy are rarely rewarded in any mountain range).

Naturally not all of us can take off four months and go racing around Europe to climb all the mountains in one big push. You might not even want to climb them all. Whatever you choose to do, this book is a great resource to call upon. Climbing a national high point is guaranteed to spice up a trip to any European country, and could provide the focus for planning future holidays.

This guide aims to answer the needs of anyone whose primary concern is getting to the top of these national high points. For the most part

View from Yewbarrow Fell of the sublime Scafell Pike (centre) and its sister Scafell (right)

13

'Hoogste Punt van Nederland' (Route 30)

the simplest and most straightforward routes are described – but not always. Speed and ease of ascent routes is balanced against the subjective merits of those routes that might initially appear more time-consuming and even more technical, but ultimately prove more spectacular and pleasurable.

USING THIS GUIDE

This book is divided into 48 chapters covering the high points of 50 European countries. Each chapter contains basic information about the country (or countries) and its (their shared) high point, including how to get there, the difficulty of the route and equipment needed, relevant map and a detailed route description (or descriptions). A sketch map showing the route/s is provided for each high point. Indications are given of the time needed to complete each route, rather than the distance, as the latter is often misleading on mountainous terrain, and distance can be difficult to

gauge accurately for many of the more far-flung routes.

Although the routes are accompanied by sketch maps, whenever possible you should take a detailed topographical map of an area. Again, when possible, details of suitable maps are given. Unfortunately, due to the remote and little-visited nature of some of the places described, it may be extremely difficult to get your hands on a decent map. When this is the case, searches online can occasionally bring up useful maps. Maps for these areas are often outdated and inaccurate and a degree of caution is therefore required. We have tried to make the route descriptions as clear as possible in case you cannot find a decent map to assist your ascent and descent. Some good map suppliers include: Stanfords, tel: 0207 836 1321 www.stanfords.co.uk; Elstead Maps, tel: 01483 898099 www.elstead.co.uk; and The Map Shop, tel: 0800 085 4080 www.themapshop.co.uk.

Difficulty
Each route has been given a difficulty grade on an ascending scale from 1 to 5:
1 Easy tourist amble
2 Standard hike
3 Hike complicated by difficulties in any of the following areas: route-finding, time, altitude, ascent, scrambling
4 Certainly requires the protection of a rope or via ferrata kit. Likely to involve exposure to steep terrain and may involve climbing, crevasses, risk of avalanche or rockfall, very low temperatures and high altitude (in addition to the difficulties of a grade 3 hike).
5 Full alpine kit required. Prolonged exposure to high altitude, steep terrain, narrow ridges, climbing, crevasses, avalanche and risk of rockfall. Likely to involve very low temperatures. If severe weather is encountered retreat may prove extremely difficult.

These ratings are based on our own experiences on the mountains. They correspond to the difficulty of the primary routes we have described on the peaks and there may well be easier alternatives. For alpine ascents the official UIAA ratings are also included.

CLIMBING GRADES

Alpine ascents are often given a descriptive mountaineering grade:
- **F** Facile – easy
- **PD** Peu Difficile – a little bit difficult
- **AD** Assez Difficile – quite difficult

Plus or minus signs are often added to these grades to signify that they are at the higher or lower end of the grade respectively. For detailed descriptions of exactly what to expect at each of these grades please consult the relevant publications in Appendix 5 (Further Reading).

Technical climbing ascents are also sometimes given a UIAA technical grade:
- **I** British Moderate
- **II** British Difficult
- **III** British Very Difficult/Mild Severe.

Looking east just below the summit of Zugspitze (Route 15) (Daniel Arndt)

Enjoyment
For quick reference a purely subjective enjoyment rating has been included. If you delight in reaching a national high point you will find that none of the peaks is wholly without merit. Naturally, a lovely sunny day with a spring in your step is likely to make an ascent fare favourably when compared to a day spent trudging through a pea-souper, soaked to the bone by rain and sleet. The ratings are as follows:

*	Fun but limited by ease
**	Fine outing
***	Jolly good hike
****	Excellent
*****	Utterly sublime and awe-inspiring.

Timing
Anyone who ascends the peaks must remember that the mountains should be enjoyed and savoured: this is not a race. Times given for routes are based on our own experiences rather than often misleading signposts. The timing ranges given cover the fast and slow ends of the spectrum for normal walkers. In instances where our ascent times have been exceptional we have adjusted timings accordingly. It should go without saying that if you have just ascended six alpine peaks in two weeks you are likely to fly up mountains in great leaps and bounds. Conversely, if you are fresh from sitting in an office nibbling your pen, you will go at a much slower pace. Obviously, route-finding difficulties or bad weather may mean that these times are exceeded.

Directions
Compass bearings are adjusted to True North. We have tried to be as accurate as possible with our directions. No guidebook can be perfect, and readers should use their own judgement when following route descriptions: remember that natural features can change (through, for example, landslides or tree felling), signposts can be removed and paths can be re-routed.

View west of the High Tatras from Rysy summit (Route 33) (Urakawa Akihiko)

THE GEOGRAPHY OF EUROPE

Europe's geography is extremely diverse, ranging from the arid plains of central Spain to the mammoth icecaps of Iceland. Describing the locations of every high point in detail is outside the scope of this book, and for this reason the major mountain ranges of Europe – where most of the peaks are located – are detailed below for prospective 'high-pointers'. (See also the map on page 9.)

The Alps
Summits include Mont Blanc, Monte Rosa, Grossglockner
This is the most extensive range in Europe and is divided primarily into the Western and Eastern Alps, with the split following the River Rhine. The Western Alps are higher and include most of the French, Swiss and Italian peaks. The Eastern Alps form a chain through Austria to Slovenia. The highest peak in the Western Alps is Mont Blanc (4808m), whereas Piz Bernina is the highest of the Eastern range. These ranges are often further subdivided.

The Apennines
Summits include Monte Titano
The Apennines form the backbone of Italy, stretching for 1000km. The name comes from the Celtic 'pen', meaning mountain top (also the origin of the name of the English Pennines).

The Balkans
Summits include Musala, Midzor
The range is separated from the Carpathians by the Danube and runs from Bulgaria through Eastern Serbia. Although the term 'Balkan' is often used to define a handful of countries, the word has traditionally been used to encompass a much wider geographical and mountain area. The range includes the subdivisions Rila, Rhodope and Stara Planina.

Caledonian Chain: UK/Ireland
Summits include Ben Nevis, Carrauntoohil
England, Scotland, Wales, Northern Ireland and Ireland contain the mini-ranges of the Lakeland Fells, the Grampians, Snowdonia, the Mountains of Mourne and Macgillycuddy's Reeks, where

their respective high points are located. These were all part of the Caledonian chain when the countries were attached to the European mainland millions of years ago. The regions are all characterised by changeable weather.

The Carpathians
Summits include Gerlach, Rysy, Moldoveanu, Goverla
The Carpathians form a 1500km-long arc from the eastern Czech Republic through Romania, Poland, Slovakia, Ukraine and Hungary. The range is the second-most extensive on the continent, and is separated from the Alps by the River Danube. Major subdivisions of the range include the Transylvanian Alps/Fagaras Mountains, the Tatras and the Eastern Beskides. Gerlachovsky stit (2654m) in Slovakia is the loftiest peak.

The Caucasus
Summits include Mount Elbrus (the highest in the range and in Europe)
The watershed of the Caucasus Mountains provides the southeastern geographical border of Europe and Asia and so the range is sometimes classed as being Eurasian. It extends through Russia, Georgia and Azerbaijan from the Black Sea to the Caspian Sea. The range is divided into the Greater and Lesser Caucasus.

The Dinaric Alps
Summits include Maglic, Triglav, Dinara
The Dinaric Alps form a chain along the coast of the Adriatic through Slovenia, Croatia, Bosnia, Serbia, Montenegro and Albania. Major subdivisions include the Julian Alps, the Prokletije range and the Mount Korab range. The highest peak is Triglav (2864m).

The Pyrenees
Summits include Pic de Coma Pedrosa
The Pyrenees form a natural border between France and Spain and encompass the tiny country of Andorra. They stretch from the Bay of Biscay to the Mediterranean Sea. The range is named after Pyrene, a Greek god of fire, and the highest peak is Pico del Aneto (3404m), which lies in Spain.

Iceberg lagoon at Jokulsarlon, used for filming 007 in 'Die Another Day' and 'You Only Live Twice' (Route 18)

Veleta from the summit of Mulhacén (Route 42)

The Scandinavian Mountains
Summits include Halti, Galdhopiggen, Kebnekaise
The range is a long string of mountains which stretches down the Scandinavian peninsula from far north in the Arctic Circle. They border the North Sea and in some places rise spectacularly up from the famous fjords of Norway. Galdhopiggen (2469m) is the highest peak in the range.

The Sierra Nevada
Summits include Mulhacén
The range is located is southern Spain and boasts Europe's most southerly ski resort, within spitting distance of the Costa del Sol. Its highest point is Mulhacén (3478m).

The Low Countries
Belgium and the Netherlands are characterised by a large proportion of land lying less than 1m above sea level, or which has been reclaimed from the sea. This flood-prone territory is reinforced by a barrage of sea-wall defences. Further inland the ground level rises considerably to the foothills of the Ardennes range where Vaalserberg (321m) and Signal de Botrange (694m) are situated. Luxembourg does not have a coastline, but also rises gently towards the Ardennes hills.

PLANTS AND WILDLIFE
A sighting of some colourful local plants or wildlife is one of the many pleasures of visiting foreign peaks. It would be impossible to generalise about the vast array of flora and fauna on offer, so a few species to look out for throughout Europe are outlined below (see also Appendix 5, Further Reading).

The Alps Deciduous trees grow in the valleys and up to 1200–1600m. Above these, pine trees thrive, although many areas have been cultivated or deforested. From 2000–3000m alpine meadows teem with glacier buttercups, gentians, alpenroses and the ubiquitous edelweiss. You would be unlucky to visit all the alpine peaks in this book and not come across animals such as marmot, ibex and chamois. Marmots, the largest member of the squirrel family, live above 1600m and are fairly shy mammals. Nesting birds include eagles, alpine choughs and ptarmigan.

Marmot on Triglav, common throughout the alps

Black newt, Triglav (Hrvojka Skokovic)

The distinctive diminutive Icelandic horse, isolated from other breeds since AD800

The Balkans Wildlife abounds here, the more unusual inhabitants being black polecats, Balkan brown bears, badgers, wild boar, hares and squirrels. Birds include green woodpeckers, grey geese and wild ducks. Fauna is similar to that of the Carpathians, with walnut and willow more common in lower areas.

The Carpathians Beech forests grow at lower altitudes; spruce and pine thrive to around 1800m. Notable mammals are the Tatra chamois, red deer, roe deer and marmots; less common are snow voles, brown bear and wild boar.

The Caucasus Lower slopes are covered by oak, maple and ash forests; birch and pine take over higher up. Lower regions also support steppes and grasslands. Wildlife includes chamois, Caucasian red deer, wild goats, mouflon (wild sheep), brown bear, Caucasian grouse

The idyllic Rila Mountains (Route 6) (Atanas Radenski)

and the endangered Caucasus leopard. Peculiar to the region is the Caucasian tur, a very large mammal similar to an ibex, which is popular with Russian hunters.

The Dinaric Alps There are vast swathes of ancient unspoiled oak, beech and conifer forests in the plains. The limestone karst plateaus are fairly barren. Wildlife includes brown bear, fox, lynx, hare, weasel, otter and marten.

The Pyrenees The eastern half of the range is wild and barren, while the west is wooded. Wildlife includes the Pyrenean chamois, Pyrenean bear (very rare), brown bear (extremely rare), red squirrel, Pyrenean desman (of the mole genus), red fox, pine marten and badger. The Pyrenean euprocte – a relative of the salamander – is peculiar to the area. Eagles (including the golden eagle), kites and vultures might also be spotted.

The Scandinavian Mountains These regions are sparsely populated and wildlife thrives even in harsh winter climates. You will undoubtedly see reindeer, which are farmed and eaten widely. Moose are common, as are roe deer. Less often seen are mountain hares, Norwegian lemmings, lynx, arctic foxes and Scandinavian brown bears. Blind worm lizards are common, and birds and fish abound. Plants must survive months of snow cover and are generally hardy alpines. Although much of Scandinavia is densely forested, the mountain regions are less so, with birch and spruce growing in the valleys.

WHEN TO GO

Included in the detailed mountain chapters are – where relevant – the recommended times of year to climb. For some high points, such as those of the Low Countries or the Baltic States, the time of your visit is completely flexible and common sense will tell you when to go to avoid the crowds or to enjoy warmer weather. For other mountains, such as the alpine peaks or those in the Tatras range, climbing the mountains outside the recommended months would be a far more serious undertaking and might require additional equipment and an awareness of avalanche risk. In these regions May to

September generally provide the best climbing conditions, but bad weather systems can strike at any time of the year.

HOW TO GET THERE

Some of Europe's high points are far more accessible than others. While most can feasibly be accessed by public transport networks, this will in some less-developed or more rural areas prove time-consuming, and sufficient allowance should be made in your schedule. Language barriers in rural areas may also add to the adventure of finding some of the places by local transport. Good links – where they exist – have been noted; conversely, we have tried to point out where there are few alternatives to taxis, hitching or hire cars. By referring to the map of ranges and the information included in each chapter about neighbouring high points you may be able to plan a trip which takes in several peaks. Whether you are driving or linking areas by public transport, do consider ferry routes as these can cut out many troublesome road miles.

It is possible to reach many European countries very cheaply by budget airlines. Flights leave from major UK airports to the principal cities of Western Europe (and now much of Eastern Europe) on a regular basis. Cities within reach of the Alps, Carpathians, Dinaric Alps, Pyrenees, Sierra Nevada and some of the Balkan mountains are served by budget airlines. Routes are too numerous to list but some useful websites are www.ryanair.com, www.sterling.com, www.jet2.com, www.flybe.com, www.easy jet.com and www.flybmi.com.

The more remote mountains of Scandinavia and Russia, by contrast, are served by regional airports and internal flights, and are consequently more difficult to reach. With a little forward planning, however, no mountains in this book should prove prohibitively expensive to visit.

Other useful airline websites include www.icelandair.com, www.icelandexpress.com (budget flights to Iceland), www.flysas.com, www. finnair.com (range of Scandinavian destinations) and www.ba.com (reasonable flights to Russia).

On top of these, it is easy to take package holiday flights to countries such as Malta and Cyprus.

HEALTH AND SAFETY ISSUES

Getting to the summits of Europe's high points has been a great adventure for us, and with any adventure comes an element of risk. Each section details the difficulties of each peak; read the mountain safety information in preparation for alpine ascents.

Most of Europe is relatively safe in comparison to further-flung corners of the globe and those using this book should be aware of the normal guidelines issued to travellers, such as not leaving valuable items on show and taking advice about local water. You are unlikely to be troubled by wild animals, but should note that some farmers' dogs in Eastern European countries, particularly those of the former Yugoslavia, can look ferocious. You should not shy away from using a stick or stone to ward off any unruly beasts, as this is the customary method. In the Alps it is possible to come across wild boar and, in the Prokletije range, bears. Catching sight of these animals is a rarity, and – while they should not be approached – they are highly unlikely to threaten hikers.

You will not require any special vaccinations for the majority of the countries in Europe, but check the current advice and make sure that your jabs are up to date well in advance of departure to countries such as Russia and Moldova. A good place to get up-to-date official travel advice is the UK government's website: www.fco.gov.uk.

FORMER YUGOSLAV REPUBLICS

Emerging from the fall of Communism (and, in most instances, civil war) the former Yugoslav Republics are Slovenia, Croatia, Bosnia, Serbia, Kosovo, Macedonia and Montenegro. Because of its proximity to these countries and involvement in political disputes, the following information also applies to Albania.

In the former Yugoslavia – and particularly in the border regions where many of the high points are located – extra precautions must be taken by visitors due to the presence of unexploded landmines and other military ordnance. Although the routes described are believed to be free of such ordnance, your safety is not guaranteed. The general advice in all the former Yugoslavian countries is not to stray off paths into the wilderness. Do not risk camping wild in unknown areas, and certainly do not cross any fences or taped-off areas.

While Bosnia is without question the most blighted country, with skull-and-crossbones warning signs an all-too-common sight, all the former Yugoslav republics have been affected by landmines. With the assistance of the European Union and the United Nations, these countries are striving to remove all the landmines which were placed during the Balkan conflicts, and a great many areas have been successfully cleared. Work is, however, ongoing. Generally speaking, areas which are thought to still contain unexploded ordnance are well signed with the universally understood skull-and-crossbones symbol. Please bear in mind that locals are extremely friendly and helpful but may not always know everything about the safety of an area. If you have any doubts about your route, shepherds on the hillsides should always be consulted as their information can be invaluable.

Mine clearance on Djeravica (Kosovo) was ongoing when we ascended the peak in 2005. The United Nations Mission in Kosovo (UNMIK) have informed us the mountain has now been declared clear. However, caution on this mountain in particular is essential. Areas across the Albanian border in this region unfortunately remain high risk.

COMMUNICATION

With so many countries, cultures and languages involved in ascending Europe's high points, communication can often prove as much a challenge as the mountains themselves. This is especially pertinent to those readers who are travelling by public transport. While the internet and Hollywood have made English the great universal language, it is by no means ubiquitous. Despite language barriers people are, in nearly all instances, more than happy to help, and much fun can be had. Being polite, shaking hands when meeting people, hand gestures and the occasional word in the relevant language can go a long way, especially if asking for directions.

In Scandinavia, English is so well taught in schools and so widely understood that travel is easy. In the Eastern Bloc countries of Russia, Serbia, Bulgaria, Macedonia and Ukraine a translation of the Cyrillic alphabet can be indispensable. The Greek alphabet is similarly constructed, although a Latin translation of place names is now the norm in Greece.

In terms of a beneficial language for travelling throughout Europe, readers may be surprised to find Russian the most useful. In Western Europe, even if English is not spoken at all, the culture is often so generic that language rarely proves an obstacle to getting about. This is not necessarily the case in Eastern Europe. A great deal of the Russian vocabulary is used or understood by people in the remote regions of Eastern Europe where English, German and Latin languages have no footing whatsoever. Simple Russian words such as *gora* (mountain – commonly used throughout the Eastern Bloc), *autobus* (bus), *vauxhall* (station), *bolshoi* (big), *malinkai* (little) and numbers can do wonders to aid understanding. Try to pick up odd words of various European vocabularies, rather than worrying about forming proficient or even grammatically correct sentences.

MOUNTAIN SAFETY

Whereas all Europe's high points should be within reach of an ordinary fit and acclimatised individual, do not tackle any of the more

Avalanche on Zugspitze (Daniel Arndt)

serious ascents without adequate preparation and technical skills. Please refer to Appendix 2 (Mountain Routes Graded by Difficulty).

While British mountains can provide any number of challenges and unpredictable weather conditions, they are much lower than the peaks of many of our neighbouring countries. Long days with large amounts of ascent are commonplace on the routes described in this book. It is essential that you prepare yourself well in advance to avoid your holiday turning into an endurance event.

Regardless of individual ability, use common sense and never underestimate any mountain. Too many 'easy' mountains bear plaques commemorating unforeseen tragedies, ill-prepared parties, utter stupidity and, dare we say it, arrogance. Competence in navigation and compass work is a prerequisite of ascending any mountain.

Mountain rescue

Be aware that mobile phone network coverage is patchy or non-existent in many mountain areas.

The international mountain rescue number is 112, and will connect you to the local service. Bear in mind that while alpine countries and Scandinavia have good mountain rescue services, many countries included in this book do not.

If a helicopter is approaching, the internationally recognised signal for assistance is to stand with both arms raised in a V shape above the head. To signal that no help is required, one arm should be raised while the other remains down at your side.

Other standard distress signals are six short blasts on a whistle (or six shouts or flashes of a torch) followed by a one-minute pause, and then six more blasts. When someone responds, there should be three answering blasts followed by a pause and then three more blasts. See Appendix 5 (Further Reading) for more information.

Insurance

Mountain rescue can be very expensive. We recommend you are insured. Some schemes come with membership, for example the Austrian Alpine Club. The BMC has an insurance scheme. Others such as Snowcard are standalone policies.

SERIOUS ASCENTS

It is often perceived that there is a huge leap from hillwalking into the realms of mountaineering, and many competent hikers are put off by the technical aspects of alpine peaks. With care and experience easier alpine routes, such as those described in this book, can be attempted. Some of the routes bridge the gap between hillwalking and mountaineering. They do not fall neatly into either category, and may involve using an ice axe and/or crampons to negotiate less steeply inclined slopes.

Novices should take a short winter or alpine mountain skills course as a starting point before tackling the bigger peaks such as Mont Blanc or Dufourspitze. Excellent winter courses including skills such as the use of crampons, ice axes, rope work and mountain safety take place in Scotland throughout the winter months; courses last from two to five days. Better still are the alpine skills courses, which take place in the Chamonix area and elsewhere in the Alps. These tend to include glacier travel skills and crevasse rescue as part of the schedule. For students and young people the subsidised Conville courses are an excellent way to learn the basics, and generally include a two-day alpine ascent. Details of these and other courses can be found on the British Mountaineering Council website www.thebmc. co.uk. Other useful contacts are the National Mountaineering Centre at Plas Y Brenin www. pyb.co.uk, Glenmore Lodge www.glenmore-lodge.org.uk, and Talisman Activities www. talisman-activities.co.uk

Although we have not required the services of a paid guide for any of the ascents, many people are happier to be guided up their first alpine peaks. There are numerous guided packages available if you wish to climb the more popular peaks such as Mount Elbrus or Mont Blanc in this way. It is possible to hire official alpine guides in France, Switzerland, Italy and Austria. It is important to understand that hiring a guide is no substitute whatsoever to knowing how to take care of yourself on a mountain. Whether or not you choose to hire a guide it is still essential to develop your own mountain skills.

Before contemplating any of the serious or alpine ascents described in this book it is therefore essential to:

- be able to move together as a roped party
- know how to set up belays and abseils if necessary
- arrest a fall with an ice axe
- use crampons confidently on mixed terrain
- have an awareness of the dangers of crevasses, avalanches, seracs and rockfall
- understand safe glacier travel techniques and basic crevasse rescue.

Please refer to the difficulty ratings of each mountain and gradually work up to the harder ascents.

Pace

Those ascending alpine-style peaks will be rewarded for employing a steady and constant pace: the tortoise always beats the hare on a mountain. When stops are made they should be brief as this, rather than your pace, is where most time is lost. In most instances early starts are essential because snow conditions deteriorate markedly as the day heats up which makes progress slower and slippier, while snow bridges across crevasses can weaken, seracs can collapse and avalanche risk is increased. As a general rule, if you suspect that you will not be clear of all snow dangers by 1pm then you should simply turn back and make another attempt on a different day.

While avoiding unnecessary weight is wise, travelling too light can be counter-productive. If camping at altitude or on snow, a tent is recommended over bivvying out. The disadvantage of extra weight (lugging tent poles, camping mats and good sleeping bags up a peak) is greatly exceeded by the benefits of a good night's sleep.

Altitude

Undoubtedly fitness is an advantage for serious ascents, but always bear in mind that no degree of fitness can get you to the top of Mont Blanc or Mount Elbrus safely. Acclimatisation is absolutely essential for any peak above 3800m and advisable for mountains above 3000m. If altitude sickness is experienced, then simply descend as quickly and safely as possible. The primary symptoms of altitude sickness are: headaches; loss of appetite; nausea/vomiting; dizziness; blurred vision and trouble sleeping.

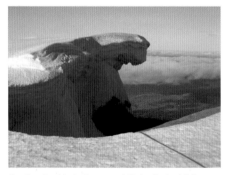

Cornice, Ben Nevis. Try to avoid being in the fall line of loaded snow features, especially as the day heats up (Scott Barnett)

The Frebouze Glacier, Grand Jorasses. With clear fracture lines and softening snow bridges, glaciers can become impassable.

EQUIPMENT

A first aid kit, compass and map should be an instinctive part of your hiking gear. On routes where you might run out of daylight, a head torch should be packed. Beyond these basics, necessary equipment is listed at the start of each route description, and falls into four broad categories:

1 None
- Sandals, sunhats and sun cream

2 Standard hiking gear
- Sturdy boots
- Waterproofs
- Fleece

3 Full alpine gear/full alpine climbing gear
- Thermal base layer
- Fleeces and waterproof shell clothing
- Plastic or leather rigid crampon-compatible boots
- UVB- and UVC-proof glacier glasses
- Possibly a helmet
- Hat
- Over-gloves
- Liner-gloves
- Gaiters

Warm lightweight clothing worn in layers which can be added or removed easily is strongly recommended over large bulky items: it is not unusual to experience temperatures as low as -25°C on the summit of Mont Blanc in the morning and wilt in the sweltering +30°C afternoon heat of Chamonix.

For serious ascents you will also need:
- high-factor sun cream (30 minimum)
- rope (30m walking ropes will generally suffice; on some routes it would be prudent to have a single 50m climbing rope)
- harness
- slings
- ice screws (at least one long 20cm+ per person)
- karabiners
- ice axe
- crampons
- deadman/snow fluke
- lightweight mountain shelter.

The deadman/snow fluke is an underused – but excellent – anchor device for alpine-style ascents. It is so named because without it, in certain scenarios, you could be a 'dead man'. The deadman is a metal plate with a length of wire tied through it. The device might well come to the rescue if an anchor or runner is required and there is no suitable ice/frozen snow in which to place an ice screw, no time to dig out a snow bollard or snow bucket, and a buried ice axe is not practical or possible. The metal plate can be hammered into snow with speed and the wire clipped into easily. Primarily used as part of a winter-climbing rack, a deadman comes into its own in the soft snow of alpine afternoons.

The use of snow stakes is not advised as these are prone to failure.

While packing a bivvy bag is often recommended for alpine summit ascents, a far more useful item is a lightweight mountain shelter. Larger than a bivvy bag, a mountain shelter usually weighs no more, can be whipped out in a sudden snowstorm, climbed under with ease and normally accommodates two people. If visibility is low and the bad weather expected to pass, a mountain shelter gives a

The Gervasutti Hut above Val Ferret, near Courmayeur in the Italian Alps. Notice camping mat: never assume you will reach a refuge or be able to stay in it

25

Zugspitze's final via ferrata section under snow, with the Eibsee beyond (Route 15) (Daniel Arndt)

great advantage. It can also double as a bivvy bag if necessary.

4 Via ferrata gear

Early mountain tourism and troop movements during World Wars I and II have left many of Europe's mountain routes protected by pitons connected by iron cables. Often these act as little more than a hand rail; in instances where they do not, via ferrata equipment is required. The basic principle of via ferrata kit is to ensure that the climber is always attached to the cable by at least one karabiner, hence the use of two leads in order to negotiate the pitons which hold the cables.

Various types of kit can be purchased or used with varying degrees of safety. Many specialist via ferrata kits are now available from well-known brands and any of these will suffice. On top of this the following items are required:

- harness
- helmet
- one screw-gate/lock-gate karabiner
- two clip-gate karabiners (preferably large as some cables can be quite thick).

While experienced climbers can make their own versions of the specialist kits, climbers should be aware that the use of slings on via ferrata routes is dangerous: slings are static, unlike climbing rope, which is dynamic.

Out-of-season/Winter ascents

An out-of-season ascent may turn a mountain – which in summer can be scaled in little more than a pair of shorts, trainers and with a compass – into a serious ascent requiring two ice axes and a full climbing rack. Avalanche awareness, even on the most straightforward ascent, is crucial in winter months.

Out-of-season ascents should only be undertaken by those who deem themselves adequately experienced for the terrain, weather conditions and dangers pertaining to each individual peak.

There are no in-season routes described in this book which require two ice axes or a full rack of climbing gear. However, safety on some routes can be aided by the use of a few wires or a couple of cams. The route descriptions specify when additional climbing gear is required.

Note that digital cameras are prone to failure in cold weather, especially at altitude.

WHAT IS EUROPE?

There is a surprising degree of confusion regarding what constitutes Europe. This is a shame and also unnecessary: Europe's boundaries have become pretty well standardised through a process of tradition based upon geographical features, and are agreed by the UN as:

> The Mediterranean in the south; the Arctic Ocean in the north; the mid-Atlantic ridge in the west; the Bosporus and Dardanelles in the southeast; the Ural Mountains and Ural River in the east and, finally, the watershed of the Greater Caucasian mountain range in the east-southeast.

These traditional boundaries are occasionally challenged by alternative economic, political and cultural perspectives. Some geographers, for example, prefer to band together areas which are culturally or politically similar: 'Latin America', for example, can be a far more useful term than North and South America or even Central America. Likewise, for countries such as Israel or Georgia, who find themselves culturally alienated from the states which surround them, a desire to belong to a continent which predominantly shares a similar set of values has great appeal. This is why we find Israel in the Eurovision song contest. But Israel is not in Europe – never has been, never will be. The same can be said of the Central Asian republics of Georgia, Armenia, Azerbaijan and Kazakhstan which are on the Asiatic plate.

In selecting the countries and high points for this book we have therefore selected states and high points which fall within the standard boundaries of Europe. Europe has three truly 'trans-continental' states. As these transcend the boundaries of Europe they need special attention: Iceland, Russia and Turkey.

Iceland The mid-Atlantic divide dissects Iceland and makes for a distinct tourist attraction on the island. One third of Iceland subsequently rests on the North American tectonic plate. Hvannadalshnukur (2111m), Iceland's national high point, is situated on the European tectonic plate. Iceland has traditionally been viewed as wholly European despite its trans-continental status.

Russia Consuming an enormous swathe of the Eurasian land mass, Russia is unquestionably a trans-continental state. Conveniently for the purposes of this book the national high point of Russia, Mount Elbrus (5642m), falls within its European land mass. If Tajikistan and Kyrgyzstan had not gained independence from Russia after the break-up of the USSR, then Russia's highest peaks would have been on the Asian land mass and, for this book, a European Russian peak (Elbrus) would have needed to act as a substitute. For those interested, the highest peak of the USSR was Peak Communism (Ismoil Somoni Peak – 7495m), in Tajikistan.

Turkey Turkey is proud of its trans-continental status: when crossing the Bosporus at Istanbul from west to east you will meet a 'Welcome to Asia' sign. Likewise, if you cross the Bosporus in an east–west direction you will meet a 'Welcome to Europe' sign. The national high point of Turkey is Mount Ararat (5137m). Unfortunately for this book, Mount Ararat is situated 2000km east of the Bosporus beside the Iranian border and thus with no stretch of the imagination could be cited as a European peak. While Turkey's portion of European land only equates to three per cent of its overall area, this does include a number of popular beach resorts and half of Istanbul, formerly Turkey's capital city. Therefore we have included the highest point of European Turkey, Mahya Dagi (1030m). Since this is not a national high point the climbing of it

Turkey: leaving Asia by crossing the Bosporus at Istanbul (Route 45)

is optional, as far as completing this list in this book. The actual summit of Mahya Dagi is covered by a NATO monitoring station, and entrance to the military compound is forbidden.

UEFA and FIFA
UEFA, the governing body of European football, has allowed some states which are not part of Europe to take part in its competitions, which has occasionally led to geographical confusion: Israel, Georgia, Armenia, Azerbaijan and Kazakhstan. FIFA, the governing body of world football, also follows UEFA's system. FIFA's other strange deviations from continental divides include Guyana, Suriname and French Guyana (each South American countries) as part of the North American federation. Likewise, Australia is now part of the Asian federation.

The Caucasus/Georgia
As the watershed of the Greater Caucasian range forms one of the distinctive land borders of Europe and Asia, the national high points of Georgia and Azerbaijan (which are on the watershed) require special attention.

Mount Shkhara (5184m) is the third-highest mountain in Europe. It is part of the Bezingi Wall (a 4000–5000m wall of mountains which divides Europe and Asia), and the mountain therefore finds itself in two continents. As the watershed falls directly over Shkhara's summit the northern half of the mountain is European (belonging to

Russia) while the southern half, belonging to Georgia, is Asian. Therefore, it is correct to view Shkhara as both European and Asian. It is, however, inaccurate to view the Georgian high point as a European one because Georgia's share of the summit is in Asia. This situation repeats itself in exactly the same way with Bazardüzü Dagi (4485m), the national high point of Azerbaijan.

A small part of Azerbaijan to the east of its national high point and north of the capital Baku lies north of the Caucasian watershed. This small portion of the country can fairly claim to be topographically part of Europe, but we feel it too insignificant to merit its own high point.

Dominions and Crown Dependencies
Territories which have dominion or dependency status are not included in this book. As dominions constitute neither full-blown parts of states nor states in their own right, they fall into a geographical grey area and often confuse sources wishing to acknowledge a nation's high point. If we were to include dominions the high point of Great Britain would be Mount Paget (2935m), 14,480km away on the island of South Georgia in the southern hemisphere.

Spain, Portugal and Denmark
Some sources place the national high points of Denmark, Portugal and Spain on their dominions.

Denmark Greenland is geographically part of North America and a fully autonomous dominion. While the Faeroe Islands are part of Europe, they too are a fully autonomous dominion with their own parliament. The highest point of the Faeroe Islands, Slaettaratindur (882m), is massively higher than Denmark's high point. Interestingly, UEFA has regarded the islands as worthy of returning their own national football team. The islands may eventually declare statehood outright.

Portugal The Azores Islands in the mid-Atlantic are dominions of Portugal and are fully autonomous with their own president. The highest point of the Azores is Mount Pico (2351m). This is higher than the high point of mainland Portugal, La Torre (1993m).

Spain Continental Spain's high point is Mulhacén (3478m) in the Sierra Nevada range. Some sources cite Spain's national high point as Mount Teide (3718m) on Tenerife in the Spanish dominion of the Canary Islands. Regardless of the dominion status however, Mount Teide is geographically part of Africa in much the same way as Spain's mainland African dominions and subsequently could not be considered European.

New States
Now that Kosovo is on the brink of a fully ratified statehood, Europe has become more stable and so new national high points should not spring up any time soon. Transnistria, a would-be breakaway republic within Moldova, functions as a *de facto* state, but looks unlikely to gain any recognised form of independence imminently. This appears also to be the case for the would-be breakaway Russian provinces of Dagestan and Chechnya. Bosnia and Herzegovina, with its majority-Serb Srpska Republic region, is certainly a long way from being convincingly settled, but it is highly unlikely the international community would allow the country to break up in the short term. As mentioned above, the Faeroe Islands may eventually attain statehood.

United Kingdom of Great Britain and Northern Ireland
Much to the chagrin of many of their inhabitants England, Wales, Scotland and Northern Ireland remain one unified state with one seat at the UN. Despite the limited devolved governments of recent years (the Scottish Parliament, the Welsh Assembly and the Northern Ireland Parliament) and each constituent 'country' returning an international football team to FIFA and competing under their respective vests in the Commonwealth Games (although not in the Olympics), these four countries remain banded together under one Union Flag and look set to remain so for the foreseeable future. For this reason, some 'high-pointers' may choose to skip climbing the individual state high points of the United Kingdom's constituent parts in favour of climbing Ben Nevis alone.

Despite the union of these four states, we have deemed it worthwhile separating them because of their distinct cultural and historical identities. We feel it would be a shame to miss out on England's Scafell Pike, Wales's Snowdon and Northern Ireland's Slieve Donard, all magnificent little mountains.

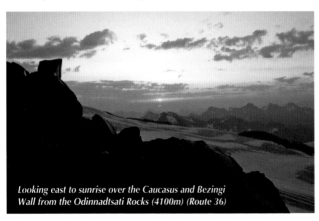

Looking east to sunrise over the Caucasus and Bezingi Wall from the Odinnadtsati Rocks (4100m) (Route 36)

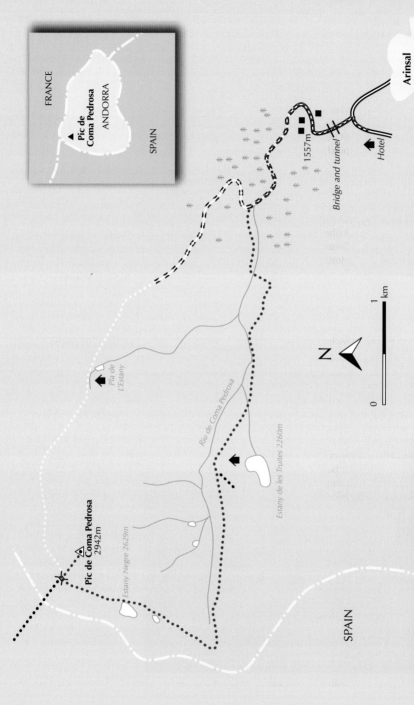

FRANCE

Pic de
Coma Pedrosa

ANDORRA

SPAIN

Arinsal

1557m

Bridge and tunnel

Hotel

Pla de
L'Estany

Riu de Coma Pedrosa

Estany de les Truites 2260m

Pic de Coma Pedrosa
2942m

Estany Negre 2629m

N

0 — 1 km

SPAIN

ANDORRA: PIC DE COMA PEDROSA

1 ANDORRA

PIC DE COMA PEDROSA 2942M

Location	Western Andorra, near ski resort of Arinsal
Start	Arinsal
Map(s)	M I Govern 1:50,000 and 1:25,000 topographic maps of Andorra can be purchased at petrol stations
Equipment	Standard hiking gear
Climbing period	May–October best
Difficulty	3
Enjoyment	****
Ascent	1400m
Time	4½hrs ascent, 3hrs descent
Water	Streams until close to summit
Accommodation	Hotels in Arinsal and refuges on the mountain
Getting there	From country's capital Andorra La Vella drive N to La Massana; turn off NW to Arinsal. Road tunnel at top of village. Park by Cresta Hotel; continue through tunnel on foot to start of route.
Public transport	Good coach links from Toulouse and Barcelona to La Vella; regular bus service to Arinsal from La Vella
Nearest high points	Mulhacén (Spain), La Torre (Portugal) and Chemin des Revoires (Monaco)

Tucked into the heart of the Pyrenees, Pic de Coma Pedrosa is a picturesque mountain which rewards hikers with a variety of terrain from meadows and hanging valleys to the arid rock and mineral-rich lakes of its upper reaches. Views from the summit are spectacular. While Andorra's streets bustle with French and Spanish day-trippers in search of tax-free goods, Coma Pedrosa provides a fitting counterpoint by lifting you above the throng into a serene tranquillity. The mountain is popular but not swarming with people; we encountered few hikers after passing beyond the chairlift area of the Refugi de Coma Pedrosa. In summer Coma Pedrosa can be climbed as a good day hike and provides no technical difficulties beyond very easy scrambling and a short section of snow walking.

ROUTE

From the top of Arinsal go through the first tunnel and immediately turn off right before a second tunnel, passing a grassy flood barrier. The first red and white route markers appear here. The road becomes a dusty dirt track. Follow this uphill into the forest.

Turn left at a sign to **Pic de Coma Pedrosa** (also pointing right to Pla de L'Estany: this is an alternative route to the summit but is not as enjoyable due to awkward boulder terrain and scree high up – see Other Routes below).

After turning left and winding up through the forest, reach another sign marking **Refugi de Coma Pedrosa** uphill to the left (close to Estany de les

Truites). More people walk to this refuge than to the summit. Ignore this diversion and continue on the main path due W across a wide valley.

At the head of the valley the path turns N (right) up to a very small tarn. To the left are the Spanish border mountains and to the right Coma Pedrosa. (The map marks a path up the scree slopes to the ridge; this is an alternative route to the summit and may prove very useful if the snow around the tarn is presenting difficulties.)

Skirt around the first tarn and along to the bigger lake of **Estany Negre**. After this the path breaks up; be careful not to follow red and white markers

At the head of the Coma Pedrosa river (2300m) looking east

Approaching the summit of Coma Pedrosa

left towards Spain. Instead follow similar markers NNE over a boulderfield and zigzag up the scree slopes to the pass on the ridge.

Once on the ridge ascend SE (right) to the summit, which is marked by a steel pole with four small steel flags. There is also a visitors' book.

Descent

Either return the way you have come, or bear off the summit SW to find a gradual route down to the small tarn S of **Estany Negre**. Rejoin the ascent route and reverse all directions.

OTHER ROUTES

OPTION 1

It is possible to cut off around 600m of ascent by taking a chairlift from Arinsal (runs in summer and begins above the Cresta Hotel) to Estany de les Truites and Refugi de Coma Pedrosa. From the cable car station, descend N to join the main route.

OPTION 2

An alternative ascent/descent marked on the 1:50,000 map goes via Pla de L'Estany. This is not recommended (although on a very hot day does provide the opportunity of cooling off in a tarn).

If however you do decide to descend this way, follow the main ascent route off the summit to the first pass.

Turn NE (right) down a steep scree slope path, then E across a long and ankle-breaking boulderfield with no path (there are occasional cairns but these are as useless as they are optimistic).

Descend SE over awkward grassy slopes down a gully to a small tarn south of the **Pla de L'Estany refuge** (you should see a grass-covered ridge to your left) – you will not see the refuge until at the tarn. From here the path is distinct and easy to follow down to Arinsal via Borda de la Coruvilla.

AUSTRIA: GROSSGLOCKNER

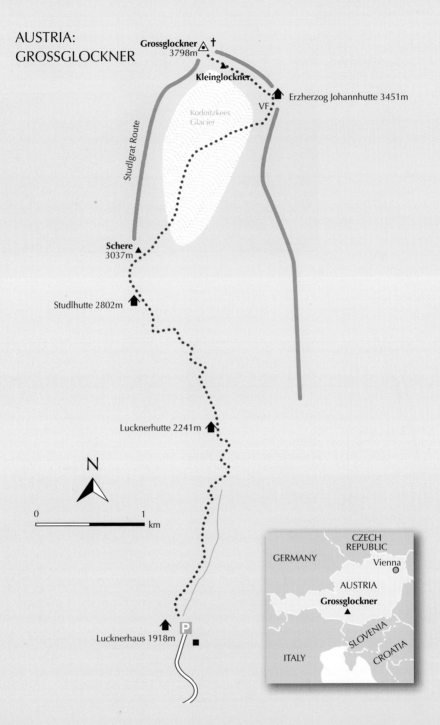

Grossglockner 3798m †

Kleinglockner

Erzherzog Johannhutte 3451m

VF

Kodnitzkees Glacier

Studlgrat Route

Schere 3037m

Studlhutte 2802m

Lucknerhutte 2241m

N

0   1 km

Lucknerhaus 1918m P

CZECH REPUBLIC

GERMANY

Vienna

AUSTRIA

Grossglockner ▲

SLOVENIA

ITALY

CROATIA

2 AUSTRIA

GROSSGLOCKNER 3798M

See Serious Ascents in the Introduction

Location	Eastern Alps in western Austria, S of Salzburg, N of Lienz, near mountain village of Kals
Start	Lucknerhaus
Map(s)	Alpenvereinskarte 40 (1:25,000) Grossglocknergruppe; mountain very popular so most topographical hiking maps of area sufficient
Equipment	Full alpine climbing gear essential
Climbing period	June–September (avoid weekends)
Difficulty	4. PD, glacier 35°, UIAA II
Enjoyment	*****
Ascent	1880m
Time	5–7hrs ascent, 4hrs descent
Water	Available at huts and from stream running off Kodnitzkees glacier
Accommodation	Campsite at bottom of Matrei a few kilometres N of Lucknerhaus road turn-off. Also Lucknerhaus or Lucknerhutte refuges at beginning of route, and three other refuge options if want to break climb into two days. Bivouacs allowed.
Getting there	From Matrei drive S in direction of Lienz on 108 for c10km to Huben. Turn left off main road and drive to Kals, signposted on a bend. At Kals head out of village, signs to Lucknerhaus. After 3km a tollbooth charges €8 per vehicle to drive last 4km. No barrier here to hinder early starts; one-day mountaineer will likely pass for free and pay on way down. No fee to park at Lucknerhaus (1918m).
Public transport	Lienz well connected to Austrian rail network, plus bus connections to Matrei, Huben and Kals. From Kals, hitch or hire a taxi. Some coach tours go to trailhead; enquire at tourist information office in Kals (part of the museum). Regular bus services run from Huben to Lucknerhaus, with links to Lienz, Matrei and Kitzbuhel (www.postbus.at for details). Taxi service also available (Venediger Taxis 04877 5369/5231).
Nearest high points	Zugspitze (Germany), Triglav (Slovenia), Grauspitz (Liechtenstein)

The highest point in the Eastern Alps, Grossglockner is a classic and accordingly popular peak. Its sharp pyramidal shape draws climbers in search of a standard mountaineering ascent and those looking for tougher challenges. The dramatic summit of Grossglockner can be seen on nearly all of its approaches. While it is a serious and impressive mountain, its standard route is not as difficult as Mont Blanc or Dufourspitze and, unlike both those mountains, it can feasibly be ascended in one day by a fit and experienced party. Many people choose to tackle it over two days, however. The mountain's only real downside is the queue which tends to develop for the narrow snow bridge between the Kleinglockner and the absolute summit; this can be one of the worst queues in the Alps, and certainly required patience on the day we went up.

Note The route described is from the Lucknerhaus because the previous 'normal' ascent from Franz Josef's Haus has become problematic due to the horrendous condition of the Pasterze glacier (global warming seems to be taking a toll here). Added to this it costs €27 to drive the toll road to Franz Josef's Haus!

Note As with most alpine peaks, an early dawn start is safest to avoid the dangerous and slower soft snow and crevasses of the afternoon. Route-finding is of no difficulty as far as the Studlhutte, so pre-dawn starts are not a problem. There is no harm in spreading the ascent over two days.

ROUTE

From **Lucknerhaus** follow either the track or the footpath on the W and E of the Kodnitz River respectively, heading due N up the Kodnitztal valley to the **Lucknerhutte** where these two parallel routes join. Clear red and white waymarkers lead up an extremely straightforward ascent, eventually zigzagging beneath the supply cable lifts to the **Studlhutte** (2802m). This should take 1¾–2½hrs. Stay on the path; you will lose time trying to cut off the dogleg by heading straight up the gully.

At the Studlhutte note the Austrian authority's warning and route sign for the classic Studlgrat climbing ascent (UIAA grade III–IV) – see Other Routes. At this point our route traverses E (right) below the **Schere** for 400m. This traverse can often be very icy, especially in early season, and crampons may be required from here. The route then turns N (left) to the **Kodnitzkees** (glacier). Do not get complacent – this glacier does have crevasses – rope up before trudging across.

Follow the snow trail across the glacier NE. With good snow cover there should be no need to remove crampons before joining the Kampl ridge below the Erzherzog Johann Hutte. Some of the rockier sections of

Grossglockner's south face

Grossglockner from lower Kodnitzkees

the ridge can be avoided by continuing upwards on the glacier for a short distance. On the ridge you will find short sections of via ferrata, but nothing too challenging.

Pass by the W (left) side of the **Erzherzog Johann Hutte**, and head N following the E side of the ridge until joining the very steep snow of the Kleinglocknerkees (glacier). Having clambered W up the snow, you will join the summit ridge proper. Ample natural belay points exist on the ridge, supplemented by cunningly added steel posts. If the snow is softening, have patience and take great care here for this is where most accidents happen (especially on descent).

Follow the ridge up to the **Kleinglockner** (3770m); with luck there should be no reason to remove crampons. At this point you are likely to meet one of the worst traffic jams in the Alps as inexperienced guided climbers struggle down a 10m descent to a sharp arete, before meeting a tricky 6m climb to the summit area proper. There is a fixed steel cable down to the snow bridge, but oddly not one across it.

Note If there is absolutely no snow on the whole ridge and crampons have had to be removed, belay the snow bridge.

A 6m climb up from the snow bridge on good holds is followed by a simple scramble to the summit, which is marked by a large ornate cross.

Descent

Descend via the ascent route. Remember to give way to those ascending. Don't hang about at the Erzherzog-Johann-Hutte but stop for a celebratory beer at the Studlhutte, since crevasses on the Kodnitzkees (glacier) open up as the day progresses.

On the Grossglockner/ Kleinglockner ridge

OTHER ROUTES

OPTION 1

If planning a two-day trip on Grossglockner an alternative longer ascent/ descent is from Lucknerhaus up the Berger valley to the Glorer Hutte (2651m) continuing on to overnight at the Salm Hutte (2638m). On the second day you eventually cross the Hoffmann glacier to arrive at the Erzherzog-Johann-Hutte on the shoulder of the summit where the primary route is picked up.

OPTION 2 STUDLGRAT RIDGE (UIAA III–IV)

An excellent sustained and serious climbing route which requires a full mixed-route climbing rack. One route starts from the Studlhutte and follows the SW ridge over Schere and Luisenkopf to the summit but there are other approaches. An extended guide to this ridge should be consulted, such as Dieter Siebert's *Eastern Alps: The Classic Routes on the Highest Peaks* (see Appendix 5, Further Reading).

3 BELARUS

DZYARZHYNSKAYA 345M

Also known as Djarzinskaya/Дзяржынская

Location	32km due W of Minsk
Start	Skirmantovo
Map(s)	Hard to come by; asking in a few petrol stations might produce general map of country
Equipment	None
Climbing period	Year-round
Difficulty	1
Enjoyment	*** (quite satisfying to reach the hill having forged your way into the netherworld of Belarus)
Ascent	5m
Time	45secs
Water	Not applicable
Accommodation	Range of hotels in Minsk
Getting there	From M6 Vilnius–Minsk or M1 Brest–Minsk–Moscow motorways take turn-off for P65 road (part of a kind of outer ring road for Minsk). Coming from N (M6), travel SW on P65 for c15km until second signpost marking Skirmantovo (ignore first). Sign also marks Yakutsky Gory, a small skiing place.
	Take road to Skirmantovo for exactly 3.8km to just before village. Look for three poles which look like spotlights (right): these are very close to the high point. Next to poles are a few farm buildings; 100m further along is another disused farm building (right) by a small track, opposite sign marking end/start of village. Park here.
Public transport	Simplest to catch train or fly to Minsk, then taxi there and back. Bus services patchy and complicated.
Nearest high point	Aukstojas/Juozapine Kalnas (Lithuania)

It should soon become far simpler to visit Belarus. Until then, one of your biggest problems in reaching this high point is actually being let into the country. Having already procured a visa, we managed to skip 5hrs of queues and still spent 8½hrs at the border of Belarus near Brest, despite being able to speak a fair bit of Russian. The Belarusian high point is, in contrast, quite a simple affair assuming you have access to a car and the energy for an 80m walk. An ability to read signs in a Cyrillic script is also very useful. The hill was once known as Svyataya but was renamed in 1954 to honour the founder of the Cheka (which later became the KGB): Felix Dzerzhinsky. Whereas Belarusians can by no means be accused of over-celebrating their high point, nevertheless they have felt this area of indistinct scrubland worthy of a surprising marble summit stone.

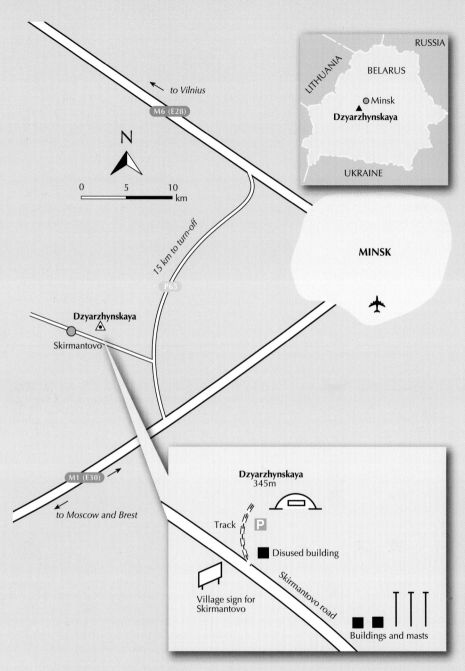

to Vilnius

M6 (E28)

N

0 5 10
km

15 km to turn-off

P65

Dzyarzhynskaya

Skirmantovo

RUSSIA

LITHUANIA

BELARUS

Minsk

Dzyarzhynskaya

UKRAINE

MINSK

M1 (E30)

to Moscow and Brest

Dzyarzhynskaya
345m

Track

P

Disused building

Skirmantovo road

Village sign for
Skirmantovo

Buildings and masts

BELARUS: DZYARZHYNSKAYA

Note If crossing a Belarus border by car, avoid joining the queue for Belarusian nationals. EU vehicles can skip the initial 5hr queue by driving to the front and asking to go through. Nonetheless expect to spend considerable time here. Home-stays for those who might eventually cross the border are offered by local *babushkas* (Russian term for elderly grandmotherly types). At the time of writing Belarus requires that all EU citizens get a tourist visa in advance, but the precise requirements change frequently; check www.belarusembassy.org for the latest information. Transit visas are also available for those passing through the country en route for Russia.

Note From a distance, the high point is difficult to separate from the surrounding landscape as everything appears to be the same height. Djarzinskaya is nowhere near the town of Djarzinsk, despite sharing its name. The roads in Belarus are, surprisingly, very good indeed.

ROUTE

Walk NWN up the track for about 80m until you see the high point. The area is quite overgrown but is well visited. The high point is in a clearing and is well marked with a boulder proclaiming a spot height and the peak's name.

Descent

By the same route.

DID YOU KNOW?

Famous native
Felix Dzerzhinsky, founder of the KGB.

Irrelevant fact
Men and women do not get on for long in Belarus! It has the highest divorce rate in Europe, and the second highest in the world behind the Maldives.

Ode to the KGB?
Dzyarzhynskaya

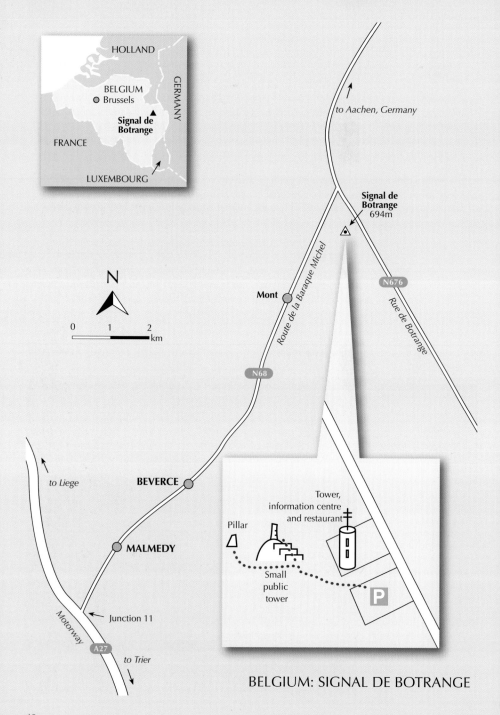

HOLLAND

GERMANY

BELGIUM
◉ Brussels

**Signal de
Botrange**

FRANCE

LUXEMBOURG

to Aachen, Germany

**Signal de
Botrange**
694m

N

0   1   2
km

Mont

Route de la Baraque Michel

N676

Rue de Botrange

N68

Tower,
information centre
and restaurant

to Liege

BEVERCE

Pillar

MALMEDY

Small
public
tower

P

Motorway

Junction 11

A27

to Trier

BELGIUM: SIGNAL DE BOTRANGE

Signal de Botrange: stairway to heaven?

DID YOU KNOW?

Famous native Adolphe Sax (1814–94), inventor of the saxophone.

Irrelevant fact Tintin, the Belgian cartoonist Hergé's famous character, was intended as a representative of Hitler's Nazi Youth and represented Hergé's Fascist leanings. In the first Tintin book (*Tintin in Russia*) Hergé presents an anti-Communist treatise.

The high fens near Signal du Botrange

Location	NW Belgium, SW of Liege in Hautes Fens (High Fens) range
Start	Rue de Botrange
Map(s)	Good road map easily available at garages
Equipment	None
Climbing period	Year-round
Difficulty	1
Enjoyment	*
Ascent	None
Time	None
Water	Bar/restaurant and public toilets at summit
Accommodation	Beverce has three campsites and youth hostel
Getting there	From Liege take A3 E to A27 (E42). Follow A27 S to junction 11, Malmedy. From here follow N68 Route de la Baraque Michel NE to Beverce and on through Mont and Xhoffraix. Few kilometres after Mont turn right (SE) on N676 Rue de Botrange, signposted to Robertville. You will soon see sign for Signal de Botrange and high point on right. Visitor centre open all week except Mondays. Two stone towers, one of which you can go up.
Public transport	Buses run directly past Signal de Botrange on St Vith–Eupen routes 390 and 394 (21mins from Eupen). Regular Malmedy–Eupen buses pass by N676 turning (500m walk to summit). Malmedy on main Belgian rail network; for up-to-date information contact Botrange tourist office.
Nearest high points	Vaalserberg (Netherlands), Buurgplatz/Kneiff (Luxembourg)

Despite reaching a decent height, the landscape which supports Belgium's highest point is broad and rises only gradually. Subsequently there is no real hill to walk up, and even the most determined will find anything other than driving to the highest point of Belgium quite frustrating. Despite this, the Belgians have designed a series of hikes and cycle routes in the area. There are also a number of cross-country ski routes – snow permitting. The only peculiarity of Botrange is that in 1934 the Belgians felt the need to build a 6m tower so that visitors could elevate themselves to the dizzy height of 700m. There is something rather arbitrary about this desire for a round number and we can only wonder at the thought process behind it.

ROUTE
No directions necessary – you're already there!

Does what it says on the tin

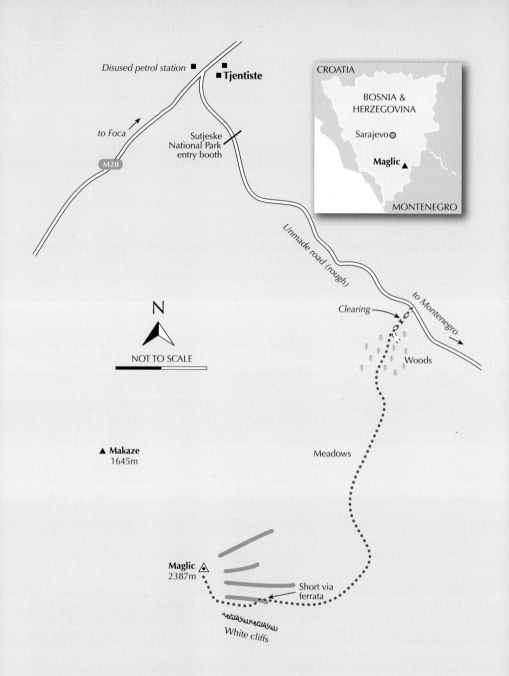

Disused petrol station ■
■ **Tjentiste**

to Foca ↗

M20

Sutjeske
National Park
entry booth

CROATIA

BOSNIA &
HERZEGOVINA

Sarajevo ⊙

Maglic ▲

MONTENEGRO

Unmade road (rough)

to Montenegro →

Clearing →

Woods

N

NOT TO SCALE

Meadows

▲ **Makaze**
1645m

Maglic ◬
2387m

Short via
ferrata ←

White cliffs

BOSNIA AND HERZOGOVINA: MAGLIC

5 BOSNIA AND HERZEGOVINA

MAGLIC 2387M

See Former Yugoslav Republics under Health and Safety in the Introduction

Location	In Central Dinaric Alps, known locally as the 'Majestic Range', close to Montenegrin border in SE of country; 100km SSE of Sarajevo and 20km from city of Foca
Start	Tjentiste
Map(s)	Very difficult to obtain
Equipment	Hiking gear
Climbing period	April–October best
Difficulty	3
Enjoyment	****
Ascent	750m (estimated)
Time	2–3hrs ascent, 2hrs descent
Water	No water on walk; available on road to trailhead
Accommodation	Nearest hotel at Tjentiste. No apparent camping restriction on mountain (but see below); good spots near start of trail.
Getting there	**Note** Road to trailhead in extremely poor condition; not a problem for 4x4s, but cars travel up at great peril to their exhausts! You have been warned. Getting to start of trail is most difficult part of trip. Because of tension in Srpska Republic roads can be diverted over very rough tracks for many miles due to bridges having been blown up. From Sarajevo take 18 SE to Foca and Brod. From Foca take 20 to Sutjeska National Park and sparse village of Tjentiste (20km). Just after sign for village you will see disused petrol station (right) and small road directly opposite. Take this for exactly 17.7km to trailhead (set your distance clock). This road is a back door into Montenegro and can be busier than expected; tarmac for several kilometres until reaching a barrier/toll booth where small charge for entry to National Park (passports needed). Road soon seriously deteriorates and winds up through forest. After 6km pass tarmac car park but do not stop; continue past small area of strange concrete monuments and up out of forest to a plateau (if start descending have gone too far). On right are some log picnic benches, collapsed wooden shelter and forest track; also small sign to Maglic placed here on a tree by the authors. Peak should be visible through trees. Park here.
Public transport	Bus to Foca from Sarajevo; from Foca bus to Tjentiste from where hiking or hitching are only options to trailhead.
Nearest high points	Bobotov Kuk and Maja Kolata (Montenegro) Dinara (Croatia)

While Bosnia is trying to pick itself up after a truly horrendous war, life is still not straightforward. Almost every building in the country outside of Sarajevo is riddled with bullet holes and it is impossible not to despair for the plight of Bosnians when as yet uncleared minefields are visible everywhere. Tensions between the predominantly Serbian Republika Srpska (which makes up a third of the country's land mass) and the rest of Bosnia are unfortunately still prevalent. The legacy of the war is hard to forget. When we made our way to Maglic in 2005, Srpskan separatists destroyed a bridge between the two republics. This necessitated our taking a 40km detour along dirt tracks simply to cross the river and rejoin our route a mile down the road. Despite these ongoing tensions, the people throughout Bosnia tend to be very friendly and welcoming to visitors. The mix of various Yugoslav cultures makes a trip to Bosnia both exciting and rewarding. Sarajevo is a vibrant cosmopolitan city which will surprise as much as it will elate. It has the ubiquitous Irish pub and more *burek* stalls (sumptuous Balkan pies) than you could shake a stick at.

Because Maglic is situated firmly inside the Serbian Republic, the mountain has become not so much a symbol of national pride as much as a forgotten focal point of a former age. The old Yugoslav flag and a monument to Tito (the father of Yugoslavia) on its summit say as much. This is a shame as Bosnians have a lot to be proud of in this national high point. A stone's throw from the border with Montenegro, the road to its trailhead serves as an illegal back-door entry into Montenegro and therefore the mountain may at first appear busier than it actually is. Maglic is characterised by the incredible 'White Cliffs of Dover' phenomenon of its inner gorge which is visually stunning and makes the troublesome journey all the more worthwhile. The route is secluded and the view from the summit sublime.

Note We have been assured by Bosnian tourist information in Sarajevo that there are no landmines in this border area around Maglic. Likewise, there have been no reports of casualties. Needless to say, extreme caution should be taken in other rural areas. While we feel it is fine to camp in this particular area, it is a worthwhile rule of thumb not to camp wild in Bosnia as landmine warning signs are an all-too-common reality. Added to this there are mined areas which remain unsigned.

Note There is another Maglic (2141m) in southeast Montenegro.

ROUTE

Somewhat surprisingly there is actually a trail up Maglic with star, triangle and circle waymarkers although these are, at times, difficult to follow. Start off S along the forest track. After 60m a marker on a tree shows an overgrown path off to the right. Take this. This is the worst part of the route – eventually the trail does become a decent path.

Taking care not to lose the markers through dense ash trees, follow the trail to emerge in rolling meadows and continue upwards passing sporadic pine trees.

The path will soon lead you into another ash and beech wood where the markers are far easier to follow. Eventually the route heads out of the woods over grassy terrain and up over a small hill where you will see the wide face of the massif (the summit of **Maglic** is the darker peak on the right). The massif is characterised by five distinct ridges (two clear outer ridges, one clear central ridge and two less distinct inner ridges to the left and right). The ascent is up the second ridge from the left.

The splendid white cliffs of Maglic

Following the path descend slightly before progressing up a small grassy gully and traversing below the middle ridge. Here you will encounter a short scramble and via ferrata section (no equipment necessary).

Keeping an eye out for waymarkers ascend the unlikely steep grassy/rocky gully which leads you safely up to the summit ridge. You are rewarded here with excellent views of the 'White Cliffs of Dover' feature and if clear, with the dramatic cliff edges that fall away into Montenegro.

Once you have reached the summit ridge you must turn right to reach the top. Take stock of your surroundings here as there is an alternative

Tito memorial and outdated Yugoslav flag on the summit of Maglic

descent passing to the left and finding your original route off the ridge can be difficult in poor visibility. Descend slightly over the crest of the ridge and continue for 400m before reaching the steep rocky summit scramble.

The scramble is not difficult and at no point is the climber seriously exposed. The summit is marked by an old steel Yugoslav flag; there is also a visitors' book and a plaque honouring Marshal Tito.

Descent
The markers which head off the summit in the opposite direction eventually lead to Montenegro. Return the way you have come, taking care not to blindly amble past the point at which you originally joined the summit ridge.

OTHER ROUTES
It is possible to ascend Maglic from the Montenegrin side. However, this involves 1700m of ascent taking an estimated 6hrs. Not recommended, but if you do want to try it:

From the town of Pluzine drive N round Lake Piva to the village of Mratinje. The route starts here and heads NW–N to the summit via the Malo and Veliko Mratinjinski lakes, Carev Do Pass and Trnovacko Lake, from where a badly marked trail takes you to the summit.

If considering an ascent from this side get hold of *The Mountains of Montenegro – A Mountaineering Guide* by Vincek, Popovic and Kovacevic – the three experts of Montenegrin mountain climbing (see Appendix 5, Further Reading). While their route descriptions are brief, the guide is a comprehensive collection of all Montenegro's mountains.

6 BULGARIA

MUSALA 2925M

Musala's north face from near Ledenoto Ezero (Ice Lake) (Atanas Radenski)

Location	80km S of Sofia, past Samokov, near ski resort of Borovets
Start	Borovets
Map(s)	1:55,000 and 1:33,000 tourist maps marking trails available in Borovets
Equipment	Standard hiking gear
Climbing period	June–October. Winter temperatures reach -25°C with very deep snow; due to nearby skiing activity ascents can be considered – dress accordingly.
Difficulty	2
Enjoyment	***
Ascent	700m from top of cable car (1600m from Borovets)
Time	2½–3½hrs ascent (at least 6hrs from Borovets), 3–3½hrs descent
Water	Available at summit, two huts on route and plenty of natural sources
Accommodation	Ample, to suit all budgets, in Borovets; good number of basic mountain refuges
Getting there	From Sofia ring road take 82 to Samokov and Borovets
Public transport	One of Europe's cheapest ski resorts, Borovets is a popular tourist destination year-round; well served by direct coach and bus tours from Sofia. The easiest way to reach Borovets is to take one of the half-hourly buses from Sofia's southern bus station ('Yug') to Samokov and then one of the half-hourly buses from there to Borovets. Alternatively, catch train to Kostenets then bus to Borovets.
Nearest high points	Mount Olympus (Greece), Mount Korab (Macedonia/Albania), Midzor (Serbia), Djeravica (Kosovo), Mahya Dagi (Turkey)

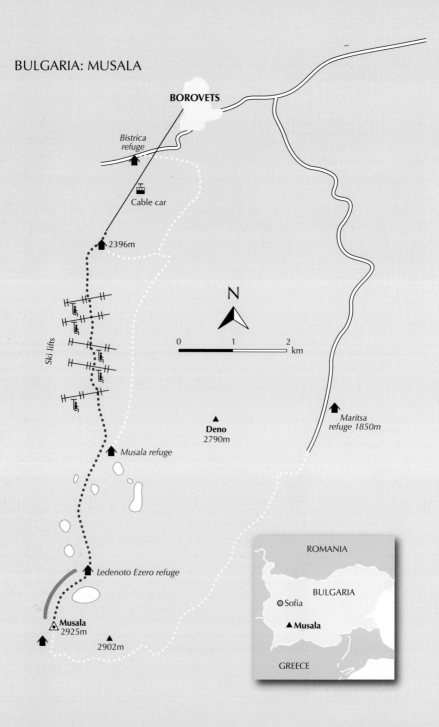

BULGARIA: MUSALA

BOROVETS

Bistrica refuge

Cable car

2396m

Ski lifts

N

0   1   2 km

Deno
2790m

Maritsa
refuge 1850m

Musala refuge

Ledenoto Ezero refuge

Musala
2925m

2902m

ROMANIA

BULGARIA

Sofia

Musala

GREECE

As the highest mountain in the Balkans, Musala attracts a great many Bulgarian and Eastern European hikers who congregate on the summit to sample fruity teas and share spirits neat from the bottle. We found fellow hikers on the mountain keen to offer more than a nip of high-percentage spirits – teetotallers beware! Despite its popularity and its proximity to the lively ski resort of Borovets, Musala and the Rila National Park are remarkably unspoilt. Bears may be encountered here but tend to keep to themselves. While day walks to the peak are straightforward enough, many Bulgarians choose to continue along the range on a four-day pilgrimage to the revered Rila/Rilski monastery. Extended stays are made easier by numerous trails and rudimentary refuges (bring your own food) and visitors will find the area serves adventurous hikers very well. Musala was known as Stalin Peak from 1949 until 1961.

Note Parking in Borovets is tightly controlled by local 'businessmen'. Park in the paid car park to avoid entanglement with the local Mafiosi.

Note The 'you are here' noticeboards on the mountain can be wildly inaccurate – trust your own judgement.

ROUTE

From Borovets you can either shorten the ascent by catching the Bistrica gondola lift to the top station or hike up the whole thing. The gondola costs €5.50 one way. Daytime opening hours during summer are 9am–4pm. By September the lift may only be operating at weekends and closed for repairs by late September. If you choose to go up by cable car, descend slightly from the cable car station past a restaurant to follow the red trail SSE. Continue on a good level traverse track that passes under five ski draglifts to the **Musala refuge**.

If the cable car is closed (or not chosen), find the well-marked E8 footpath which leaves the road S of Borovets near the **Bistrica refuge** and continue up the Bistrica valley – the building of a ski run has sadly altered

The distinctive blue triangle of the Ledenoto Ezero – or Everest – refuge (Atanas Radenski)

the nature of the path – eventually joining the main route at the **Musala refuge**.

Head down once again to the lake on your left and pick up the red marked path that winds up over rocky and shrubby terrain past several more lakes. After roughly 45mins you will reach the unmistakable large blue triangular **Ledenoto Ezero** refuge (now known as the Everest refuge).

Go past the refuge towards the nearby lake; from here the peak and its summit buildings should be visible even in cloud to the SSW. The ascent from the lake appears prohibitively steep but is tamed by a relatively easy path which emerges at the summit.

The summit is marked by a triangulation point, an ecological observatory and a weather station (with a one-room emergency refuge) selling very sweet Bulgarian tea. Expect also to be offered a celebratory shot of vodka by Musala's numerous Bulgarian pilgrims.

Descent
By the same route.

OTHER ROUTES

Due to the popularity of this mountain a good number of viable alternative ascents are possible, although these tend to be less well marked. One of these is the green trail that starts from the **Maritsa refuge**, but a 4x4 or high-clearance vehicle is required to drive there. The long road to Maritsa leaves the main Borovets–Dolna Banja road 0.6km E of Borovets. The beginning of the road passes through a lumberyard. Its surface is initially hard clay and rubble, but quickly degenerates into a very rugged boulder-strewn mess.

The ascent from Maritsa should take 3½–4½hrs. It is easy to lose the green route markers as the path goes through heavy undergrowth. Heading up from here does have the benefit of avoiding the crowds until the summit. The ascent is 1200m vertical height.

Follow the track S from **Maritsa** past the turn-off to the Zaravica refuge and stay on the track until it ends; in doing so you will pass two inaccurate National Park information boards.

An overgrown path continues from here and is oddly the most difficult section of the route to follow. Keeping an eye out for the green and white waymarkers, head WSW through pine-bush canopies. You should pass three main streams and two small streams before reaching the wide fluvial plain of the upper Golijama Marica.

If you find yourself at the lake you have gone too far S. Look out for a small cairn and take the right fork across the fluvial plain. A steep zig-zagging ascent leads you up to the ridge beneath the craggy SE face of **Musala**.

Once on the ridge you will join the more distinct red route N of the Preslapa Pass and ascend northwards to the summit.

Note In poor visibility the beginning of the descent to Marica is difficult to identify. If you have gone too far and reached the Preslapa Pass, the simplest thing is to bear due E down the scree slopes and continue to trust your bearings until you come across the path.

DID YOU KNOW?

Famous native
Stefka Kostadinova, Olympic gold medalist and female high-jump world-record holder 1987 to present (2.09m).

Irrelevant fact
The Turks call Bulgaria 'Bulgaristan'.

DINARA 1831M

See Former Yugoslav Republics under Health and Safety in the Introduction

Location	In Dinaric Alps, 25km from town of Knin, inland from Split near Bosnian border
Start	Glavas
Map(s)	1:30,000 map published by SMAND available locally in Zagreb and other major cities
Equipment	Hiking gear
Climbing period	Year-round; some snow in winter
Difficulty	2
Enjoyment	***
Ascent	1300m
Time	2½–4hrs ascent, 2½hrs descent
Water	No permanent water on route
Accommodation	Nearest hotel is Mihovil just outside Knin on Split–Zagreb road (Split 1–1½hrs away by road)
Getting there	From Knin take E71 (1) towards Split for 15km via Polac Pass (when clear of cloud excellent views of Dinara's impressive 7km-wide SE face). Continue to small village of Kijevo. In centre turn left on narrow tarmac road directly opposite post office, signed Ustina, with smaller sign marking Dinara. Continue for 6km to start of hamlet of Glavas. Park by concrete bus shelter with rough faded map of Dinara on side. Alternatively, may be safer to drive into village to park. Ask permission to do so (people seemed friendly).
Public transport	Bus shelter at Glavas implies possible to get there from Knin by public transport, but not advised; you will have to deal with unhelpful staff at Knin bus station before getting anywhere. Far more likely catch bus from Knin to Kijevo then walk 6km to start of route. Knin well served by bus and train links from Split on Croatian coast. If bus driver very helpful may be possible to go direct to Kijevo from Split as route passes this way.
Nearest high point	Maglic (Bosnia and Herzegovina)

A summit ridge of mesmerising karst limestone paving and craters makes a visit to Croatia's high point enticing. Dinara does not appear to hold the same national importance for Croatians as, for example, Triglav does for the Slovenes. A visit to Dinara will take you into one of the more remote areas of the country, where the spectre of war and ethnic cleansing looms large, providing a stark contrast to the tourist hotspots of the Dalmatian coast. Needless to say, these problems are now firmly in the past. The mountain boasts a refreshing mixture of landscapes,

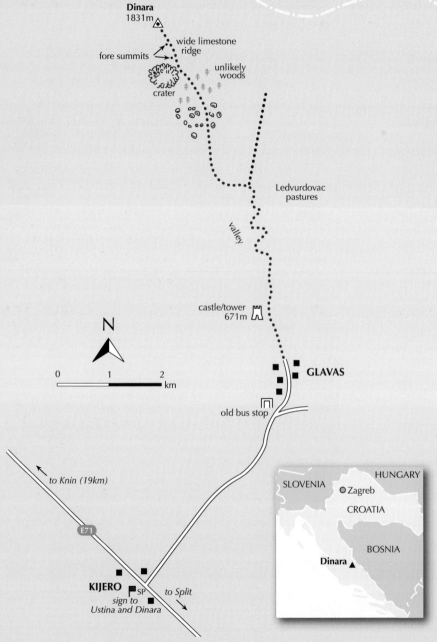

CROATIA: DINARA

BOSNIA

Dinara
1831m

wide limestone
ridge

fore summits

unlikely
woods

crater

Ledvurdovac
pastures

valley

castle/tower
671m

GLAVAS

old bus stop

N

0   1   2
km

to Knin (19km)

E71

KIJERO
SP
sign to
Ustina and Dinara

to Split

SLOVENIA   HUNGARY
      Zagreb
         CROATIA

         BOSNIA

Dinara

rising from the arid plains of Knin through meadows, an unlikely copse and swathes of tumulus. Climbing the mountain is slightly complicated by a lack of signposts, but remains an enjoyable long walk. That said, we were encouraged to discover a rudimentary map of Dinara painted in profile on a bus shelter at the start of the route.

Note The route is marked by red and white target signs but care must be taken not to lose them. The summit is much further than is visible at the outset.

ROUTE

Take the track left of the bus shelter for 400m to the village. From here, follow the clear markers gradually uphill towards a ruined **castle tower** directly N. The path is indistinct here but will soon improve. Pass on the right of the castle.

Continue on a broad ridge before following markers that lead you into a valley. After a long gradual walk NNW, the path zigzags steeply out of the valley before continuing on a gentle stony trail.

Eventually meet a marked path junction in a wide grassy area (the **Ledvurdovac pastures**). The main path continues straight ahead to two farm buildings. Ignore this and turn left (W) to Dinara. The path is again less distinct here. After 400m, the route swings right to follow its original N–NNW bearing.

Enter a gorge strewn with limestone karst and continue through what can only be described as '**the unlikely woods**'.

After the woods you will reach the summit ridge, though there is still a way to go. Continue right (NNW) along the ridge above a giant meteor-like crater. In clear weather you will be able to see the summit cross in the distance. There are two small false summits. After the first, you will find yourself descending a little for around 80m.

The bus shelter at Glavas with a painted profile map of Dinara (the '4.00h' is generous)

The route to the summit is simple enough now and follows the ridge through interesting flora and limestone formations. The summit has two parts: one with a cross and a slightly higher one 50m before it with a triangulation point and plaque. There is a visitors' book with a **Dinara** stamp.

Above left:
Cross on Dinara's second summit, with main summit beyond

Descent
By the same route.

OTHER ROUTES
Other routes up the ridges on the SE face of Dinara do exist, but it may be very difficult to find the starting points.

Above right:
Descending into the 'unlikely woods' amidst karst formations

MOUNT OLYMPUS (CHIONISTRA) 1951M

Location	Central Cyprus, equidistant from Paphos and Nicosia in Troodos Mountain range
Start	Troodos
Map(s)	Free from visitor centre on way up
Equipment	None
Climbing period	Year round
Difficulty	1
Enjoyment	* (summit ruined by military base)
Ascent	120m from Artemis trail
Time	Circular walk of summit with detour to top takes 1–1½hrs
Water	Café and toilets open year-round at visitor centre
Accommodation	Three campsites in National Park
Getting there	Hire cars are ludicrously cheap in Cyprus. Olympus is well served by roads from all main cities on Greek Cypriot side; close to junction between B8 and B9 roads and well signposted. Follow road up to summit from visitor centre. On route you will see wooden sign for 'Artemis' trail; park here.
Public transport	Simplest way to reach Olympus by bus is to book on excursion with tour operator in any of major resorts. Make sure you have plenty of time to potter about. Buses run to Troodos but times and services intermittent; taxi from Troodos should be quite reasonable.

No photos! The NATO monitoring station on Mount Olympus

The island of Cyprus has always been part of Europe although, like Rhodes, its proximity to Asian Turkey places it on the periphery of the continent in terms of physical geography. However, its cultural, political and historical ties are soundly aligned with Europe. This certainly remains the case on the larger and 'politically legal' Greek side of the island. Its highest point, conveniently situated on this Greek half, is a slight disappointment. A good tarmac road leads all the way to the top, where unfortunately a NATO golf-ball listening post and military base is situated (the golf ball sits on the actual summit). Photographs are formally not permitted, but people (ourselves included) seem to get away with taking them, in standard tourist fashion. Unless you are a military commander in the Cypriot army or James Bond, you are unlikely ever to stand on the actual highest point outright of Cyprus. For most highpointers a few metres from the summit will have to do. In late January to early March there may be enough snow to allow the ski lifts to open, which would spice up a trip to the mountain. There are six pistes. While the summit can be driven to, we recommend a circular walk in the Troodos National Park around the peak with a quick detour to the top to make a day of it.

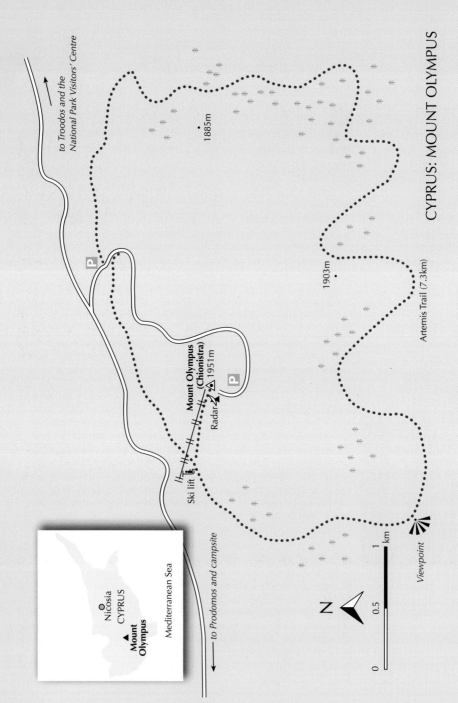

CYPRUS: MOUNT OLYMPUS

to Troodos and the
National Park Visitors' Centre

1885m

1903m

Artemis Trail (7.3km)

Mount Olympus
(Chionistra)
1951m

Radar

Ski lift

to Prodomos and campsite

Mediterranean Sea

Nicosia
CYPRUS

Mount
Olympus

Viewpoint

N

0   0.5   1   km

Piste-less: on the ski run below the summit of Mount Olympus

ROUTE

To make a walk out of this 'drive-up' mountain, we recommend the Artemis trail (7.3km); a map can be obtained from the visitor centre.

Follow the circular Artemis trail anticlockwise (W) below the golf-ball listening post.

After crossing the creek and heading round the promontory, break off to the left (S) following the ski-lift pillars. This will bring you out on a piste which leads up to the E side of the listening post. Walk past the listening post on either the N or S sides, eventually joining the road. This is as high as you can get in Cyprus.

From here wind your way down the piste northwards to rejoin the Artemis trail. Follow the trail anticlockwise around the mountain until meeting the road where you have parked.

OTHER ROUTES

There are plenty of other marked trails in the National Park. Mountain biking up the mountain from the base would be a tremendous challenge and quite a satisfying ascent. Mountain bikes can be hired at various locations on the island. From Limassol a cycle ride to Olympus could be done in a day, but this would be a colossal undertaking and two days would be more realistic.

Caught out! Aphrodite's birthplace at Petra tou Romiou

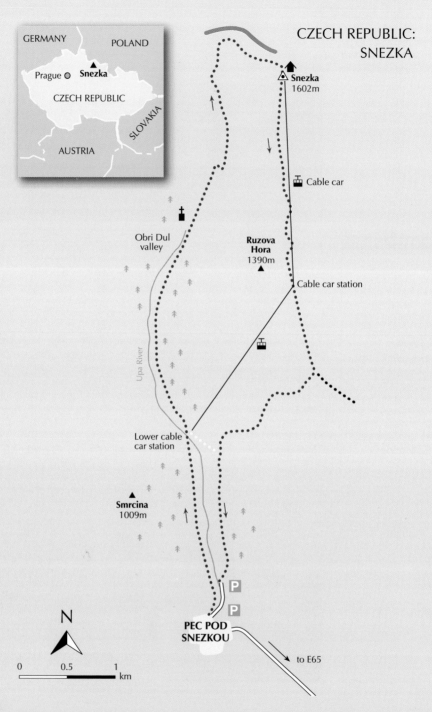

CZECH REPUBLIC:
SNEZKA

GERMANY

POLAND

Prague ⊙ **Snezka**

CZECH REPUBLIC

SLOVAKIA

AUSTRIA

△ **Snezka**
1602m

🚡 Cable car

Obri Dul
valley

**Ruzova
Hora**
1390m
▲

Cable car station

Upa River

Lower cable
car station

Smrcina
1009m

P

P

**PEC POD
SNEZKOU**

to E65

N

0   0.5   1
▬▬▬▬▬▬▬▬
                    km

9 CZECH REPUBLIC

SNEZKA 1602M

Location	Karkonosze Mountain range, Bohemia, Northern Czech Republic on Polish border 193km NE of Prague
Start	Pec pod Snezkou
Map(s)	1:50,000 walking maps available from shops and kiosks in Pec pod Snezkou
Equipment	Standard hiking gear
Climbing period	April–November best; avalanche risk in winter months; Pec pod Snezkou a ski centre so plenty of skiing available
Difficulty	2
Enjoyment	***
Ascent	900m
Time	1½hrs ascent, 1hr descent
Water	Café on summit; in summer streams can dry up, so take plenty of water
Accommodation	Possible to stay in old Communist-style hotel on Polish side of summit
Getting there	From Prague follow 10 (E65) N towards Polish border. After passing through town of Desna turn right (E) on 14; follow this for 50km to Mlade Buky. Turn left (N) to Pec pod Snezkou; route starts here. Circular trail possible.
Public transport	Easy to get to Karkonosze National Park in summer. Train from Prague to Trutnov via Hradec Kralove and Jaomer; from Trutnov bus to Pec pod Snezkou.
Nearest high points	Gerlachovsky (Slovakia), Rysy (Poland)

Snezka from the Polish side (Milan a Zaneta)

63

With a post office, hotel and café on the summit, Snezka is not a remote or challenging peak. It does, however, offer splendid views and a relaxing circular walk on good paths. Added to this, you can send a Snezka-stamped postcard from the summit, or even better sample 'acid cucumbers' from the café menu (a brilliant translation of gherkins!). Despite the mountain's rather tame appearance, there remains a sizeable risk of avalanche in winter, especially from the Obri Dul face. A chairlift carries more sedentary Czechs to the top so they can gorge themselves on sausages. We mistakenly opted for a 'delicious' lunch of acid cucumbers accompanied by a little trough of lard in the Czechs' highest café.

ROUTE

There are two primary routes from Pec pod Snezkou to the summit. While the Obri Dul route is described for the ascent and the route over the spine of Ruzova Hora for the descent, there is no reason why you should not swap these around (most people ascend and descend via the Obri Dul valley below the tremendous W face of the mountain).

Follow the W side of the Upa River NW to the **lower cable car station**.

Continue to follow the route NW then N to the chapel at **Obri Dul**. The route crosses to the E side of the Upa River and snakes upwards below the impressive SW face of **Snezka** to the summit ridge.

Once you have met the ridge, and therefore the Polish border, follow the path steeply SE–S until you meet the summit. Here you will find a hotel, a café and a post office. There are a number of monuments and a 'distance from' sign.

Czech side of the Snezka summit in winter

All roads lead to the Slaski Dom: view from the top of Snezka

Descent
Follow the route due S from the summit beneath the chairlift. The path here is clear and well maintained.

The path passes by the summit of **Ruzova Hora** 1390m and the chairlift junction. Continue in a SSE direction to the refuges of Ruzuburky and Sovi Bouda. Here a clear path descends, initially westwards before turning southwards to the Obri Dul valley. You can continue through the forest to **Pec pod Snezkou** or descend to the valley floor and rejoin your ascent route at the cable car station.

OTHER ROUTES
It is possible to ascend the mountain from the Polish side. Go to Wroclaw, then on to Jelenia Gora, and from there to the mountain town of Karpacz.

From Karpacz follow the Lomniczka River S. The route begins on the W side of the river. After 1km cross to the E side of the river. The route stays with the river all the way to the summit ridge.

Once you have met the ridge, and therefore the Czech border, follow the path steeply SE–S to reach the summit.

DENMARK: MØLLEHØJ

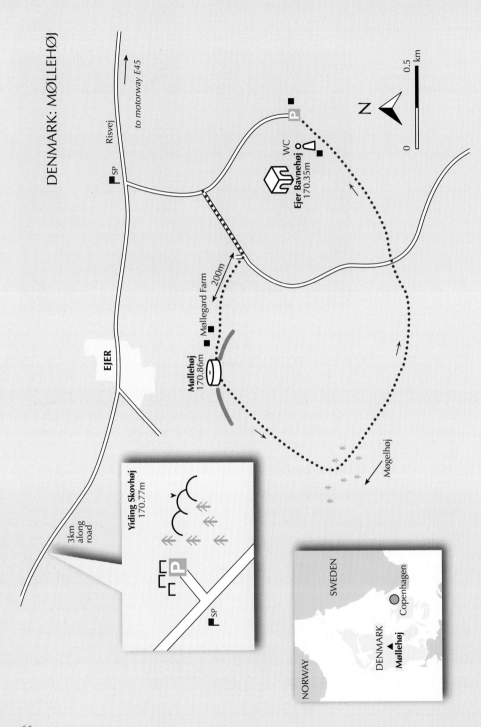

to motorway E45

Risvej

SP

EJER

3km along road

Yiding Skovhøj
170.77m

P

SP

Møllehøj
170.86m

Møllegard Farm

200m

P

WC

Ejer Bavnehøj
170.35m

Mogelhøj

N

0   0.5   km

NORWAY

SWEDEN

DENMARK
Møllehøj

Copenhagen

Location	Jutland (continental Denmark), North Horsens, S of Arhus
Start	Møllehøj
Map(s)	Good road map; maps showing circular walk from Ejer Bavnehøj to Møllehøj available at information point on Ejer Bavnehøj
Equipment	None
Climbing period	Year-round
Difficulty	1
Enjoyment	*** So ridiculous is the controversy over Denmark's highest point that much fun can be had visiting all three sites
Ascent	20m
Time	3mins
Water	Toilet and restaurant at Ejer Bavnehøj
Accommodation	Plenty of campsites in area
Getting there	Take junction 54 off E45. Follow signs W for 0.6km to Ejer Bavnehøj and park.
Public transport	Train to Horsens, from where bus service to Ejer and Ostbirk

If getting to the highest point of each country sometimes makes you feel like you are a playing an enormous board game, then the hunt for Denmark's high ground will do little to lessen that feeling. One has to hand it to the Danes: although their high point is – with the exception of Monaco and the Vatican – the lowest in Europe, they are very proud of it. They have gone to great lengths to ensure that visitors stand on the exact hallowed spot, measuring down to the last centimetre.

If only every country was as thorough with its national high point as Denmark! The Danes' highest point has been in dispute between three locations all in the same area. For many years Ejer Bavnehøj (170.35m), less than 300m from Møllehøj (170.86m), was regarded as the highest natural point in Denmark. Subsequently the Danes built a giant viewing tower on its summit, complete with a lift for the disabled. Then some bright spark in early 2005 worked out that a farmer's hill nearby was actually a whopping 49cm higher! Subsequently Møllehøj was recognised as the official highest point of Denmark. Yding Skovhøj, a burial mound in some nearby woods, attains a height of 173m. Ah ha, you might think, then it is higher. But the Danes are real sticklers and have a separate measurement for the 'man-made land' of the burial mound and the 'natural land' beneath. Recent research has shown that Yding Skovhøj's natural land lies an incredible 9cm lower than Møllehøj at 170.77m. Why an ancient burial mound is not, after many centuries, regarded as part of the land is hard to fathom, but we trust the Danes' logic and cite Møllehøj as the highest point. Nonetheless, bearing in mind the miniscule differences in height and the proximity of the three locations, we strongly recommend visiting all three in case the Danes change their minds – and all three points have signs stating they are the highest point in Denmark!

DISPUTE

Some sources may cite the highest point in Denmark as being on the Faeroe Islands. The Faeroes are a crown dependency of Denmark and therefore do not fit the European high point criteria (see What is Europe? in the Introduction). Their highest point is Slaettaratindur 882m.

ROUTE

After a brief ascent of the steps up the monument of **Ejer Bavnehøj** you will see some farm buildings 200m W; 5km further NW you will see **Yding Forest**. The panoramic viewing plaque on Ejer Bavnehøj marks them both. Follow the track down to a wooden gate.

Head up towards the farm building. You may have to negotiate a small electric fence which has been put in place to segregate the cows, but you are allowed to walk here.

On the S side of the barns there is a millstone. This is Møllehøj, the highest point of Denmark. From here the knoll with trees on it 200m S (confusingly named Møgelhøj) appears higher. It is not, but walk over there anyway if you choose.

Rachel (and the highest cows in Denmark) on Møllehøj, with Møgelhøj beyond

It's all green to me: atop the ancient burial mound of Yding Skovhøj

Descent
By the same route.

OTHER ROUTES
To reach **Yding Skovhøj** leave the car park and follow the Risvej road W for 3.5km towards the forest. Here you will see a sign for Yding Skovhøj and a couple of picnic benches on your right. Head into the wood a short distance and search for the highest ground. You will find three burial mounds. The highest is the central one, Yding Skovhøj. It is very overgrown but has no trees on it.

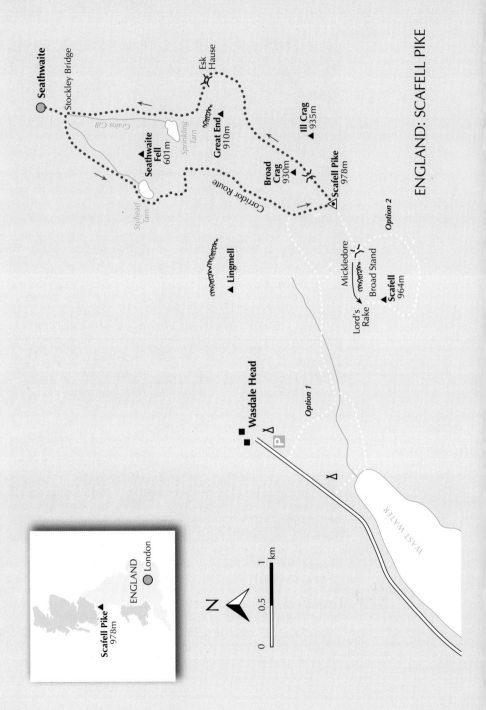

ENGLAND: SCAFELL PIKE

Seathwaite
Stockley Bridge
Grains Gill
Esk Hause
Sprinkling Tarn
Great End 910m
Seathwaite Fell 601m
Styhead Tarn
Corridor Route
Broad Crag 930m
Ill Crag 935m
Scafell Pike 978m
Lingmell
Option 2
Mickledore
Broad Stand
Lord's Rake
Scafell 964m
Wasdale Head
Option 1
WAST WATER

ENGLAND
London

Scafell Pike 978m

N

0   0.5   1
km

Scafell Pike 978m

11 ENGLAND

SCAFELL PIKE 978M

Not to be confused with its sister peak Scafell 964m

Location	Lake District, Cumbria, NW England
Start	Seathwaite
Map(s)	Ordnance Survey 1:25,000 Outdoor Leisure 6 (SW) and Outdoor Leisure 4 1:25,000 (NW) or 1:50,000 Ordnance Survey The Lake District
Equipment	Standard hiking gear
Climbing period	Year-round
Difficulty	2
Enjoyment	****
Ascent	850m
Time	From Seathwaite 2–2½hrs ascent, 2–2½hrs descent via Great End
Water	Plenty on route
Accommodation	Campsite at Seathwaite; Lake District has many youth hostels (red triangles on OS maps)
Getting there	Take M6 to Junction 40; then A66 westbound to Keswick, coming off at first turning. Follow signs for Seatoller/Rosthwaite on B6289 which follows E side of Derwentwater southwards up Borrowdale. Turn off left (S) before Seatoller, signed Seathwaite. Park here (spaces hard to come by on summer weekends).
Public transport	Penrith is on West Coast mainline and well served by train; bus to Keswick, then another to Seatoller in Borrowdale (service times vary with seasons)
Nearest high points	Ben Nevis (Scotland), Mount Snowdon (Wales)

Set in the splendid Lake District National Park, Scafell Pike offers a number of good hikes in what we consider Britain's most beautiful area. Rugged crags and fells rise magnificently from the numerous lakes and tarns which punctuate the region in such a picturesque manner as to leave the hiker with the suspicion that they may well be walking through a series of living watercolours. Whatever the weather the Lake District defines beauty, and although rainfall figures are high the region is deservedly regarded as the jewel in the crown of the English landscape. Guaranteed to fill the soul with glee (if not a little rainwater) it is quite understandable how those two poetic revolutionaries, Coleridge and Wordsworth, found themselves compelled to express their new Romantic form of poetry in this Lakeland country. While such a rewarding landscape draws hordes of tourists to the villages in the National Park all year round, walks in the hills remain far less populated and are infinitely more pleasurable experiences.

The location of Scafell Pike is a good one. Visitors on clear days are rewarded with spectacular views outwards across the Irish Sea to the Isle of Man and Ireland, and inwards to the heart of the Lake District's many splendid peaks. As Scafell Pike is served by a number of

Scafell Pike (centre), Scafell (right) and Wastwater from Yewbarrow Fell

excellent footpaths and can be ascended from all directions, a circular route is described here which is slightly less crowded and so more enjoyable. If you are tempted by a detour to Scafell (see Other Routes) the fastest and most straightforward route up the mountain is recommended, leaving from Wasdale Head at the northern end of Wast Water via the col at Lingmell.

Note For those interested in good face climbing, the Lake District has an abundance of excellent multi-pitch routes at all standards (see Appendix 5, Further Reading).

ROUTE

From Seathwaite follow the path southwards on the E side of the river to **Stockley Bridge**, which is reached after 1000m.

At the bridge the path splits. Take the westward path as it climbs steeply up from the river. Eventually join and cross the Styhead River before reaching Styhead Tarn.

From **Styhead Tarn** continue to the head of the valley. Care is needed here in poor visibility as the route can be easily lost. Trend W for 150m. Here the path splits. Take the traverse 'Corridor Route' which trends southwards.

There is a short steep scrambled descent before the path starts to head southwestwards to meet the head of Piers Gill. Here a steep scree-covered path rises to your left. Go past this until you meet a small wall. The path fades out until reaching a T-junction with the Wast Water ascent via Hollow Stones.

Turn left (SSE) following the clear well-cairned path to the summit of **Scafell Pike**. The summit is marked by a large circular cairn which has a war memorial to 'Those men of the Lake District who fell for God and King, for Freedom, Peace and Right in the Great War 1914–1918'. The second-highest mountain in England (Scafell 964m) is 1km SW of you.

Well done! Get yourself back to Keswick for a pint of Jennings ale!

Descent

From the summit follow the path northeastwards steeply down to the col between Scafell Pike and Broad Crag.

Follow the path upwards and over the shoulder of **Broad Crag**, passing between the summit pillar of Broad Crag and **Ill Crag** on the SE side. The terrain is briefly quite angular here.

Trend NE towards **Great End**. When the path clearly forks after 800m take the right-hand fork eastwards down a clear and stepped path to the col of **Esk Hause**. Follow the path downhill NNE for 300m.

Take the clear path northwestwards downhill. This will pass beneath the impressive face of Great End, a good spot for winter ice climbing but only rarely possible these days as a result of global warming.

Roughly 400m before reaching **Sprinkling Tarn** take a clear path north-eastwards down **Grains Gill** to Seathwaite via **Stockley Bridge**.

View of Scafell Pike from just above Broad Stand

OTHER ROUTES

Start	Wasdale Head
Enjoyment	***
Ascent	700m
Time	1½–2hrs ascent, 1hr descent
Accommodation	Campsite and inn at Wasdale Head
Getting there	Wast Water is particularly laborious to reach. By car take junction 36 off M6 and A590 W via Ulverston to Grenodd. Take the A5092 to Grizebeck, then A595 to Gubbergill near Seascale, then minor road right to Irton. Follow signs to Nether Wasdale, then Wasdale Head and Wast Water. Free car park at N end of lake by Wasdale Head Inn.

OPTION 1 FROM WASDALE HEAD

ROUTE
From **Wasdale Head** follow the road S for 300m.

Take the path signed Scafell Pike ESE for a further 300m until crossing the river. The path then trends SSE to Lingmell Gill.

At Brown Tongue the path forks. On ascent take the right-hand fork to **Mickledore**. The upper reaches of the route to Mickledore are steep and a little scree-worn. The impressive crags of both Scafell and Scafell Pike border your ascent to the right and left respectively.

The Mickledore saddle is small and unmistakable. To your right (SW) you will see the tricky **Broad Stand**, a minor but troublesome crag which prevents easy ascents of England's second-highest peak (see Scafell below). For **Scafell Pike** follow the cairned path NE toward to the summit.

Descent
Follow the alternative route northwestwards to Lingmell Col and continue to follow the clear stepped path westwards back to Wasdale Head.

OPTION 2 TO SCAFELL 961M
While no natural route up Scafell Pike should go via Scafell, many walkers will be tempted by a brief visit to the summit of Scafell, England's second-highest mountain. Because a 'brief' visit has often led walkers into great difficulty, some short notes on Scafell are provided here.

Having ascended to the summit of Scafell Pike, a cursory glance at an OS map may suggest a quick ascent of Scafell via Mickledore. Hikers should be warned that the direct route from Mickledore involves the ascent of Broad Stand.

Broad Stand is a very short but tricky enough climb. Due to the polished nature of the footholds, the exposure of one move and the potential of flash sweeps of rain, Broad Stand should not be climbed without the back-up of at least a 10m rope and two cams of variant size in order to arrest a slip. Too many hikers have been embarrassed by the need for rescue from this 'scramble', and too many more have slipped and fallen to severe injury or death.

Begin by entering the obvious narrow crack in the face at the Mickledore col. Once you emerge from the crack, scramble up to the left on smooth holds before rounding the edge of the slab and ascending again on smooth holds to a slanting plateau and square recess. Most accidents occur on the tricky climb off this. Either climb the overhanging right corner or use the very smooth crack on the left end of the plateau, ideally placing a cam or two in the crack to arrest a slip. From here an easy scramble up the gully and ridge lead to the summit plateau. The summit of **Scafell** is marked by a large cairn and excellent views of the Irish Sea, the Isle of Man, Ireland and Scafell Pike are offered on clear days.

An alternative technically easier and safer way up and down Scafell goes via Foxes tarn. Descend steeply down the scree path southeast from Mickledore losing a frustrating 120m of height until a cairned path breaks off right. Ascend this southwest until reaching Foxes Tarn (the smallest named tarn in the Lakes). Continue to follow the cairns to the large summit cairn.

Deep Gill, a steep scree-filled rake, offers a viable descent down the north face from the summit plateau (not recommended in ascent). It can be found 250m NNE of the summit cairn and is, itself, marked by a cairn. It is not much fun on the feet but does remove the re-ascent to Mickledore. In the lower section of the gill follow the obvious path off left which bypasses the worst of the gully.

The famous Lord's Rake ascent and descent is still marked on 1:25000 Ordnance Survey maps, but due to recent rockfall it is unreliable and discouraged.

Note There is a faint traverse path below Scafell Pike crag from the base of the Mickledore screes to the saddle between Ling Fell and the Pike handy for those returning to Seathwaite.

ESTONIA: SUUR MUNAMAGI

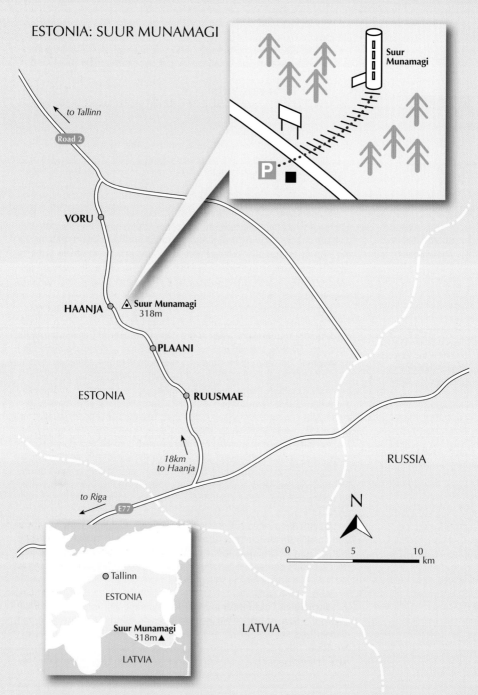

to Tallinn
Road 2

VORU

Suur Munamagi
318m

HAANJA

PLAANI

ESTONIA

RUUSMAE

18km
to Haanja

to Riga
E77

Suur
Munamagi

RUSSIA

N

0   5   10
km

Tallinn

ESTONIA

Suur Munamagi
318m▲

LATVIA

LATVIA

SUUR MUNAMAGI 318M

Location	SE corner of Estonia, S of Voru just off main Riga–St Petersburg road (E77)
Start	Haanja
Map(s)	Good road map of Baltic States
Equipment	None
Climbing period	Year-round
Difficulty	1
Enjoyment	*
Ascent	30m
Time	3mins
Water	Café in the tower
Accommodation	Campsite in Haanja
Getting there	From Riga on E77 turn left (NE) 4km after Estonian border on road to Ruusmae; unsurfaced after 2km, but remains excellent. After 6km reach Ruusmae; continue N to Plaani, then 8km to Haanja. Just as sign for Hannja reached, note café and parking area left. Park here.
Public transport	From Voru on main Baltic rail network take bus to Haanja via Soodja; if not running taxi would be reasonable
Nearest high points	Gaizinkalns (Latvia), Aukstojas/Juozapine Kalnas (Lithuania)

Of the three Baltic peaks, this one surely has the most enticing name: literally translated it means 'big egg mountain'. It is also the most tourist-friendly, complete with a newly built light-house-style tower on the top and a café. Disappointingly there is no plaque or trig point other than the tower, and the surrounding forest prohibits views unless you pay to go up. Nearby are walking trails, picnic areas, skiing in winter and a campsite. Although not the most memorable high point you will visit, it is a pleasant enough excursion.

ROUTE

Across the road from the car park you will see an information board with prices and opening times of the summit tower (the tower is hidden in the woods). Go up the obvious paved footpath to the summit, passing by an impressive carved wooden troll. There is no view unless you pay to go up the tower.

The tower is open: 1 April to 31 August, 10am–8pm every day; 1 September to 31 October, 10am–5pm every day; 1 November to 31 March, 12–3pm weekends only.

Descent

By the same route.

Famous natives
Kristina Smigun, the first Estonian woman to win a Winter Olympic gold medal, she did so in cross country skiing.

Irrelevant fact
Estonians keep winning the world wife-carrying championships, held in Finland. They have won every year since the event's inauguration in 1997, mainly due to the skill of that well-known master wife-carrier Margo Uusorg!

A long way from the sea: the lighthouse-style tower of Suur Munamagi

Also known as Haldi

Kingdom of snow: the frozen summit of Halti

Location	Most NW point of Finland on Norwegian border; 120km ESE of Tromso; near Kilpisjarvi (Finland) and Skibotn (Norway)
Start	Guolasjavri Lake
Map(s)	Raisduottarhaldi Norge 1:50,000 1733IV – order before travelling to Finland. May be available from Sten Oil petrol station on E6 S of Skibotn.
Equipment	Standard hiking gear
Climbing period	Mid-June to mid-October suitable. In March and October especially very high chance of seeing aurora borealis; in June sun will not set.
Difficulty	3 (navigation and angular terrain)
Enjoyment	***
Ascent	550m
Time	4½–6½hrs ascent, 4–6hrs descent
Water	Last permanent water at start of route
Accommodation	Possible to stay in small bothy at trailhead: visitor's book, stove, but only two beds. Sami reindeer herders generally very friendly and helpful – no problems camping. Skibotn a good base with chalets and campsites.
Getting there	From Skibotn – where E8 meets E6 (two petrol stations, supermarket with stuffed wolves inside, plenty of campsites and chalets, bank) – drive N

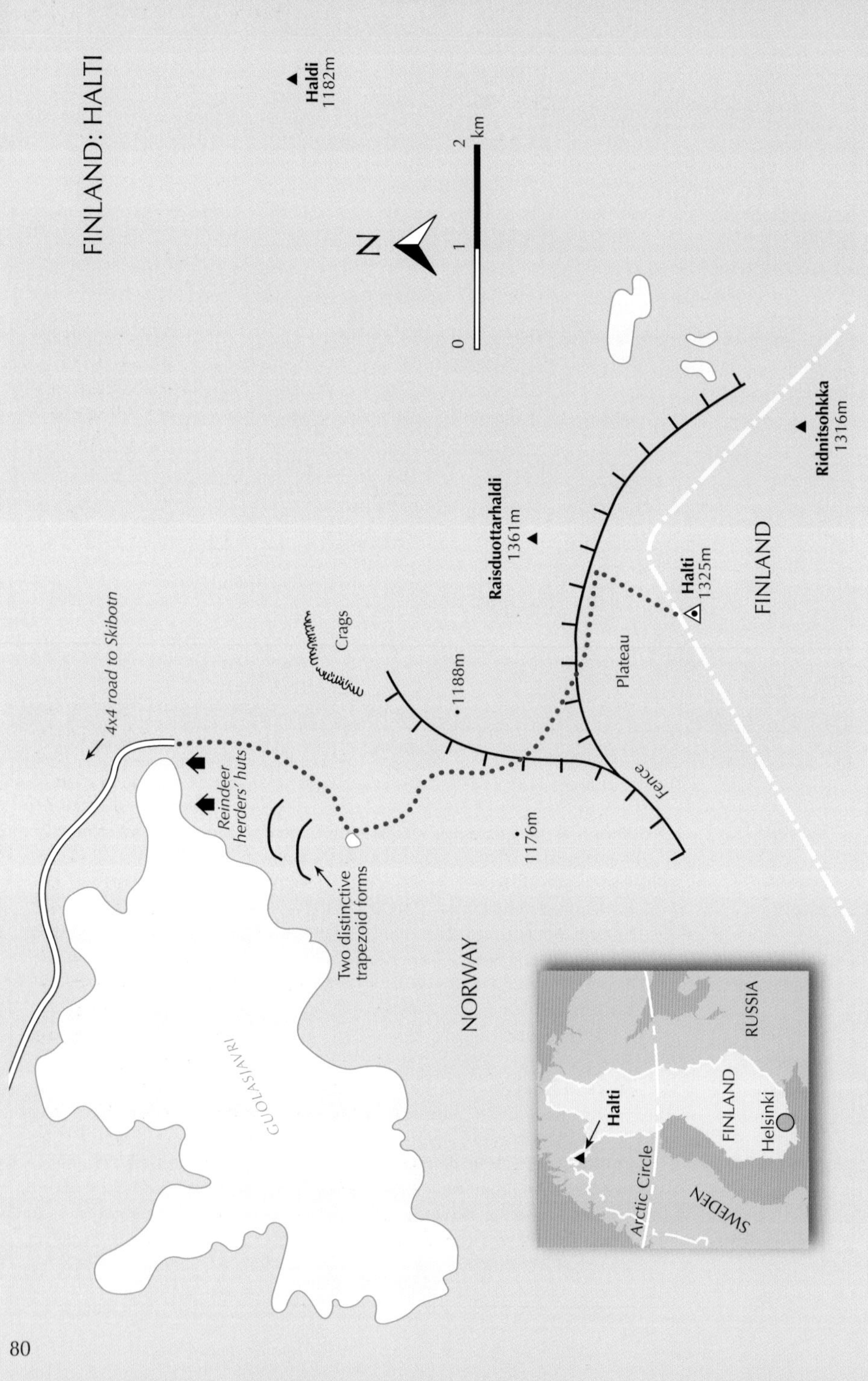

FINLAND: HALTI

Haldi
1182m

N

0   1   2 km

4x4 road to Skibotn

Reindeer
herders' huts

Two distinctive
trapezoid forms

Crags

Raisduottarhaldi
1361m

•1188m

Fence

Plateau

Halti
1325m

•1176m

GUOLASJAVRI

NORWAY

FINLAND

Ridnitsohka
1316m

SWEDEN

Arctic Circle

Halti

FINLAND

RUSSIA

Helsinki

Public transport

along E6 to Odden, then SE to very small town of Britavarre (petrol station, shop for last-minute supplies). Leave E6 at Britavarre and turn S to Ankerlia and Guolasjavri (lake); road quickly turns into a high-quality unsurfaced track which winds up Guolasjohka (valley), passing over dramatic wooden canyon bridge (from Britavarre c25km). Guolasjavri Lake is reached eventually; road forks. Take left fork (small sign marks Halti 6km away – actually c8km). After 300m reach excellent well-equipped emergency shelter. Continue around lake to trailhead to find two bothies used by reindeer farmers in spring/autumn (also large herds of reindeer). Park here. Fly to Tromso or Andselv in Norway; from Tromso buses run year-round to Skibotn, from where various buses run N along E06 via Britavarre; likewise buses run N through Britavarre from Andselv. If approaching from Kebnekaise, catch train from Kiruna to Narvik. Norway's internal railway terminates at Bode, though good bus links to Narvik. Buses run N from Narvik along E06 to Britavarre. Taxi, hitchhiking or walking only options to reach trailhead from Britivarre. If hitchhiking, do not end up on SW side of lake. Alternatively, Kilpisjavri can be reached by bus from Tromso via Skibotn (mid-June to September).

Nearest high point   Kebnekaise (Sweden)

Three hundred miles inside the Arctic Circle, Halti is the most northerly national high point in the world. There is not a tree to be seen here, but the barren sub-Arctic landscape is as insuppressibly endearing as it is desolate. The odd herd of reindeer and even the occasional herder might be encountered near the lake at the foot of the mountain; but once that is left behind Halti provides a brief foray into true wilderness. While a cursory glance at a map suggests this is an easy peak because of the short ascent and distance, reality is another matter. Unfortunately the terrain on Halti is characterised by perhaps the worst ankle-breaking boulderfields we have ever encountered, and progress can be very frustrating. Nonetheless exceptional views of the massive Guolasjavri and Pitsusjavri lakes tend to lift the spirits whenever heads are raised from the tedious task of carefully placing every footstep.

The summit is difficult to separate from the broad rolling debris of the higher Raisduottarhaldi in Norway (1361m), and as such route-finding can be exceptionally difficult. The highest part of Halti is actually in Norway, spitting distance from the border stone – though when you get there you will realise this is truly splitting hairs. There exists no dispute for the Finns in regards to Halti; with its fantastic views and remote setting, it is unequivocally regarded as the highest mountain in Finland. The summit of the nearby Ridnitsohkka (1316m), the country's second-highest mountain, is the highest entirely in Finland and is not too difficult to visit. There are two essential routes up Halti. From the Finnish side a well-marked trail punctuated by refuges takes three to four days to hike to the summit and return. However, from the Norwegian side the summit can be ascended in one day. The latter route is described below.

Note If you are trying to get up the track to Guolasjavri Lake in early or late season you may require a 4x4 car and winter tyres (snow chains are not permitted on public roads in Scandinavia).

In the height of summer there should be no trouble getting to the trailhead by ordinary car (though watch your exhaust). In winter months the route is only passable by snowmobile.

Note Due to the geographical location of this mountain, the climber should be prepared for extreme weather conditions and serious night-time temperature drops, especially in early and late season. Navigation is very difficult on Halti and accurate compass reading a must. Acknowledge the position of Magnetic North, which differs greatly from True North due to the proximity of the North Pole. The area is susceptible to white-out, freezing wind, freezing fog and blizzards. Pleasant sunny days can disappear in minutes. Avoid the assumption that climbing Raisduottarhaldi first, or following the ridge, will be easier – it will not. Please note that many hikers have been lured in the direction of Ridnitsohkka (1316m) because that mountain has a large pole on it. Avoid this common error by simply not descending at all.

ROUTE

From the small bothy walk 50m SE to a makeshift gate in the fence. There is a faint farm track here which soon runs out. Follow this SW and continue, remaining within close sight of the two large **trapezoid crags** (852m and 898m), until you reach a very small **lake** (grid ref: 078 925). This may be frozen or snow-covered, and is your last clear natural marker.

From the lake ascend in an exact SE direction. You will soon encounter the ankle-breaking boulder terrain that blights all of Halti and the surrounding peaks. Aim to pass between the spot heights of **1176m** and **1188m**. The 1176m rise is more distinctive, and has a thin white cairn, which can be seen as you gain height (if in doubt err ESE). Continuing in this direction you should eventually intersect the legendary **reindeer fence** – a potential lifesaver.

This fence will lead you to the pass between the Norwegian and Finnish Haldi/Halti. Even in good visibility do not lose sight of it. In poor visibility you should virtually cling to it (while terrain at the fence is awful, it is no better anywhere else). Follow the fence, which will seem to lead you too far S–SW. The fence eventually forks, with one part heading SSW, the route you need to follow heading upwards E–ESE. In good visibility you will be able to identify the worst of the fence's downhill dogleg and head it off.

Follow the left fork of the fence E-ESE to the plateau. In poor visibility your guard against getting lost is to stop if the fence starts to descend. You should now be within 100m of the small ponds marked on the plateau; these, even in summer, are difficult to identify. Straight ahead on an ESE bearing are the three lakes below the 1124m spot height. **Raisduottarhaldi** is on your left (N-NNW), and difficult to distinguish from its rolling plateau. Turn right (S-SSE) and keep to the SE-facing ridge in poor visibility. Continue over difficult slow boulders/snow for 800m. The summit cairns cannot be seen until you are within 30m. Make sure you do not go too far along the ridge (if you start to descend you are going wrong).

The summit of **Halti** is marked by a very large yellow-painted cairn. On top of this is a boundary stone with Suomi (Finland) carved into it and its Rr 303 B marker. Very close by is a large metal box holding a visitors' book. Surprisingly many people have made this intrepid journey, more often from the

Finnish side; our numbers were 81376 and 81377. Simply leave your name, nationality and number; do not take up unnecessary space. Despite these high numbers we have been up the mountain twice and not seen a soul.

Descent
In poor visibility descend the way you came up. In good weather simply leave the summit on a NNW bearing until you intersect the fence.

With good visibility in summer, – and especially if you have extended your walk to reach **Ridnitsohkka** 5km to the SE – the terrain in the Huortnasvaggi (valley) N of **Raisduottarhaldi** is far easier going than the debris field of the mountain proper. Traverse round the E face of Raisduottarhaldi, taking care not to descend to Hajit Lake.

OTHER ROUTES

KILPISJAVRI–HALTI

Map(s)	Halti, Kilpisjavri (1:50,000, Genimap, Wsoy Ulkoilukartat)
Time	3–4 days
Distance	98km (round trip)
Getting there	Kilpisjavri is on E08 (21) between Skibotn and Muonio

From the Finnish side you can procure a map from Kilpisjavri petrol station – though we strongly recommend purchasing one before setting off, or at other petrol stations on route, as these can sell out. A small tourist office in the village is open in summer, and there are plenty of chalets and suchlike. From late October to April Kilpisjavri is virtually a ghost town as most inhabitants migrate S for the winter. If the tourist office is closed try the customs house outside of town on the border with Norway where, with a small deposit, you can gain keys to the many refuges on route. It is possible to shorten the excessive hike from Kilpisjavri to Halti by flying from Kilpisjavri Lake to Pitsusjavri Lake, but this service is not regular; enquire at the tourist office in the town.

Guolasjavri Lake with the Halti massif beyond

Mont Blanc from the Grand Montet, near the Petit Verte (Greg Parsons)

14 FRANCE AND ITALY

MONT BLANC/MONTE BIANCO 4808M

See Serious Ascents in the Introduction

Location	Mont Blanc towers over towns of Chamonix in SE France and Courmayeur in Italy
Start	Nid d'Aigle
Map(s)	IGN 1:25,000 sheets 3531ET St Gervais les Bains and 3630OT Chamonix Mont Blanc; former shows Gouter route (both maps place summit in France: see below). Sheet 107 1:25,000 Monte Bianco Massif, Instituto Geografico Centrale (places summit on border).
Equipment	Full alpine gear
Climbing period	June, July and August best, but most crowded
Difficulty	5 Gouter route PD with climbing to II and 40° snow. Grand Mulets F.
Enjoyment	*****
Ascent	1500m from mountain railway station to Gouter hut; 1050m to summit
Time	6–7hrs Nid d'Aigle to Gouter hut, 4–5hrs to summit
Water	Due to popularity of mountain and al fresco toilet facilities at huts, do not drink natural water below Gouter hut. Take plenty and buy water at huts. Huts are manned May–September, with a small area left open in winter.
Accommodation	Tourist information office in Chamonix, plus mountain tourist office; nights at refuges can be reserved here. Places reserved months in advance, but confirmation system applies and bed space can arise at short notice. Any refuge booking restricts climber to set climbing period (better to wait and see what weather is doing; mountain weather reports in both tourist offices in Chamonix, in Argentiere's tourist office and top ticket office on Nid'Aigle railway).
Getting there	Chamonix has railway station; good bus services throughout the Chamonix valley. From Chamonix two choices to start of route: a) drive or take bus c30km to Le Fayet or St Gervais les Bains (free car park) from where mountain railway to Nid d'Aigle departs; b) drive or take bus for 10km to Les Houches cable car (connects with mountain railway). Start from Nid d'Aigle station.
	Note Mountain railway very popular with day-trippers so don't be surprised if you cannot get on first available train, especially in descent; booking certain trains possible
Nearest high points	Dufourspitze (Switzerland), Chemin des Revoires (Monaco)

The grand monsieur of Europe, Mont Blanc was the birthplace of mountaineering. Its majestic snow-draped summit is a siren call to the hearts and ambitions of Europe's would-be mountaineers that is impossible to ignore. An ascent of this particular peak – unlike any other on our European high points list (and perhaps like no other in the world) – will change forever the

Mont Blanc's west face (Greg Parsons)

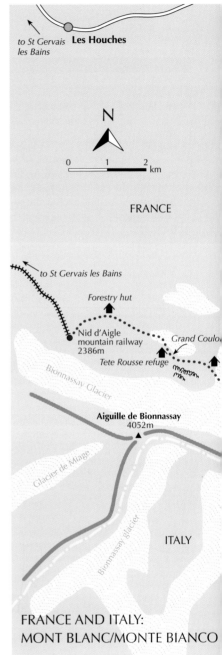

climber's understanding and perception of mountaineering. It is possible to climb far higher, and to tackle far more difficult and technical peaks, but Mont Blanc lies at the very roots of mountaineering. The mountain fascinates just as much today as in the 18th century when the clamour for its first ascent – achieved by Gabriel Paccard and Jacques Balmat in August 1786 – encouraged the pursuit of mountaineering.

Mont Blanc can challenge the mountaineer to brave steep forbidding slopes and knife-edge ridges, often needing to beat a path through dramatic blizzards and sudden tumultuous storms, or dodge violent rockfalls and leap crevasses. For the mountaineer who overcomes these challenges there awaits the glistening prize of the unmarked summit. There is something poetic in the absence of a summit marker: Mont Blanc towers over everything around it and while the summit is small, it is unmistakable. You could almost imagine the summit uttering in a husky French accent: 'I am the summit of Mont Blanc – I do not require an introduction.' Mont Blanc is ultimately a mountain of great personality. Although you might be among the hordes that flock to its slopes aspiring to reach the summit, you can feel quite humbled by its vast snowy expanse.

In good weather Mont Blanc can present climbers with a pleasant and straightforward ascent which will leave them wondering how so many people die on the mountain every year. Yet at other times the mountain can unleash an untold wrath upon the poor souls edging up its shoulders. The mountain should not be underestimated and

**FRANCE AND ITALY:
MONT BLANC/MONTE BIANCO**

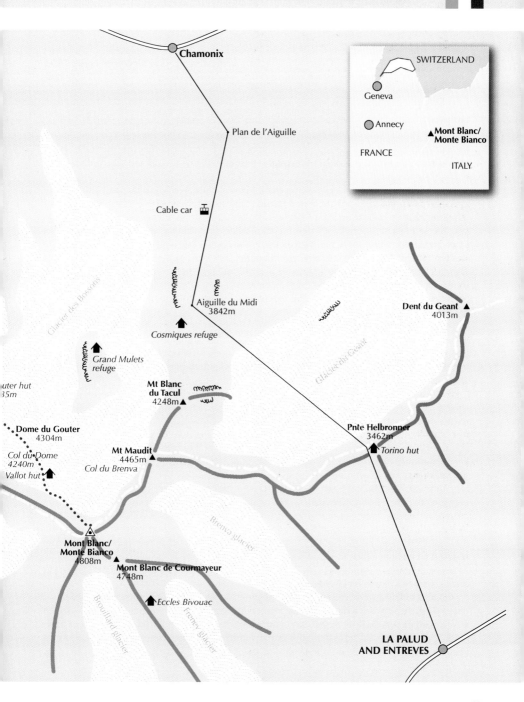

Chamonix

SWITZERLAND

Geneva

Annecy

▲ Mont Blanc/
   Monte Bianco

FRANCE

ITALY

Plan de l'Aiguille

Cable car

Aiguille du Midi
3842m

Dent du Geant ▲
4013m

Cosmiques refuge

*Grand Mulets
refuge*

Glacier des Bossons

Glacier du Geant

uter hut
35m

**Mt Blanc
du Tacul**
4248m ▲

Dome du Gouter
4304m

Pnte Helbronner
3462m
Torino hut

Col du Dome
4240m
Vallot hut ◀

Mt Maudit
4465m
Col du Brenva

Brenva glacier

**Mont Blanc/
Monte Bianco**
4808m

Mont Blanc de Courmayeur
4748m

▲ *Eccles Bivouac*

Brouillard glacier

Freney glacier

**LA PALUD
AND ENTREVES**

weather reports should be treated with caution. We set out to the summit following a prediction of excellent weather only to be met with a vicious storm which had to be sat out in the Vallot emergency shelter before our ascent could be completed. Mont Blanc has a knack of surprising its mountaineers.

DISPUTE

The designation of Italy's highest point has, in some quarters, become farcical. Essentially, most Italians view their highest mountain as 'Monte Bianco'. In our view, they are correct to do so. However, as confusion persists it is necessary to explore the issues and the oft-cited claims to Italy's highest point.

The highest point in Italy is by rights Mont Blanc (Monte Bianco). When Italy attained the majority of its unification in 1861 it was agreed at the Turin Convention that year that the summit of Mont Blanc would be shared between France and the newly unified Italy. Italian mapping shows a shared summit, but over time the French mountaineering community has sought to claim the summit wholly for France. On French maps the border follows Mont Blanc's western ridge to 4740m before curving around the cliff faces of the Italian side (reaching its highest point at Mont Blanc de Courmayeur, 4748m). Subsequently modern French mapping shows the summit to be entirely within French territory. In defence of the French, Mont Blanc (the world – outside Italy – refers to the mountain by its French name) is culturally very much a French mountain. It was the French who initially concerned themselves with its ascent. It was two Frenchmen, Paccard and Balmat, who first scaled its heights. These two – along with Horace Bénédict de Saussure who put up the reward for the first ascent and was the third person to climb it – paved the way for modern mountaineering. In addition, ascents from the Italian side are severely technical and prohibitive, and the three primary ascent routes all approach the summit from France.

Even if French mapping is viewed as the be all and end all of Mont Blanc, the question as to whether Mont Blanc de Courmayeur can be regarded as an individual peak is a matter of opinion and definition. The UIAA (Union Internationale des Associations d'Alpinisme, essentially the closest thing to a mountaineering governing body), now regards Mont Blanc de Courmayeur as a summit in its own right, but in reality it is little more than an 18m raised knobble on a tributary shoulder of Mont Blanc proper. Viewing the point as a distinct mountain is debatable.

Some sources choose Gran Paradiso (4061m) as Italy's highest mountain. While there are ample higher border points than Gran Paradiso (regardless of which country's mapping is referred to), Paradiso remains the highest mountain and mountain massif with its summit entirely in Italy. It is undoubtedly a great alpine mountain which lives up to its name (Great Paradise) by leading climbers up the pleasant waterfall-bordered hike of its lower hills to the thrilling exposed rocky ridge of the summit (marked by a mini Madonna statue and an unmarked snow area further along). Regardless of the high point dispute, it is a very good acclimatisation and practice peak for an ascent of Mont Blanc (see Some Disputed High Points).

Finally, if the French mapping is adhered to and Mont Blanc de Courmayeur dismissed on the grounds that it is not a mountain, the highest undisputed shared summit in Italy is Nordend (4609m) on the Monte Rosa massif. Nordend is an exceptional fairytale peak. When seen from the summit of Dufourspitze (4634m) it is difficult to believe the mountain is real, let alone assailable. Over 100m of ascent separates Nordend from the Dufourspitze ridge. On all maps

The popular acclimatisation peak of Mont Blanc du Tacul (Greg Parsons)

the Swiss/Italian border goes directly across its summit. Information which refers to the summit of Monte Rosa/Dufourspitze as partly in Italy is inaccurate; the highest summit of Monte Rosa is entirely inside Switzerland. The highest point of the Dufourspitze ridge – which touches the Italian border – is known as Grenzgipfel (4618m), but this is not a peak in its own right.

Note The Gouter route is described below as the primary route as the Grand Mulets route is not always open due to the poor condition of the glacier. The Gouter route is more dramatic and rewarding. However, a descent via the Grand Mulets, if open, should be considered.

Note Before attempting to climb Mont Blanc we recommend you climb at least two alpine peaks, one over 3200m and one over 3800m (ideally over 4000m) for acclimatisation purposes. If you are based in Chamonix, mountains such as Petit Mont Blanc, Aiguille de Tour and Mont Blanc de Tacul are suitable. Spending a night at high altitude and then descending will also stand you in good stead. Brush up on your alpine skills – if in doubt there are plenty of short courses available in Chamonix. Likewise, if you intend to bivvy out on the mountain, do not do this for the first time on Mont Blanc.

Most people take two days for the ascent and descent of Mont Blanc, but there is no reason why you should not spend an extra day on the mountain, and if you can allow for extra time your success will not be as dependent on the weather. A further benefit of staying at the Tete Rousse refuge or the forestry hut is that you can cross the extremely dangerous Grand Couloir in the early morning, rather than later on when the chance of rockfall is greater.

ROUTE

From the **Nid d'Aigle station** at 2386m take a track S for 250m before turning off left to head NE up a zigzagging path into a scree gully with a ridge on your left. After around 1.5km reach a small **unmanned forestry hut**. It is possible to stay here but there are limited beds and no facilities. You should be carrying sufficient water as there is no permanent clean water source here.

At the hut turn right (SE), heading over boulderfields to a clear ridge. In good weather you may be able to see the Gouter hut looming more than 1000m above you. It appears deceptively close. Head up the ridge following a clear path until you come to the **Tete Rousse glacier**. On the right-hand side of this is the Tete Rousse hut; you may see many tourists with no equipment crossing the glacier to reach it.

Unless you are staying there, there is no need to go to this hut. Ignore the first tracks across the snow and head a little further up the ridge to a second track bearing SE up to the top right of the small glacier. Snow conditions will dictate whether or not crampons are worn at this point.

After ascending for a few minutes you will find yourself at the infamous **Grand Couloir**. Although the 50m crossing is not difficult, this is where most accidents happen on the mountain and **helmets should be worn** at all times. The important thing is to cross quickly, particularly later in the day – do not stop to adjust clothing (we have witnessed people doing just that). If rocks are falling wait for a break.

After the couloir continue scrambling up the rock spur ESE for 700m to the **Gouter hut**. The route is strenuous but enjoyable and never very difficult. There are some fixed cables and pitons, but confident mountaineers should not need to rope up but conditions vary so climbers should use their own judgment and helmets should be kept on until the Gouter refuge.

Sleep at the Gouter hut or at the bivouac camp on the plateau just above it (dusk to dawn only). Climbers usually set off at 2am the next morning but this is too early – if you made good progress you would reach the summit in the dark. Rope up in the chaos of the hut and follow the line of twinkling head torches SE up the broad slopes of the Dôme de Gouter. Keep a steady pace and avoid unnecessary energy-sapping stops.

At the top of the **Dôme de Gouter** (4304m – tick off another Alpine 4000er), descend briefly to the **Col du Dôme** from where you will see the Bosses ridge leading up in a southeast direction to the summit. A short steeper section leads to the small **Vallot shelter**. This is designated for emergency use only but climbers often use it to sit out bad weather – do not plan to bivvy here.

From the shelter, the ridge gradually narrows and leads up over two snow humps, the Grande Bosse and Petit Bosse. Between these is a narrow ridge across a saddle, which is very dangerous in windy conditions. Take care

Rachel on the Col du Dôme, with the Vallot Hut and Mont Blanc beyond – our water and Smarties were still frozen!

Mont Blanc du Tacul (4248m) with the Aiguille du Midi in the distance on the right

here and when passing other parties on the ridge, which becomes much sharper from here. Pass a group of rocks, La Tournette, on your right.

Keep heading up the sharp ridge until you the reach the small plateau of the summit. The summit is not marked but you are way above everything in sight: you will know when you are there.

S is Mont Blanc de Courmayeur. Only attempt to continue to this peak in perfect weather.

Descent

By the same route. If you made good time to the summit, it is feasible to descend all the way to the mountain railway and down to the valley in the afternoon, even stopping for a celebratory lunch at the Gouter refuge. If this is done even greater care and awareness of rockfall in the Grand Couloir is essential.

OTHER ROUTES

OPTION 1

An alternative ascent/descent is by the technically easier (graded F) but much longer Grand Mulets route (described here in descent). Afternoon descents of the Grand Mulets route have a high objective risk due to an increased chance of serac fall and avalanche, especially whilst crossing the Petit Plateau. Check its condition at the Office de Hautes Montagnes in Chamonix. If the glacier is in a bad state climbers are often deterred from taking it. The Grand Mulets descent route provides better shelter from the elements than the Gouter route and will deliver you to the Plan de l'Aiguille station of the Midi cable car and down to Chamonix. As crevasses and navigation form the greatest dangers, make use of the Vallot hut if bad weather comes in or visibility is poor.

Follow the ridge back down to the **Col du Dôme**. Instead of going back over the Dôme, turn right (NE) to Le Grand Plateau. Only use this descent if tracks are visible in the snow (preferably ascent tracks). After 4km of plodding along the snow you will reach the Grand Mulets refuge on the rock spur to your right. From here a path with a rail leads down to the Bossons glacier. The first part of this, La Jonction, is the most heavily crevassed and is best crossed before the snow gets too soft. The route takes you N and then NE across the glacier (there may be ladders across certain crevasses) to the cliffs under the Aiguille du Midi. There is a danger of stone fall here.

Continue down the right-hand edge of the glacier until you meet a steep good path on rock which takes you down to the disused Gare de Glaciers cable car station. From here traverse NE, eventually crossing the bottom of the Glacier de Pelerins. Follow the marked path N sharply down for another kilometre to reach the Plan de L'Aiguille station.

OPTION 2

Another route for more experienced mountaineers is the classic ascent/descent from the Aiguille du Midi cable car station via the peaks of Mont Blanc de Tacul and Mont Maudit. (The Mont Maudit traverse provides a stiffer physical and technical ascent/descent of Mont Blanc, which may require an abseil from the Mont Maudit saddle and should only be considered as a viable alternative by competent mountaineers.)

Descend NE from the summit of **Mont Blanc**, keeping your distance from the cliffs on your right. The route becomes steeper down the Mur de la Cote into the Col de la Brenva. Continue on the broad ridge N keeping away from possible cornices on the right over two snow humps to the saddle of **Mont Maudit**. From here descend a long steep snow slope to the distinctive Col Maudit before ascending gradually over the W shoulder of **Mont Blanc du Tacul**, thereby bypassing its summit. From the shoulder descend steeply to the Col du Midi; after crossing this ascend 300m to the **Aiguille du Midi** cable car station.

OPTION 3

There is also an Italian approach to Mont Blanc from Val Veni via the Gonella refuge which meets the other routes at the **Dôme de Gouter**.

15 GERMANY

ZUGSPITZE 2962M

See Serious Ascents in the Introduction

The magnificent Bavarian Alps (Daniel Arndt)

Location	In limestone Wettersteingebirge range, Bavarian Alps, on German/Austrian border 97km SSW of Munich near town of Garmisch-Partenkirchen
Start	Hammersbach
Map(s)	Austrian Alpenvereinskarte 4/2 Wetterstein-und Mieminger Gebirge 1:25,000 best (German maps will suffice)
Equipment	Via ferrata gear (note cables often chunky so large karabiners should be used). Crampons generally essential; ice axe not required; rope not essential, but short walking rope handy, especially if unconfident on steep ground.
Climbing period	June–September best
Difficulty	4
Enjoyment	*****
Ascent	2200m (over short distance)
Time	6–8hrs ascent (descend via funicular to save knees)
Water	Permanent water to 2100m; café and bar on summit
Accommodation	Possible to stay overnight at two Hoellental refuges on route and at Muchner Haus on top of mountain. Campsite in Garmisch and one near Ehrwald.
Getting there	From Munich take A95 (E533) and 2 to Garmisch-Partenkirchen. Continue to village of Hammersbach, 4km SW (reasonably priced long-stay car park)
Public transport	Mainline train station at Garmisch-Partenkirchen; smaller one in Hammersbach where route begins. Check weather at station in Garmisch and tourist information in centre of town
Nearest high points	Grauspitz (Liechtenstein), Grossglockner (Austria)

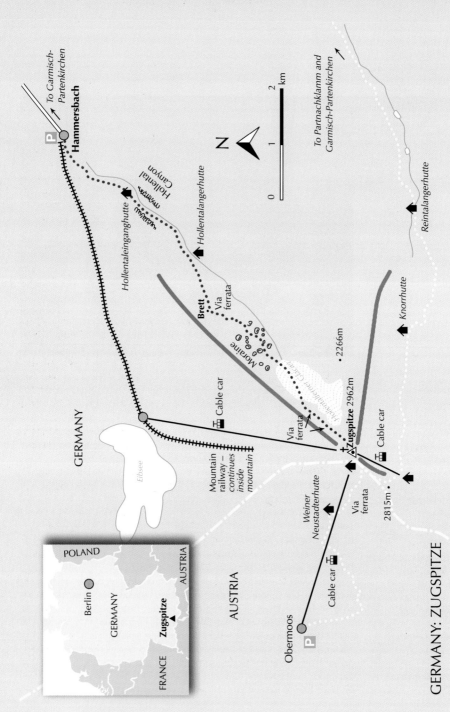

To Garmisch-Partenkirchen

Hammersbach

Hollentaleinganghutte

Hollental Canyon

stream

Hollentalangerhutte

2 km

1

N

0

To Partnachklamm and Garmisch-Partenkirchen

Reintalangerhutte

Brett

Via ferrata

Knorrhutte

Moraine

2266m

Hollentalferner Glacier

GERMANY

Elbsee

Cable car

Via ferrata

Zugspitze 2962m

Cable car

Mountain railway – continues inside mountain

Weiner Neustadterhutte

Via ferrata

2815m

Obermoos

Cable car

AUSTRIA

POLAND

Berlin

GERMANY

Zugspitze

AUSTRIA

FRANCE

GERMANY: ZUGSPITZE

The jewel in the crown of the Bavarian Alps, Zugspitze is a veritable trove of thigh-slapping delights. With a cable car to the peak and a gift shop adorning the summit, you might not expect much of Germany's highest mountain. Climbers will therefore be pleased to discover that Zugspitze offers a sensational climb, one of the most spectacular we made summiting the high points of Europe. From the northeast it is possible to ascend the whole mountain passing through splendid gorges, a majestic hanging valley and over a glacier without ever glimpsing the funicular, cable car or visitor complex close to the summit. It is a quite surreal experience to emerge from a dramatic 600m cliff climb to the airy summit and meet crowds of astonished Japanese tourists waving at you. Even more surreal is the 75-year-old funicular railway which climbs steeply to 2600m through tunnels in the heart of the mountain. Via ferrata (German *klettersteig*) cables and tunnels built into the mountain to aid troop movements in World Wars I and II allow a sensational ascent through impossible gorges and up exposed cliff faces that will leave climbers elated. Having reached the summit follow Bavarian tradition with a well-earned glass of beer.

There are three standard routes. The fastest and most dramatic is described below; it also happens to be the most beautiful.

ROUTE

Walk S uphill on the road to the centre of **Hammersbach** where a bridge crosses the Hammersbach River. Take the signposted path on the left (E) side of the river.

Follow the broad and clearly marked path to the **Hollentaleingangshutte**. This is the entrance to the **Hollental canyon** (and a refuge) where you pay €2.50. The toll-booth opens at 6am and the gorge is closed during the winter until May (there is a longer route avoiding the gorge, but this is not recommended).

Continue through spectacular and very wet tunnels inside the gorge while waterfalls pound down around you. Once out of the canyon, the trail ascends gradually to the **Hoellentalangerhutte** (1381m).

Just after the refuge, take the path which turns right and crosses the river on a wooden bridge. Follow this path up the valley, climbing through meadows to steeper rocky terrain.

After 1km the path splits, with the left fork leading to the Hoellental glacier and the right to the mountain Riffelspitze. Stop and prepare your via ferrata equipment before taking the left fork.

The short ferrata section begins with a ladder and continues with good protection up a steep face called **Brett**.

As the terrain becomes less steep, the ferrata ends and a good path leads up 1.5km of easy scree slopes to the **Hollentalferner glacier** at the head of the valley.

The route is well trodden so there should be a clear trail in the snow of the glacier. The glacier is not very steep and there are few crevasses, but do not be complacent. Near the top of the glacier the path bears NW to the rock face on your right where an iron ladder marks the start of the second via ferrata section. Take care crossing from the edge of the glacier to the rock face as the bergschrund (crevasse) is massive here and alarming drops are common.

The medium-grade via ferrata route now leads SW for 600m vertically to the summit on very good protection. The route is prone to ice and snow so crampons may be necessary, especially in early and late season.

You should see the summit cross (though not the visitor centre) looming above you as you climb higher. Follow the cables until you reach the top.

The summit of **Zugspitze** is unmistakable. The café, bar, cable car station and even a museum are all in the building 40m away: good for a celebratory beer and a few souvenirs!

Descent

As the climb up is long and fairly strenuous, many people will want to descend by cable car and mountain railway to Eibsee or Hammersbach, €25 one way or €44 for a return trip. The last train down leaves at 4.30pm and the last cable car to Eibsee leaves at 4.45pm. Tickets can be purchased in the souvenir shop on the summit.

The first via ferrata section on Brett

Above left:
Zugspitze's summit cross
(Daniel Arndt)

Above right:
Looking east down
the Reintal valley
(Daniel Arndt)

You could retrace your steps on the way down – possible in one long strenuous day, or make it a two-day trip.

Another alternative is to take the Reintal E4 path (see below) back to Garmisch-Partenkirchen after spending the night at the summit refuge or camping on route.

OTHER ROUTES

OPTION 1

The Reintal route is longer but does not involve crossing a glacier or via ferrata.

Start at the Olympic Stadium in Garmisch-Partenkirchen and follow the narrow Partnach canyon, which also has an entrance fee. The well-marked path continues up the Reintal River valley WSW to the **Reintalangerhutte** at 1366m. The trail then climbs more steeply to the **Knorrhutte** at 2052m, before continuing W over less steep ground to the mountain railway station. From there some easy scrambling is required to reach the summit.

OPTION 2

A further route option starts from the Obermoos cable car station NE of the Austrian village of Ehrwald.

A short but steep ascent on the E4 path in a NE direction towards the peak and goes via the **Wiener Neustadter refuge**. Take via ferrata equipment for this ascent.

GREECE: MOUNT OLYMPUS

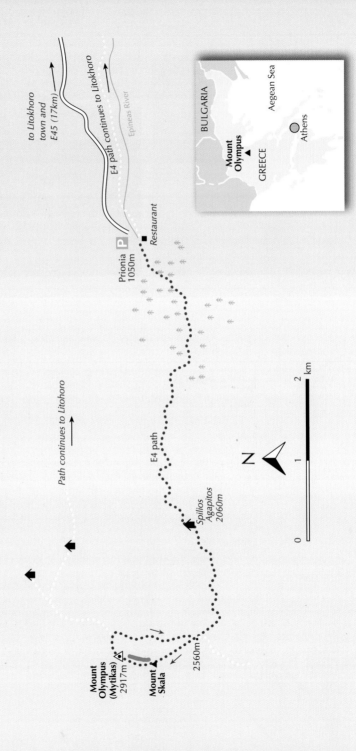

to Litokhoro
town and
E45 (17km)

E4 path continues to Litokhoro

Epineas River

BULGARIA

Aegean Sea

Mount
Olympus

GREECE

Athens

Prionia
1050m

P

Restaurant

Path continues to Litohoro

E4 path

Spilios
Agapitos
2060m

N

0   1   2 km

Mount
Olympus
(Mytikas)
2917m

Mount
Skala

2560m

16 GREECE

MOUNT OLYMPUS 2917M

Location	E coast of Greece, N of Larissa, S of Thessalonica and Katerina; close to town of Litokhoro
Start	Prionia
Map(s)	Walking maps easy to buy in Litokhoro; tourist information office provides excellent free 1:20,000 map of mountain
Equipment	Normal hiking gear; winter climbs require full alpine kit
Climbing period	mid-May–October; in winter extremely deep snow and corresponding risk of avalanches, while scrambling up Mytikas can become tricky ice climb. Any winter attempt requires full alpine gear; progress very slow without snowshoes.
Difficulty	3
Enjoyment	✶✶✶✶
Ascent	1900m
Time	5–7hrs ascent from Prionia, 4–5hrs descent; many tourists misled by information leaflets giving optimistically fast ascent times
Water	None after Spilios Agapitos refuge
Accommodation	Several refuges on mountain; places can be reserved through tourist information office in Litokhoro (note refuges locked from October to April). Litokhoro has number of hotels. Proud of Olympus's World Biosphere Reserve status, the Greeks have banned any camping on mountain.
Getting there	Take route 1 from Thessalonica or Athens to Litokhoro junction; follow road to centre of Litokhoro. At roundabout turn right; follow winding mountain road for 18km to Prionia (car park and small restaurant). Alternatively possible to climb Olympus from Litokhoro on E4 path which follows Enipeas River W via Dionysus monastery to Prionia (4–6hrs).
Public transport	Litokhoro on main Athens–Thessalonica rail line; station at sea level c2hr walk from town. Taxis often appear when train passes through. In summer occasional buses/coaches take walkers from Litokhoro to Prionia (check tourist information); hitching to Prionia should not be too troublesome.
Nearest high points	Musala (Bulgaria), Mount Korab (Macedonia and Albania)

As the ancient home of the Greek Gods, Mount Olympus is one of the world's most famous mountains. It is accordingly a popular ascent. While climbing Olympus is not beyond the means of most hikers, the summit involves surprisingly exposed scrambling. Often turbulent weather combines with this to remind climbers of the mythical presence of Zeus breathing down their necks. Legend has it that Mount Olympus was the home of the Greek gods. Despite completing both a winter and summer ascent, we have yet to have a face-to-face meeting with Zeus, but don't let that stop you from keeping an eye out.

Because Olympus rises uninterrupted from the sea those wishing to challenge themselves further will find this one of the few high mountains in Europe for which an ascent from sea level is a practicality (allow two to three days).

Note Because of the large amount of ascent involved and better mountain weather conditions in the mornings, we recommend making this climb a two-day trip and staying at one of the excellent refuges. You can book refuges in advance or from Litokhoro tourist information. The paper napkins at Spilios Agapitos refuge mark the summit heights incorrectly.

ROUTE

From **Prionia** head W past the restaurant following the exceptionally clear E4 trail through the forest to the **Spilios Agapitos refuge** (also known as Refuge A) (2½–3½hrs). If the weather is clear you will have excellent views of the sea, summit cliffs and surrounding waterfalls. You will also pass warning signs for the deadly plant belladonna (the top choice for old-fashioned murderers in crime fiction).

At the Spilios Agapitos refuge head straight up from the patio to eventually emerge above the treeline. Ignore a path branching off which is signposted 'Refuge C' (also known as Refuge Ch. Kakalos).

At 2560m the path splits again. Both routes go to the summit, giving an excellent circular route option. (Both ascents are of a similar difficulty and length; the E4 ascent via Skala is described, but it is equally fulfilling to go the other way).

Ignore the right-hand fork and follow the sprayed sign to E4 and **Mount Skala** (the first peak on the summit ridge). The path soon fragments a little but as long as you're heading upwards all is well. Eventually reach the top of Skala marked with cairns – from this point the route is mainly scrambling.

Mytikas (2918m) provides some good scrambling to reach the home of the Gods (Wade Schwartzkopf)

Up with the Gods and looking out to sea on Mount Olympus

The hole in the wall on Skala (both images Wade Schwartzkopf)

Descend steeply from Skala for 10m. Pass beneath a stony column (higher than Skala) then cross a narrow gap before starting another brief descent (50m height loss).

Follow the red and yellow markers and ascend the mildly exposed route to **Mytikas** (the highest point of Olympus). The summit is marked by a scruffy concrete pillar and an old Greek flag.

Descent

To descend via the alternative route, follow the red markers N off the summit. These eventually lead W down a long steep gully. The path then becomes a fantastic traverse S under the summit ridge for 40mins and joins the E4 route.

OTHER ROUTES

For longer treks in the Olympus National Park, refuges can be found on paths to the N and S of the mountain, with two of them close by the peak to the NE.

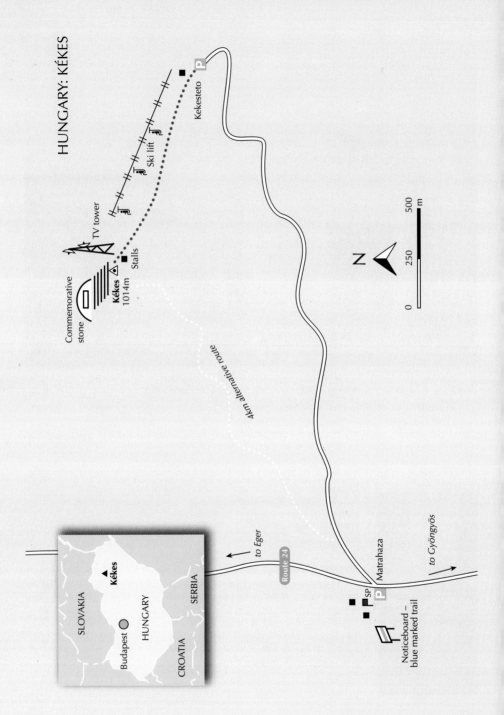

HUNGARY: KÉKES

Commemorative stone

Kékes
1014m

TV tower

Stalls

Ski lift

Kekesteto

4km alternative route

N

0   250   500
              m

SLOVAKIA

Kékes ▲

Budapest

HUNGARY

CROATIA

SERBIA

to Eger

Route 24

Matrahaza

SP

Noticeboard –
blue marked trail

to Gyöngyös

KÉKES 1014M

Also known as Kékestető

Kékes' old tower (Mark Leaver)

Location	In Mátra range, near tiny village of Kékestető, 90km NE of Budapest; between Budapest and Miskolc, close to Gyöngyös
Start	Kékestető
Map(s)	General road map of Hungary. Information board showing trails in area at Mátraháza car park.
Equipment	None. Skis can be hired in winter.
Climbing period	Year-round
Difficulty	1
Enjoyment	*
Ascent	300m
Time	30mins
Water	Café on summit
Accommodation	Plenty of small hotels in villages in this popular area
Getting there	Take M3/E71 road from Budapest or Miskolc. Turn off at Gyöngyös on 4 towards Eger through Mátrafüred to Mátraháza. Either park here or, if feeling idle, at Mátraháza turn off right onto smaller road uphill signposted to Kékes and Kékestető – small village near top of mountain – use car parks here.
Public transport	Gyöngyös well served by buses direct from Budapest; more from city of Hatvan. From here number of buses run to Mátraháza and occasionally to Kékestető. Mátraháza can be reached from N: train to Hatvan from Budapest, then train to Recsk, from where buses run to Mátraháza.
Nearest high points	Gerlachkovsky stit (Slovakia), Rysy (Poland), Goverla (Ukraine)

Hungary does not boast the high peaks of its neighbours Austria and Slovakia, and Kékes disappointingly is not located in a spectacular range. A television tower, numerous trinket stalls, a small ski 'resort', a car park and a café adorn the summit area. It is not in any way remote. Despite this, the mountain makes an amusing afternoon trip and good walks can be planned in the area. A winter visit would probably be the most rewarding, making most of the short ski runs. With a height not dissimilar to Ben Nevis, Kékes could not be more different from the UK's highest mountain. After ascending Kékes, it is easy to comprehend how Hungarians might assume that there are no proper mountains in Britain.

ROUTE

It is possible to drive nearly all the way to the summit, park up and amble up the final section of the ski run. However, as with Vaalserberg in the Netherlands, having come this far you might as well make a small hike of it. Park at Mátraháza car park, cross the road and after 100m or so on the road up to Kékestető follow blue markers left. These lead to the wide grassy ski run. Hike up here to the unmistakable summit with its huge television tower. This route is roughly 4km long with 300m ascent. Longer marked trails in the National Park area can also be planned.

Descent

A short ski descent to Mátraháza (and drag-lift ascent) would be fun and possible in winter.

Kékes marker stone
(Mark Leaver)

18 ICELAND

HVANNADALSHNUKUR 2111M

See Serious Ascents in the Introduction

Location	SE Iceland just outside Skaftafell National Park on edge of Vatnajokull ice cap
Start	Sandfell
Map(s)	Skaftafell 1:100,000 (Landmaelingar Islands); purchase before leaving Reykjavik
Equipment	Full alpine climbing gear (crampons, ice axe, 25m rope, deadman, compass essential)
Climbing period	May–September ideal. Winter ascents possible, but extreme cold and brief hours of daylight
Difficulty	4
Enjoyment	****
Ascent	2100m
Time	11–15hrs round trip (much less if skiing down)
Water	Last water at roughly 700m; in summer allow at least 1 litre per person beyond this point
Accommodation	Campsite in Skaftafell National Park with showers and visitor centre. Visitor centre (open until 3pm) has printed weather report in English; small supermarket during summer months (June–August). Petrol station with café 4.8km along road from Skaftafell; has small supermarket (open year-round) selling useful supplies including variety of camping gas canisters. Campsite with hot pool at Svinafell 4km before Sandfell. Permanent water source at Sandfell c200m N of parking area.
Getting there	From Reykjavik take Route 1 via Vik and Skaftafell. Turning for Sandfell parking area (200m off route) c16km beyond that for Skaftafell.
Public transport	In summer months simple to get to Skaftafell National Park by public and private buses. Sandfell c12km further along Route 1 from Skaftafell. Hitching in Iceland fine, but little traffic.

Iceland bills itself as the land of fire and ice, and it does more than live up to this dramatic description. Perched on the edge of Europe's largest ice cap, an ascent of Hvannadalshnukur requires passage through an island punctuated by explosive geysers, thunderous 100m waterfalls, natural hot springs, boiling mud pools, icebergs, lava fields, active and dormant volcanoes and lunar and Martian landscapes.

The mountain itself isn't too bad either. Attaining Hvannadalshnukur's summit involves the climber in making an impressive crossing of a 3.2km glacier in an extinct volcanic crater and making a final steep 250m ascent beside blue ice cliffs. From the summit the world appears to curve as you look out to sea. Our visit to Iceland and its high point was one of the most

ICELAND: HVANNADALSHNUKUR

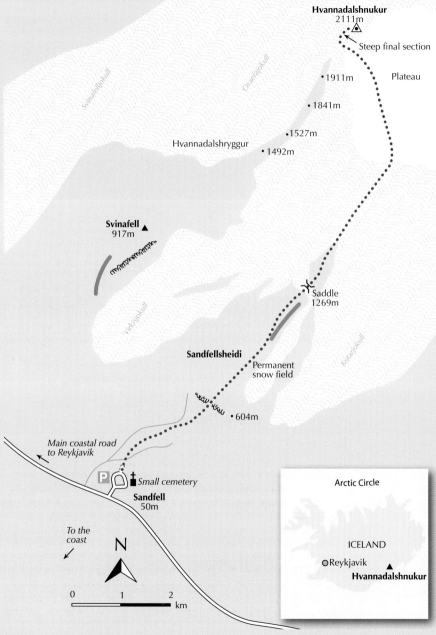

Hvannadalshnukur
2111m

Steep final section

•1911m   Plateau

•1841m

•1527m

Hvannadalshryggur   •1492m

Svinafell ▲
917m

Svinafelljokull

Oraefajokull

Virdjsjokull

Saddle
1269m

Kotarjokull

Sandfellsheidi

Permanent
snow field

•604m

*Main coastal road
to Reykjavik*

P ☩ ■ *Small cemetery*

Sandfell
50m

*To the
coast*

N

0   1   2
km

Arctic Circle

ICELAND

⊙ Reykjavik   ▲

Hvannadalshnukur

Touching the void: the featureless crater of Hvannadalshnukur

thrilling experiences in compiling this book, and setting plenty of time aside for it is strongly recommended.

Note Iceland is *very* expensive, especially for food, so bring supplies if you are on a budget. From mid-May to mid-July a head torch is not needed for the mountain as it never gets fully dark.

Note A compass, an essential piece of equipment on any mountain, is indispensable on Hvannadalshnukur. **If you are without a compass or GPS on this mountain do not climb it.** Tracks are quickly covered by spindrift, visibility seems to drop from 100 per cent to 10m in seconds, and there are very few features by which to navigate once Sandfell is left behind. Take continuous compass bearings in case visibility is lost. Magnetic North is 16° W of True North (2007) in Iceland; our directions are based on True North.

ROUTE

From the parking area follow a distinctive wide track NNW–N. After 100m this joins a thinner but more distinct path. Immediately you have to cross a wide fast-flowing stream. Make sure boots are dubbed and gaiters are on.

Cross another smaller stream and follow the distinctive path as it winds up Sandfell and out of view of the car park. Occasionally the way is a little scree-ridden, but overall the route is excellent here. At roughly 600m the path leaves the stream behind – take this opportunity to fill up with water, as this is the last source for a long time.

At 700m the path passes beneath a lava-formed arch and out onto the gradual spine of **Sandfell**. (Make a note of the distinctive slate crag on your left to sign your descent.) Here the path disappears and cairns mark your way up the spine of Sandfell. **Note** The 1:100,000 map shows little relation

View from Sandfell of the Skeidara delta with a sandstorm and the Atlantic in the distance

to the varied terrain on Sandfell itself. Avoid coming off the spine and onto the snow as this will slow ascent. Aim for the distinctive saddle at 1200m on the main ridge, which will undoubtedly require some snow walking before it is reached.

Once at the saddle, rope up with knotted rope – there are plenty of crevasses to be wary of – especially on the summit ascent. If you have a view, take a compass bearing of the peak; it should be 18–20° E of True North. Avoid the temptation to follow this bearing for too far as it will pass you over the crevasse-ridden head of the Falljokull glacier. Keeping the remainder of the ridge in view, work your way up the gradual, but seemingly endless, 700m snow ascent to the crater on a NNE–NE bearing. There are many false dawns until you eventually reach the crater itself. (Again to aid your descent make a note of the distinctive Svinafell to the SW and Rotarfjallshnukar crag to the E; likewise, time your progress across the crater.)

Frustratingly, the crater is not as flat or as distinctive as could be hoped when looking at the map. In good visibility this will not be an issue. Take a compass bearing of the peak: if you have no view head due N. If in doubt, correct to 5°W (meeting the summit ridge too far W is not a problem as the summit stands on the NE end and navigation with the ridge in view is no problem). Remember, the crater undulates, but long continuous height loss means you have erred from the crater's edge – adjust your position. Continue for 4km. The snow-swept crags of Dyrhamar, SE of Hvannadalshnukur's summit, are also a good marker to help negotiate the crater.

With a bit of luck you will reach the distinctive 250m summit climb of **Hvannadalshnukur**. The S face is distinctively steep, but will not trouble. Two large crevasses may require care in the crossing; later in the season they are likely to be visible. In early summer, you should have a good view of the dramatic blue ice cliffs on the NE face of the summit. The rock beneath the ice is likely to be revealed as the summer progresses. A good snow ramp leads through the unpronounced cornice onto the wide summit ridge. Progress E to the unmarked summit and avoid going too close to the edge as it is liable to be heavily corniced.

Descent

As ascent, taking special care when leaving the summit ridge. If you descend to find yourself faced with a glacier covered in crevasses, you have veered too far SW and are looking at the wretched Virkisjokull. Head E to avoid it and back onto the crater. Do not rely on following your tracks as these cover quickly.

OTHER ROUTES
Sandfell is the standard route.

OPTION 1
One alternative was once possible up the northern edge of Virkisjokull glacier. We ascended the mountain in early May and can confirm this route was impassable even early in the season.

OPTION 2
Another alternative – but rather environmentally unsound route – is to drive (permission needed) by 4x4 up to 700m from Hnappavellir (12km further along the road from Sandfell). A route can then be worked up to the crater.

Isolation: over 3km visibility from the Hvannadalshnukur crater

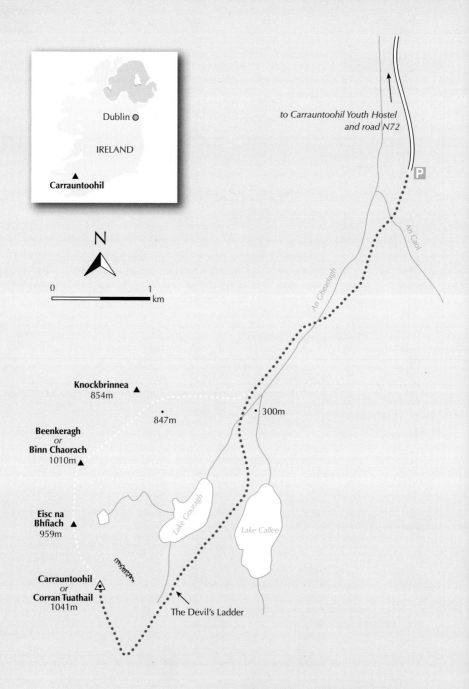

Dublin ⊙

IRELAND

▲ Carrauntoohil

N

0   1
km

to Carrauntoohil Youth Hostel and road N72

P

An Caol

An Cheadagh

Knockbrinnea ▲
854m

• 847m

• 300m

Beenkeragh
or
Binn Chaorach
1010m ▲

Lake Gouragh

Lake Callee

Eisc na
Bhfiach ▲
959m

Carrauntoohil
or
Corran Tuathail
1041m

The Devil's Ladder

IRELAND: CARRAUNTOOHIL

CARRAUNTOOHIL 1041M

Also known as Corran Tuathail; also listed as 1039m

That way, to be sure!

Location	MacGillycuddy's Reeks, near Killarney, SW Ireland
Start	Cronin's Farm
Map(s)	Ordnance Survey of Ireland 1:50,000 MacGillycuddy's Reeks
Equipment	Standard hiking gear; compass very useful for descent
Climbing period	Year-round. In height of winter may be ice on N-facing Devil's Ladder and Binn Chaorach ridge: climbers should equip themselves appropriately.
Difficulty	2
Enjoyment	***
Ascent	900m
Time	2½hrs ascent, 2–2½hrs descent
Water	Plenty up to 550m
Accommodation	Two campsites and B&B on W side of mountain at Lake Acoose (Chausis). Youth hostel and campsite open year-round at Climber's Inn in Glencar (W side).
Getting there	From Killarney follow Killorgen road (N72) for 9.5km. At petrol station turn left following sign to The Gap of Dunloe and pass through village of Beaufort. Take third right towards Glencar. After 3.5km tiny filling pumps right. Road to Carrauntoohil second left just after small bridge and signposted. Car park another mile or so at end of road (private land belonging to Cronin's Farm); €2 fee for parking, café with toilets in summer. Tourist route starts here.
Public transport	Killarney on main Irish rail network and well served by bus. Possible to get close to Beaufort by catching Killarney–Killorgan bus, then hitch or hike to mountain (hitch-hiking very popular in Ireland). Alternatively taxi to start of route from Killarney not too expensive. Telephone box at Cronin's Farm for calling return taxi.
Nearest high point	Slieve Donard (Northern Ireland)

Lake Gouragh

The summit of Carrauntoohil is said to be in cloud for 300 days of the year, but do not let that put you off. We have been up the mountain on both a dry summer's day and a wet winter's day, and both were fulfilling experiences. If raining, think of the drops beating the ground as providing a musical accompaniment like the black shoes of the *Riverdance* ensemble as you work your way up the impressive terrain, for this is a land of poetic musing and watercolours. The mountain honours its guests with wonderful strokes of green hues lifting the eye from placid dull grey lakes to the dark shiny crags of its upper slopes. The summit is marked by a wrought-iron cross and a small wind shelter.

While the Devil's Ladder ascent is described as the primary route, the Coomloughra Horseshoe is strongly recommended (see Other Routes), as it is both more challenging and more impressive.

ROUTE

From the car park follow the clear path SW up Hag's Glen, initially passing through the farm until meeting the ancient track.

After meeting a red arrow which points right the route descends towards the Gaddagh River. There is no obvious crossing point and after heavy rainfall it can be quite difficult. Make sure the river is crossed before the wire fence is met. Working your way up the steep banking at the other side of the river, an unlikely excellent ancient track is met. Continue to follow this on the river's W side.

Before reaching **Lake Gouragh** and **Lake Callee** the track re-crosses the river at an obvious ford, then leads up between the two lakes to the head of the valley.

As the valley narrows the route becomes less obvious as numerous ways have been picked through the boggy ground; a slight descent is made here.

Waterfall below the Devil's Ladder

The Devil's Ladder will soon be met. The route is not cairned or as obvious as might be expected for such a popular hike. The Devil's Ladder is slightly to the right (W) side of the valley head and is a reasonably steep, though shallow, gully with large boulders. If it has been raining, numerous streams will be running down it.

The hiking here occasionally turns into scrambling and, although tough work, you will soon reach the flat grassy saddle of the ridge by a large cairn.

From the saddle follow the path and cairns NW to the summit, marked with a large iron-girder cross and a small wind shelter. On rare clear days you will be rewarded for your efforts with excellent views of Dingle Bay.

Descent

While a descent via the ascent route is recommended in poor visibility or bad weather conditions, the best views of the mountain would be forfeited. A descent via Ireland's second-highest mountain Binn Chaorach (Beenkeragh) 1010m is recommended.

Exit the summit to the NW and descend to **Eisc na Bhfiach** (959m – short steep hike/scramble up to this). The ridge is quite exposed.

Follow the ridge northwards, climbing to the summit of **Beenkeragh** (Binn Chaorach) (1010m – a height gain of 60m).

Great care is needed here in poor visibility. Using your compass descend on a NE bearing towards the two knobbles of **Knockbrinnea** (854m and 847m) and pass between these two points.

The faint track fades here. Descend on a 70–75° easterly compass bearing, bounding down the heather-dressed hillside to rejoin the track in Hag's Glen near the river crossing. Cross the river and follow the track back to Cronin's Farm.

OTHER ROUTES

THE COOMLOUGHRA HORSESHOE

Ascent	1250m
Time	6–7hrs
Water	Last source Cottoner's River (440m)
Getting there	Follow directions as for primary route, but instead of taking final turn to Carrauntoohil continue on road following signs to Glencar. After T-junction, turn left and continue for exactly 2km to Breanlee. Parking very limited; early arrival wise. 100m S of Breanlee sign advertises Glencar Inn right and gate on left with 'No Parking – Private' and 'Kerry Mountain Rescue' signs. Gate often locked; although no stile is a permissive route for ramblers. Route starts here.
Public transport	As for primary route, though hitch or taxi from Killorgen easier or cheaper than from Killarney

For those wanting to avoid the crowds and prepared to give Ireland's highest mountain an extra hour or two, the Coomloughra Horseshoe offers an exceptional hike of the highest quality. It incorporates Ireland's second- and third-highest mountains and is wholeheartedly recommended. The only downsides are the 100m height loss between Caher (Cathair) and Carrauntoohil's summits and the steep descent from the summit of Cnoc Íochtair.

ROUTE

Hop over the fence at the right of the gate and follow the track. After a couple of initial bends a long steep hike up the hill gains 300m (vertical height) very quickly.

The track bends to the right and leads up to the Cottoner's River below Cnoc Íochtair (Eighter).

The river is crossed by a bridge and then followed to the 'hydro dam' and Lake Iochair. The dam is a small stepped construction with only a tiny iron pump visible. (Here hikers have the option of following the horseshoe in the opposite direction to the one described; both clockwise and anti-clockwise routes have their advantages.)

Follow the track SW away from dam. The ground here is boggy and a route needs to be worked to the end of the Caher ridge where the path is picked up again.

Head up onto the ridge. The going is good and gradual with the path and ridge easy enough to follow. Eventually you will reach Caher's fore summit (975m) where there is a small stone shelter. Care should be taken when close to the cliffs between the fore summit and Caher's true summit (1001m).

Descend due E over Caher's third summit (983m), eventually reaching the narrow col between Caher and Carrauntoohil. From here stay with the exposed ridge as it swings northeastwards and up to the summit of **Carrauntoohil**, marked with a large iron cross.

Exit the summit to the NW and descend to **Eisc na Bhfiach** (959m – a short steep hike/scramble up to this). The ridge is quite exposed and great care should be taken here.

Follow the ridge northwards, climbing to the summit of **Beenkeragh** 1010m (a height gain of 60m).

From the summit descend N–NW to the col below the twin summits of Skregmore (Screig Mhor) 848 and 851m. The track is clear enough and the occasional cairn helps guide the way here.

From Screig Mhor descend due W to the col below Cnoc Íochtair and then again work your way to the summit, the final one of the horsehoe.

From here the descent to Iochair Lake is steep and troublesome on the knees. A number of thin trails can be followed ESE from the summit.

On meeting the Cottoner's River, a crossing can be made via the dam, which has a handy wire grid to aid grip or via an obvious natural bridge below. The track is followed back down to Breanlee.

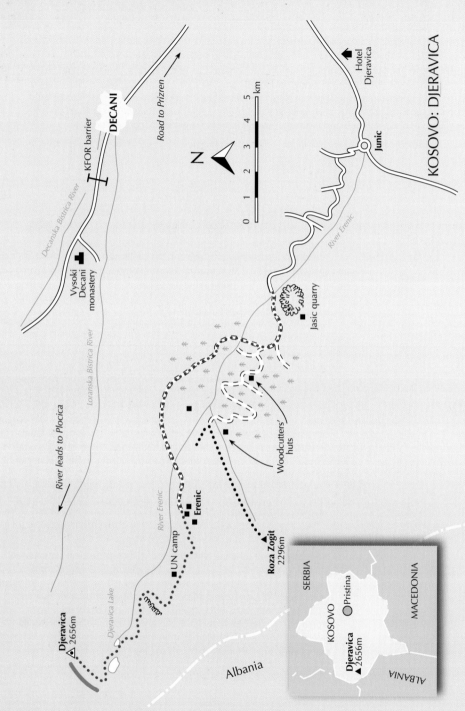

KOSOVO: DJERAVICA

Road to Prizren

DECANI

KFOR barrier

Decanska Bistrica River

Vysoki Decani monastery

Loranska Bistrica River

River leads to Plocica

River Erenic

Djeravica lake

Djeravica
2656m

UN camp

Erenic

Roza Zogit
2296m

Woodcutters' huts

Jasic quarry

River Erenic

Junic

Hotel
Djeravica

Albania

N

km
0 1 2 3 4 5

SERBIA

KOSOVO

Pristina

Djeravica
2656m

ALBANIA

MACEDONIA

20 KOSOVO

DJERAVICA 2656M

Also known as Daravica or Derovica
See Former Yugoslav Republics under Health and Safety in the Introduction

THERE IS A RISK OF LANDMINES ON THIS MOUNTAIN

Location	Prokletije range, W Kosovo (southern Serbia), stone's throw from the Albanian border. S of Pec (Peja), near town of Decani (Decanj).
Start	Jasic
Map(s)	Not available. Old Belgrade maps compiled in 1960s outdated, have inaccurate border markings and nearly impossible to come by.
Equipment	Standard hiking gear
Climbing period	April–October. Winter ascents not recommended due to snow cover.
Difficulty	3
Enjoyment	****
Ascent	1500m
Time	2½–3hrs ascent from trailhead, plus 4–6hrs ascent if hiking from Jasic
Water	Plenty up to lakes just below summit ridge
Accommodation	Decani natural base; good-sized town with ample internet cafes, dentists, UN/police station and two hotels. From Pec one hotel passed just before town; 'Jerane' on right as enter (very friendly staff, excellent food). Incredibly a large hotel, the 'Djeravica', on road to Junic, but very isolated.
Getting there	**Note** Only possible to get to trailhead by vehicle if driving high-clearance 4x4: even then beyond driving capabilities of most motorists. No normal car could get to head of Erenic River and its small settlement; be extremely wary of taxi drivers who claim otherwise. Taxi drivers seem to think most people are looking for illegal entry into Albania; be careful of miscommunication.

From Decani drive S on main road towards Prizren for c10km until turning signposted 'Junic'. Follow road to centre of Junic, meeting line of taxis. Normal car can be driven over very poor rubble roads as far as quarry at Jasic, but route to this very difficult to find; turn right at centre of Junic, but then too many turn-offs to describe. If determined to take a car, negotiate with a taxi to lead you to the quarry. Again, be wary of taxi drivers who might offer to guide you; unlikely they have ever been to trailhead and have no idea what they are talking about. If driving a car, or fearful of driving 4x4 up world's worst and most difficult road, park at Jasic and remove all valuables.

At best 2hrs to drive from Jasic to trailhead (we hitched a ride with two local woodcutters, 1hr 45mins). If driving 4x4, follow track upwards from quarry over huge boulders and deep mud troughs, winding slowly up the mountain through forest on precarious traverses. Occasionally route will descend; ignore tracks leading off main one. Eventually reach wide muddy plateau which you exit to left. Just after track will split (left track ascends to small woodcutter's settlement). Take right fork, which will eventually cross the Erenic and lead steeply up opposite side of valley before descending steeply and zigzagging down to river, which you cross back over then follow for 300m to reach trailhead.

At Jasic quarry (760m) you will hear the River Erenic right (river will, if needs must, guide you home). If here early morning try and hitch-hike up mountain, offering small payment. As forest road has number of tracks coming off it in various directions, nearly all leading to dead ends, hitch-hiking a good plan. Might also be prudent to take tent and prepare to spend two days on mountain.

If walking from quarry try to follow main track. Great number of *Romancing the Stone*-style logging mud-chutes short-cut laborious ascent of road, so use river as reference point if leaving track for long periods (you will feel very isolated and lose possibility of hitch-hiking). Logging paths provide much steeper, but infinitely quicker, route to trailhead. At very best hope to get to trailhead in 4hrs; more likely to take c6hrs.

Note If you get lift with woodcutters who take you to settlement in the forest high up on S side of Erenic valley, make your way NW to Erenic River and follow it to trailhead. Do not be distracted by sprayed names on steep path that heads SW up impressive Rosa Zogit near broad clearing and woodcutter's house. This mountain also has river flowing down it, tributary of main valley river.

Public transport   Pec, Decani and Junic can all be reached by bus, with transfers in that order. From Junic take taxi to quarry of Jasic. By asking local farmers may be able to hire horse or donkey in or around Junic; a viable option to trailhead (and even along quite a lot of the route).

Nearest high points   Maja Kolata/Bobotov Kuk (Montenegro), Maglic (Bosnia and Herzegovina), Korab (Macedonia and Albania), Midzor (Serbia)

Formerly a very popular peak, there were large battles between Serb forces and Kosovan/ Albanian fighters on Djeravica in 1998. During the late 1990s Serbian forces, aiming to prevent Albanian/Kosovan troops from crossing the border, placed a number of landmines on the mountain. When we climbed Djeravica in 2005, UNMIK were in the process of clearing these and appeared to be near completion. We interacted fully with UNMIK at the time and can assure readers that our route is safe. We have since contacted UNMIK and they have declared the mountain clear of landmines on the Kosovan side. Nonetheless, bear in mind that this mountain has had landmines on it. We therefore stress that we cannot take responsibility for those mountaineers who wish to proceed. Extreme caution remains a prerequisite; report any suspicious objects to UNMIK immediately. Do not wander off the path and certainly do not venture across the border into Albania. The local population of Decani, though friendly and helpful, know very little about the mountain that overshadows them. We spoke to the mayor of the town in 2005 – along with numerous other residents – who all assured us there were no landmines on the mountain, only to come across UNMIK while we were up there.

Aesthetically Djeravica's upper slopes are reminiscent of a Lakeland peak and offer similar difficulties. Getting to the trailhead, however, is another matter, and will inevitably involve a struggle. Like Montenegro's Maja Kolata, Djeravica's situation in the Prokletije range, close to the Albanian border, will make it feel like one of the most remote mountains in this book. Deep dark forests, the world's worst mud tracks and the presence of quirky Albanian/Kosovan woodcutters only add to that feeling of remoteness. This is now very much a Kosovan peak: the Albanian flag flies from nearly every hut but will no doubt soon be replaced.

DISPUTE

In a state of *de facto* independence since the 1999 Kosovo conflict when the UN and NATO undertook responsibility for Kosovo's security and borders, Kosovo declared full independence in February 2008. At the time of going to print, this independence has been recognised by the US, UK, France and Germany amongst many other states. Only Russia, with its historical ties to Serbia, remains staunchly opposed. Full UN ratification is now inevitable, and we therefore have no qualms about regarding Kosovo as a state in its own right. Subsequently, while Djeravica was once Serbia's highest mountain, the loss of the Kosovan territory means that Midzor (2169m) on the Serbo–Bulgarian border is now Serbia's highest mountain.

ROUTE

As of August 2005, the settlement at the start of the route had eight buildings – some of these without roofs. Locals seem to refer to this settlement as Erenic. There are no trees here. The settlement stands at the head of a 500m-long flat fluvial plain in the valley. Djeravica is the mountain to the right (NW) of the settlement.

From '**Erenic**' follow the path up a steep hill, which leaves the Erenic River (you will rejoin it later), bearing off slightly southwards. The path remains in the valley proper. Overall the route will bear W–WNW. The UN

Shepherd left to guard the UNMIK vehicles at Erenik settlement

119

has beaten out a very clear and distinct path through the heather. If you are not on a clear path at this point, you are not on route.

The path will lead you past the remnants of UNMIK's first camp, identified by ordered white rocks setting out clear camping areas. There is also a white signboard here. Follow the path onwards.

At a right turn downwards into a small heather gully you will see a wooden water feeder protruding from a stream. Here the path doubles back on itself slightly before leading N–NNW. This moment is crucial. Do not continue straight up towards the ridge at the head of the valley. Following the path burnt through the heather you should come across either **UNMIK's camp** (United Nations Mission in Kosovo) or, if they have left, their stone tent markers.

From UNMIK's second camp head NW in the direction of Djeravica and the ridge to the left (W side) of the summit. A less distinct wide grassy footpath should be followed here. Again, if you are not on a footpath, you are not on route. This will lead you to some small dark crags.

The path will lead you straight up the crags, traversing to the right (N). The path becomes harder to follow here. You will soon reach a marshy pond; continue past this until you reach **Djeravica Lake** (2400m), which borders the upper part of the mountain. There is another lake to the left (S) of this one which you will see clearly from the ridge.

Traverse around the left bank of the lake (there is a short stepping-stone section), until following the path W from the centre of the lake. After 300m the path splits. Take the right fork. Unfortunately the path fades away here

Below left:
Nearing the summit of Djeravica

Below right:
Djeravica summit stone

Djeravica Lake (2400m)

as hikers have seemingly always failed to reach agreement on which is the simplest way up to the ridge. Make your way onto the ridge, aiming for the point at which the steep mountainside joins the head of the valley (N).

From the head of the valley it is only a short steep ascent to the top of the mountain. You will find the path again and amazingly some of the old faded target markers from before the war. The route trends slightly to the right (S) side of the ridge.

The summit is marked by a mushroom-shaped concrete trig point. Its shabby vandalised exterior is ironically exhilarating. Take your time to enjoy the view and some lunch.

Descent

Return exactly the same way to the Erenic settlement. If descending from here on foot, follow the track. Once on the right (S) side of the Erenic River, follow the horse-drawn logging mud-chutes steeply down the valley. These will halve your descent time. With a small bit of jogging we managed to get from the Erenic settlement to Jasic in less than 2hrs taking advantage of these short cuts. Once back down from the mountain have a good meal and celebrate.

OTHER ROUTES

Before the war there were two routes up Djeravica: the Junic/Erenic route described above, and another route via Vysoki Decani monastery.

To reach the monastery now you must pass through a very intimidating K-For military checkpoint. From there forest roads lead up the Loranska Bistrica to Kurvala and Plocica. From Plocica two trails lead up the mountain. As there were battles here also, including the ransacking of the monastery, we do not expect this route to be any safer or easier in the short term.

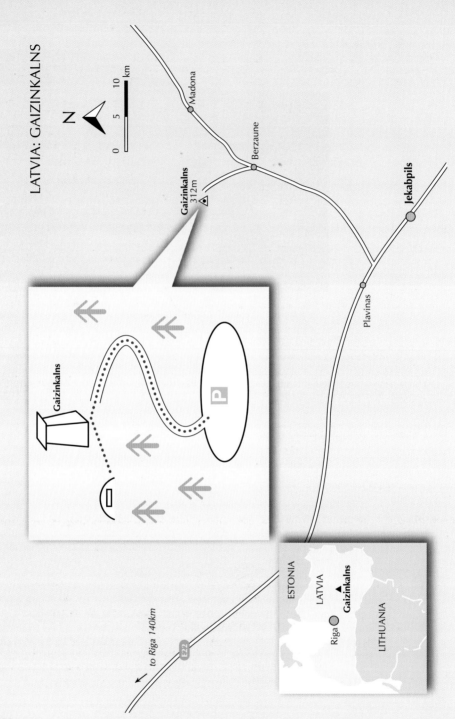

LATVIA: GAIZINKALNS

N

0 5 10 km

Gaizinkalns
312m

Madona

Berzaune

Jekabpils

Plavinas

Gaizinkalns

P

to Riga 140km

E22

ESTONIA

LATVIA

Riga

Gaizinkalns

LITHUANIA

21 LATVIA

GAIZINKALNS 312M

The condemned Gaizinkalns tower: you might need more than a hard hat!

Location	100km E of Riga, 12km W of town of Madona
Start	Gaizinkalns
Map(s)	Good Baltic road map
Equipment	None
Climbing period	All year, skiing in winter months
Difficulty	1
Enjoyment	*
Ascent	30m
Time	5mins
Water	Not applicable
Accommodation	Nearby Gaizinstars Hotel; other options in Madona
Getting there	Gaizinkalns signposted from junction of P37 and P81, SW of Madona. From village of Berzaune follow 12km of unsurfaced, yet excellent, road, passing Gaizinstars Hotel en route. Continue to end of track where giant red tower and red and white antenna. Park here.
Public transport	Madona on main Latvian rail network and well served by buses from Riga; Madona to Gaizinkalns 16km. Simplest way from there is taxi; enquire about bus services which, though sporadic, may draw you closer.
Nearest high points	Suur Munamagi (Estonia), Aukstojas/Juozapine Kalnas (Lithuania)

Gaizinkalns is home to Latvia's first 'ski resort'. This was opened in the 1960s and has just one run down a short hill. Gaizinkalns means 'weatherwise', and the hill is so-called because it is said that the forecast for the rest of the country can be made by observing its weather. The surrounding scenery is characterised by shallow valleys and deflated hills, with sporadic farms and woods; pleasant if uninspiring. On the rounded 'summit' stands a crumbling giant red tower, visible from far away. This is bricked-up to forbid people climbing it – ignore this and the multi-language 'keep off' signs at your own peril (the concrete literally crumbles beneath your feet). We do not expect this structure to remain standing for long. The summit is also marked by information boards and a plaque to commemorate a presidential visit in the 1930s.

ROUTE
Walk up the grass and turn left to reach the 'summit'.

Descent
By the same route.

*A plaque commemorates
a presidential visit
in the 1930s*

22 LIECHTENSTEIN

GRAUSPITZ 2599M

Location	E Switzerland, W Liechtenstein on Swiss border near Swiss town of Landquart and village of Malans
Start	Jenins
Map(s)	Schesaplana (Landeskarte Der Schweiz 1156) 1:25,000
Equipment	Standard hiking gear for main route; rock-climbing gear for alternative technical route (see route description)
Climbing period	June–September
Difficulty	3
Enjoyment	***
Ascent	1100m
Time	6–8hrs round trip if cable car used (considerably longer if hiking from valley)
Water	Last water at Walenbach River 700m below summit
Accommodation	Rough camping disapproved of in Liechtenstein and Switzerland; good campsite off A13 at junction 15
Getting there	Follow Swiss motorway A13 (E43) to Junction 15 Landquart. Coming from S turn right at second roundabout in Landquart and continue to large village of Malans. Turn left at ibex statue/fountain towards Jenins; cable car station on right (N) as exit village. Start early and purchase return ticket on small cable car (15 Swiss fr; for up-to-date opening times phone +(41) 813 224764; open height of summer 8am–5pm, 7am–6pm weekends.) If cable car station closed, marked trail winds up through forest beneath cables. Navigable narrow forest track enables vehicles to go much higher up mountain, but public access prohibited. Rubble track heads steeply uphill out of Jenins and continues for over 19km up mountain.
Public transport	Landquart has mainline railway station; simple to catch taxi to Jenins
Nearest high points	Zugspitze (Germany), Grossglockner (Austria)

Few people ever seem to grace the summit of Grauspitz, despite the sublime alpine scenery in which you might almost expect to find Heidi chasing around, or yodellers calling across the valleys. Because of the lack of visitors, the route up Grauspitz is quite difficult. There is no marked trail on its upper reaches and the mountain's summit section is characterised by loose awkward boulders and littered with spent mortar shells – it seems the Swiss army have formerly considered Grauspitz a kind of firing range. It should go without saying, but do not mess around with the bombs! The only logical route up the mountain is from the Swiss side. While the mountain is bafflingly unpopular, fortunately there exists the Alpibahn cable car which goes from Malans (605m) to a station at 1801m on the southwest slopes of Mount Vilan. This allows convenient access to the mountain area and removes 1400m of tedious ascent. The easiest route up the mountain is described below, but we recommend the quicker technical route (see Other Routes).

LIECHTENSTEIN: GRAUSPITZ

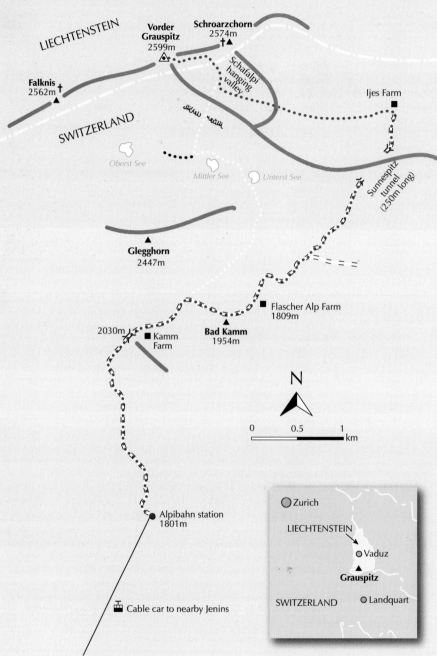

Vorder Grauspitz 2599m

Schroarzchorn 2574m

LIECHTENSTEIN

SWITZERLAND

Falknis 2562m †

Schafalpi hanging valley

Ijes Farm

Oberst See

Mittler See

Unterst See

Sunnespitz tunnel (250m long)

Glegghorn 2447m

Flascher Alp Farm 1809m

2030m

Kamm Farm

Bad Kamm 1954m

N

0   0.5   1 km

Alpibahn station 1801m

Cable car to nearby Jenins

Zurich

LIECHTENSTEIN

Vaduz

Grauspitz

SWITZERLAND   Landquart

Grauspitz, with Falknis lurking beyond (David Alexander)

Note The Alpibahn cable car map inaccurately marks Falknis as 2599m. Falknis is 2562m and very close to Grauspitz.

Note Grauspitz's adjacent peaks of the Schroarzhorn and the popular Falknis both have a white summit cross. Avoid the temptation to be distracted by these.

Note The route described essentially takes you away from the mountain before bringing you back in. Do not get confused by hikers plodding onwards to the three popular lakes, Oberst, Mittler and Unterst, and also those ascending Falknis.

ROUTE

From the **Alpibahn station** take the clear track left (NW) through classic 'Heidi country', following signs to Kamm and Falknis.

Continue N up the track to the **Kamm Pass** (2030m). Here you will see a small wooden house.

From the Kamm pass follow the track down past the **Bad Kamm** and **Flascher Alp** farms to (1780m). Here the track splits. Take the left fork uphill towards the Ijes dairy farm. If the weather is clear you will see the imposing craggy ridge of Grauspitz as you pass underneath **Glegghorn**. You should also have a view of the large red scree cirque 'Schafalpi' – the summit and fore summit of Grauspitz are on the left of the cirque.

On route to Ijes pass through the **Sunnespitz ridge** by way of a fairly dark 250m tunnel (a torch is useful here).

At **Ijes** turn due W (left) up the first wide valley. Avoid bearing off to either side and aim for the centre of the ridge at the head of the valley (due W). Where the right-hand ridge meets the head of the valley is also fine. The terrain here is tedious, particularly on descent.

22 LIECHTENSTEIN

At the head of the valley (2370m) you will find yourself on a narrow ridge above a short hanging valley that leads into the red scree of the **Schafalpi** cirque. There is no point trying to traverse around the extremely loose terrain.

Descend into the cirque before ascending WNW out to reach a grass-covered pass between the **Schroarzhorn** (2574m) and the high point **Vorder Grauspitz** (2599m).

Note The Schroarzhorn has a white steel cross on its summit. Avoid the temptation to go there before ascending Grauspitz, as descent from the summit of Schroarzhorn to the pass is extremely dangerous due to the ludicrously exposed ridge, very loose rock and sheer drops.

The north face of the Schroarzhorn, Grauspitz and Falknis from Liechtenstein (David Alexander)

Once on the ridge turn left (SW). The E side facing onto the cirque is less exposed than the W side at first. The rock here is extremely loose, and any footmarks you are likely to find will be those of ibex. Stay with the ridge until you reach the fore summit marked by a small cairn tower. The summit of **Grauspitz** is 60m to the W and marked by a large sprawling cairn. From here the ridge begins to descend slightly and continues to Falknis, but as far as we can tell it is impassable. Falknis also has a summit cross.

Descent

Descend the way you came up. If late for the cable car station, you might be able to hitch-hike a farm vehicle down to Jenins as the descent is long and very tedious. If resolved to descend on foot, follow the marked trail down from the Alpibahn station – avoid walking down the road to Jenins.

Note If using the Schesaplana map, a dotted path ascending to the summit of Sunnenspitz from E of **Unterst See** (lake), grid ref 764 212, does not exist. It is probably a mapping fingerprint.

OTHER ROUTES

TECHNICAL ROUTE

Equipment	Climbing shoes, 20m+ rope, large slings, harnesses, a small selection of gear placements, helmet
Difficulty	British standard 'Difficult' to 'Very Difficult'
Ascent	900m

The standard ascent of Grauspitz via Ijes dairy farm is understandably a frustratingly indirect route to the summit. This alternative route is perhaps the most direct possible, but will require reasonable climbing experience. It should not be attempted in rain or bad weather.

ROUTE

Follow the route above to the **Kamm Pass**, then head down the track for 100m. On your left you will see a yellow sign marking a muddy path which traverses beneath Glegghorn to Unterst lake. You subsequently lose very little of the height gained to the Kamm Pass. Follow this path to **Unterst See** (NNE).

From the lake head due W up a clearly walked path to the second lake (**Mittler See**).

At Mittler See the **Schafalpi cirque** is due N. On the left side of the cirque is the summit of Grauspitz and on the N side of the cirque is the Schroarzhorn with its white steel cross (2574m). Staying dead centre, head straight up the scree fall to the mouth of the cirque. You will see the cases of mortar bombs dropped in training by the Swiss army on this route. Rope up here.

Continue up 'Difficult' short climbs and scrambles to one final short pitch of 'V-Diff' standard. The rocks are very loose here and great care should be taken placing protection.

Having overcome the last steep climb, follow gentler grassy terrain due N into the cirque. Pick up the main route from here (descend, then ascend WNW out of the cirque).

Grauspitz from Unterst Lake

129

LITHUANIA: AUKSTOJAS/JUOZAPINE KALNAS

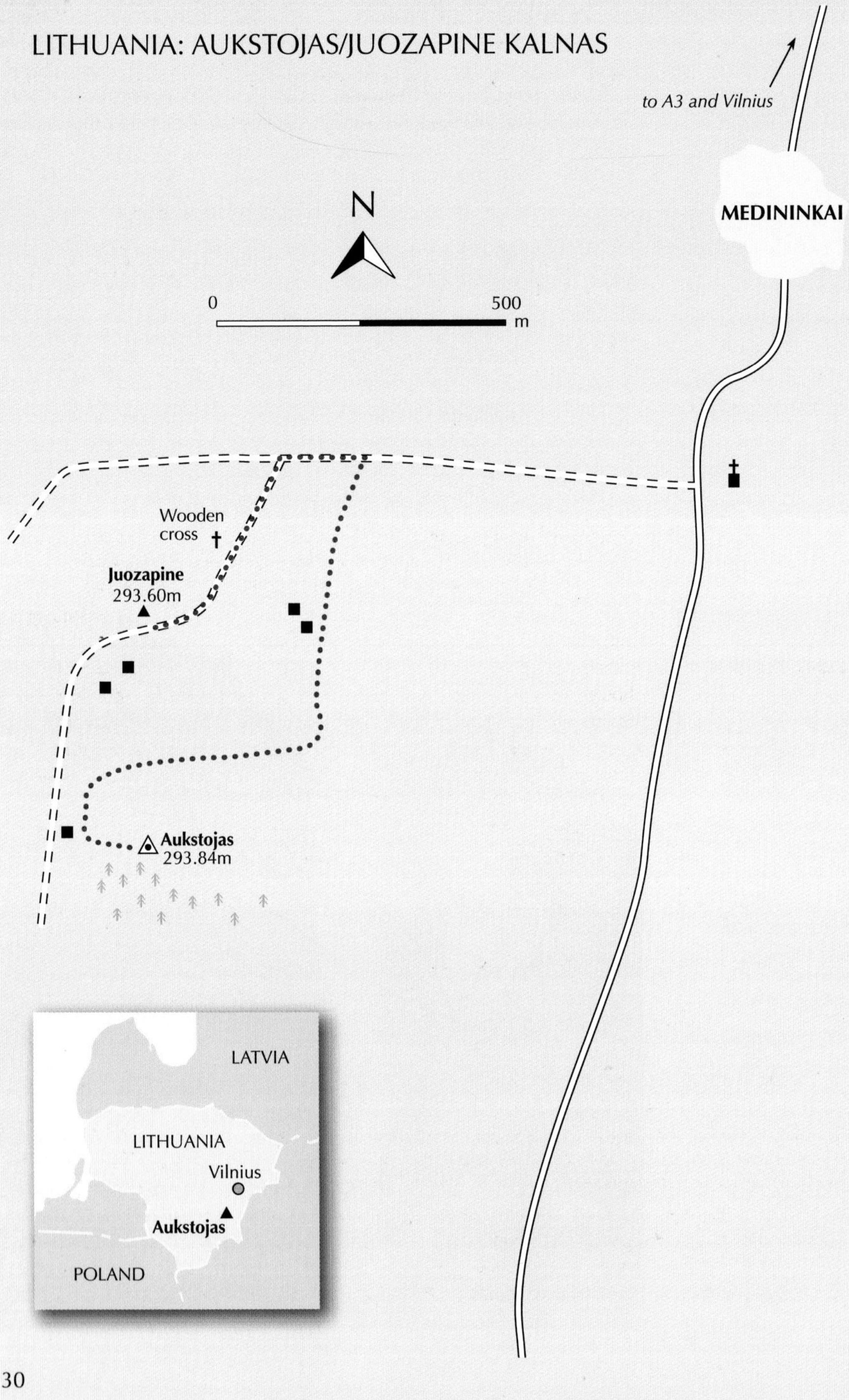

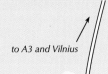

to A3 and Vilnius

MEDININKAI

N

0   500
                                              m

Wooden
cross   †

Juozapine
293.60m
▲

Aukstojas
293.84m

LATVIA

LITHUANIA

Vilnius

Aukstojas ▲

POLAND

AUKSTOJÁS/JUOZAPINE KALNAS 294M

Location	30km SE of Vilnius, near Belarus border, close to Medininkai
Start	Medininkai
Map(s)	Good Baltic States road map; if cycling (see below) Vilniaus Apylinkes IV 1:50,000 Briedis, 2007 (marks new high point)
Equipment	None
Climbing period	Year-round
Difficulty	1
Enjoyment	*
Ascent	10m
Time	5mins between two high points
Water	Not applicable
Accommodation	Best to stay in Vilnius: accommodation to suit all budgets
Getting there	From Vilnius take A3/E28 towards Minsk. Turn right on first turning to Medininkai. In village centre turn right to Juozapine. After passing impressive church, and just beyond walled area, signpost marks Juozapine Kalnas on right. Drive until see big wooden cross on left and track leading to it. Park here.
Public transport	In theory getting to Medininkai (few hundred metres from the two hills) should be easy. Roughly four buses a day run direct to Medininkai from Vilnius bus station, but inconsistent (signed to 'Turgeliai' or 'Keipunai'). Check up-to-date times with bus station information centre. At the time of writing first bus goes from stands 12 or 13 (not adjacent) at 7.10am; tickets purchased from driver. Last bus back to Vilnius 7.37pm. By taxi c€25 from Vilnius, but pre-arrange fare (make sure driver understands includes return, and meter off). In summer (long warm days) hire bicycle from tourist information on Vilnius Grad: 88.5km round trip, but after Vilnius left behind terrain very flat. Cycling along direct main Minsk Road (A3) not recommended: busy with many lorries.
Nearest high points	Gaizinkalns (Latvia), Suur Muna Magi (Estonia)

Of the Baltic three, Lithuania's high point is the silliest. Very much like the Danish mix-up, for years Juozapine Kalnas was regarded as the highest hill in Lithuania and a plaque and a large boulder stone attested to this grand status. However, after survey work by Vilnius University, some bright spark said, 'Hang on, I think that hill over there is slightly higher.' The 'hill over there' is Aukstojas, about 300m away from Juozapine and separated from the former high point by a couple of fields. Juozapine looks and feels slightly higher than the new national high point, and in order to guard against a reversal we recommend visiting both hills and, just to make sure, a visit to Lithuania's third-highest hill, Zybartoniu Kalnas, might be wise. Heights for the respective points vary. The latest data has Aukstojas at 293.8m, Juozapine at 293.6m and

Zybartoniu Kalnas at 293.4m. While Aukstojas and Juozapine are but a stone's throw away from the Belarusian border, we found that the relaxed atmosphere of the Medininkai area in Lithuania was light years away from the brusque and often forbidding style of Belarus.

ROUTE

Walk along the track and up to the wooden cross. The highest point of the hill is a mound which covers a water silo further along. It appears a trig point has been removed from here. There is also a large boulder with 1252 carved onto it, presumably to commemorate the commencement of the Lithuanian state. The 'summit' of Juozapine now has a new noticeboard which explains about the change in high point and shows a clear route to the Aukstojas marker stone, which is easy to see due S of Juozapine.

The route essentially avoids traipsing over crops and through either of the two farms by skirting the edge of the fields. Do not follow the continuation of the track as this leads to the further farm, and would involve passing through the farmyard to reach the stone. Common sense is all that is required to get you there without upsetting either farmer. In winter with deep snow cover it is probably best to follow the track to the farm and ask permission to pop across to the stone. The farmer is friendly enough.

Medininkai church

DID YOU KNOW?

Famous native
Virgilijus Alekna, who won Olympic gold medals for the discus in 2000 and 2004.

Irrelevant fact
Lithuania was the first former Soviet republic to declare independence. It did so in 1990.

Aukstojas summit stone

Aukstojas is marked by a boulder and another noticeboard on the edge of the forest.

ZYBARTONIU KALNAS
The third-highest hill in Lithuania is so close to the height of Aukstojas that you may feel it prudent to visit it as well. Zybartoniu Kalnas is 9km due W of Juozapine Kalnas.

Getting there Follow main road out of Medininkai towards Keipunai. Turn right 1.5km after Juozapine turning. Follow road for 3km until reaching a T-junction. Turn right, then immediately left. Follow road for another 3km until crossroads is reached. Turn right, follow road for 3km. On left a track by a farm leads into Kruopines National Park and up to third-highest point.

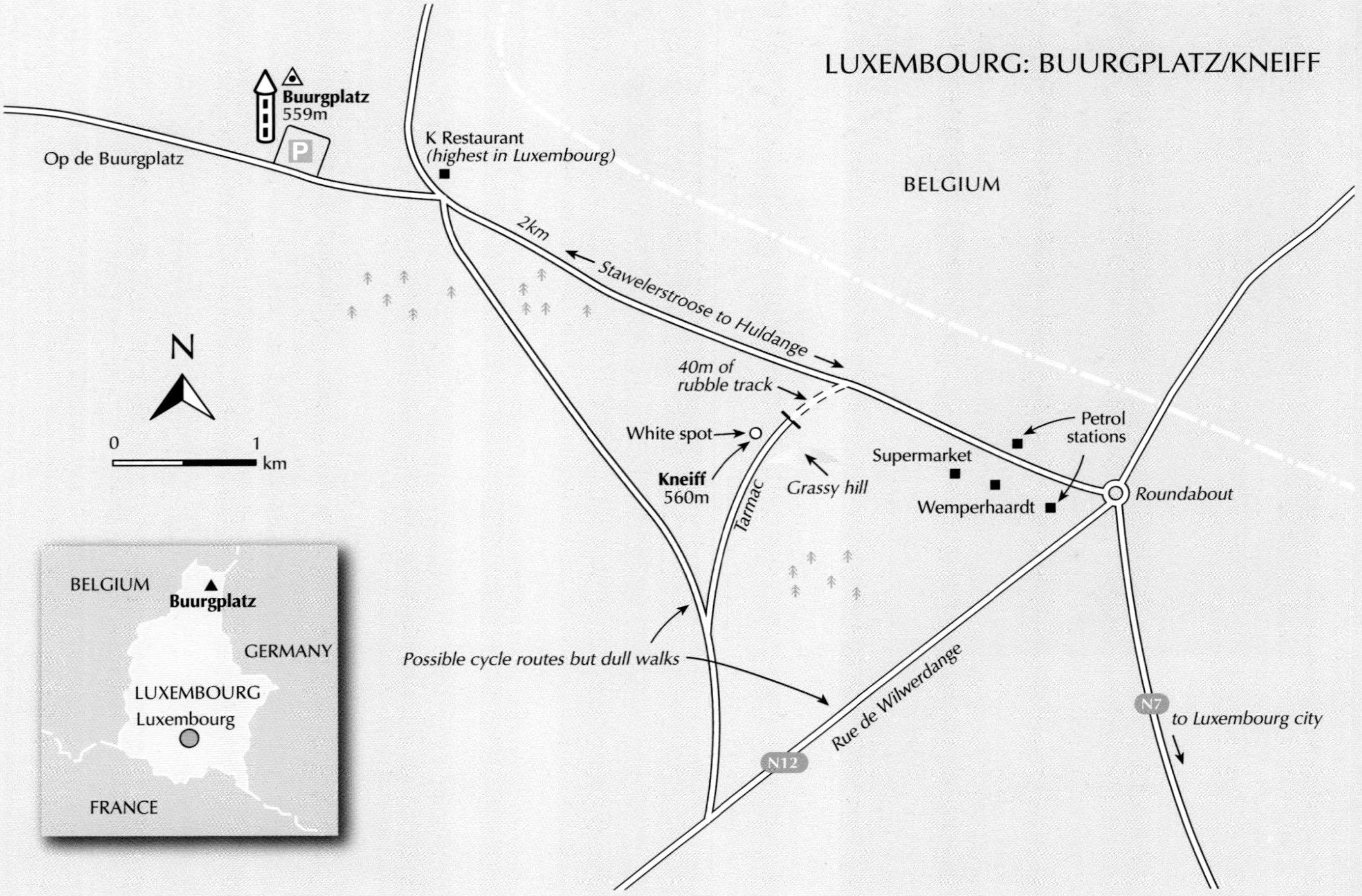

LUXEMBOURG: BUURGPLATZ/KNEIFF

BELGIUM

to Luxembourg city

N7

Roundabout

Petrol
stations

Wemperhaardt

Supermarket

Rue de Wilwerdange

N12

Grassy hill

Stawelerstroose to Huldange

40m of
rubble track

Tarmac

White spot

Kneiff
560m

Possible cycle routes but dull walks

2km

K Restaurant
(highest in Luxembourg)

Op de Buurgplatz

Buurgplatz
559m

P

N

km
1

0

BELGIUM

GERMANY

Buurgplatz

LUXEMBOURG

Luxembourg

FRANCE

Buurgplatz tower

The modest Kneiff summit stone

Old 'summit' cross at Buurgplatz

Location	Northern Luxembourg near Belgian border and Wemperhaardt
Start	Buurgplatz
Map(s)	Good road map
Equipment	None
Climbing period	Year-round
Difficulty	1
Enjoyment	*
Ascent	None
Time	None
Water	Cafe
Accommodation	Youth hostel at Wiltz or campsite at Clervaux
Getting there	From Luxembourg take A7 (E421) N towards Ettelbruck. Road eventually merges into N7; follow this N to Weiswampach and Wemperhaardt. At Wemperhaardt roundabout take Stawelerstroose road NE (signposted Salmchateau and Gouvy). Less than 0.6km along K Restaurant at Buurgplatz is on right; turning left leads to Buurgplatz tower and parking.
Public transport	From Luxembourg city catch train N to Troisvierges on line 10. Regular bus service from Troisvierges (Irish pub) to Buurgplatz.
Nearest high points	Signal de Botrange (Belgium), Vaalserberg (Netherlands)

The high point of Luxembourg is located in the rolling hills of the country's northernmost region; where forest borders farm, and farmland borders low-price fuel stations, where tractors rake across the land and cows munch tirelessly on the rich green grass; where life is slow and endearingly peaceful; a pleasant escape from the overall hustle and bustle found in this corner of Europe. The search for Luxembourg's highest ground will lead you into a dispute between the traditional high point, Buurgplatz, and an unverified claim for a nearby hill called Kneiff. The situation is very much as it was for the Danish high point in 2005. Still generally regarded as the highest point in Luxembourg, the hill Buurgplatz comes with a proud tower and a plaque. The claim for Kneiff may be inaccurate, and may soon be shown to be so. If one could be made, a 400m-long spirit level would probably settle things far better than any surveying equipment. As the height difference between the points is minimal cover your bases by visiting both. A small forest prohibits views of Buurgplatz from Knieff.

ROUTE
You're already there!

KNEIFF
Midway between the Wemperhaardt roundabout and the turning for Buurgplatz, an unsurfaced farm track leads up for 60m to a tiny little white concrete marker on the right and the small hill of Knieff beyond it. The track turns to tarmac as Kneiff is reached. Driving on the road is not prohibited.

DID YOU KNOW?

Famous native
Joseph Bartel, Luxembourg's only Olympic gold medallist, who won the 1500m at the 1952 Helsinki Olympics.

Irrelevant fact
Luxembourg presently has the highest domestic product per capita in the world.

MOUNT KORAB 2764M

Cited as 2753m in some places and also known as Golem Korab
See Former Yugoslav Republics under Health and Safety in the Introduction

Location	Macedonian/Albanian border western Macedonia, N of Lake Ohrid
Start	Strezimir
Map(s)	Not officially available, might be found on internet
Equipment	Standard hiking gear
Climbing period	**First Sunday in September**
Difficulty	2
Enjoyment	***
Ascent	1400m
Time	3½–4hrs
Water	Streams on approach to summit climb. Shepherds at old watchtower will direct you to free-running water. Beware of summer droughts.
Accommodation	Number of well-advertised home-stays available in ski resort Mavrovo at S end of Mavrovsko lake. Mavrovi Hanovi has couple of small hotels and cafés.
Getting there	Take M4 (E65) W from Skopje to Tetovo, then 26 (E65) S to Gostivar. After Gostivar take 19 W to Mavrovi Hanovi on Mavrovsko lake. At dam S of Mavrovi Hanovi take right-hand (W) road to Durbar. Follow this downhill for 9.6km to turning on right; starts with bridge across river. Tarmac continues for c200m before turning to rubble; with care just about driveable with normal car. Continues for 19km; first military checkpoint after 7km; further 12km to Strezimir. After 3–4km steep hairpin turn out of river valley. Eventually reach another steep hairpin bend and small bridge below Strezimir watchtower; park unless in 4x4. Strezimir (starting point) is large white house with guard dogs, military positions made from sandbags and razor wire.
Public transport	As part of organised September climb, Skopje Climbing Club hires several coaches to start of route. If restriction lifted (see below), possible to get to Mavrovi Hanovi from Skopje by direct bus. Enquire at information desk for up-to-date times. At the time of writing four buses leave at 8am, 10am, 1pm and 2.15pm. May prove easier to get to Mavrovi by catching train to Tetovo, then bus. From Mavrovi Hanovi take taxi to trailhead.
Nearest high points	Djeravica (Kosovo), Maja Kolata (Montenegro), Mount Olympus (Greece), Musala (Bulgaria)

The summit of Mount Korab is shared by Albania and Macedonia, and as such provides each country with its highest point. As ever with the high points of the former Yugoslav republics, a fantastic mountain which should offer a great hike is spoiled by complications! Because of its situation on the border of two countries drawn into minor conflict in 2001, Korab remains

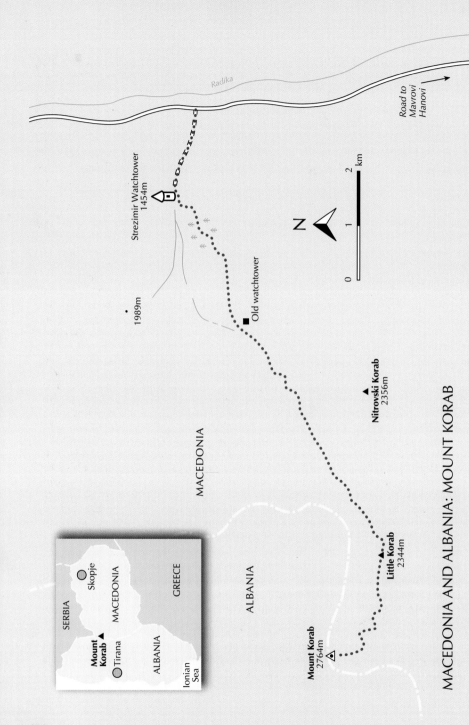

MACEDONIA AND ALBANIA: MOUNT KORAB

Mount Korab, from Macedonia: the highest point is on the left end of the ridge

a politically sensitive mountain. Residual rumours of landmines placed on the Albanian side of the mountain by the Macedonians are also a concern. While these rumours might prove entirely unfounded, no attempt to ascend the mountain from Albania should be made without extensive research. As of October 2007, Korab is officially closed from the Macedonian side for all but one day per year. The border area is presently under the jurisdiction of the Macedonian police, and security is provided by the Macedonian military. As such access to the mountain is severely restricted. Border guards here are not prone to bribery or easy persuasion. The Macedonian government has, however, acquiesced to both national and international pressure from hikers wishing to ascend the mountain. In conjunction with Skopje Climbing Club, there is now the rather bizarre scenario of a mountain open day. The simplest way to ascend Korab is to climb on this open day with the military escort provided and 1000+ climbers on the first Sunday in September. For further information log on to the Skopje Climbing Club website www. korab.org.mk. The special circumstances under which we ascended the peak are unlikely to be repeated in the foreseeable future.

The mountain itself is pleasant and remote, with only a handful of shepherds, both Macedonian and Albanian, working the hills. Bears are common, if shy, inhabitants of the lower slopes (you are far more likely to see their berry-seed excrement than the animals themselves). The walk leads through exceptional karst scenery, provides no real technical difficulty and is a great 'two for one' peak. On exceptionally clear days – and with keen eyesight – both the Ionian and Aegean seas can be spied from the summit, giving historians cause to believe Korab was climbed by Alexander the Great's father Phillip II of Macedon around 350BC.

DISPUTE

Korab is categorically the highest mountain in both Albania and Macedonia, with the summit and its dual-flag trig point situated soundly on the border. The border is not disputed. Some sources refer to a high point of Macedonia as Mount Rudoka, while attributing the height 2747m to this peak. That height bears no resemblance to the far lower Mount Rudoka but does correspond with Macedonia's second-highest mountain, Mount Titov.

Note The likelihood is you will have no route-finding to do as you will be escorted. The route is described below in case restrictions are lifted. If they ever are, do not attempt this mountain in poor visibility as getting lost could be fatal.

This ark does not float: church in the lake at Mavrovi

DID YOU KNOW?

Famous native (Macedonia) Mother Teresa (Agnes Gonxha Bojaxhiu), of Albanian ethnicity, was born in Skopje. Actress Labina Mitevska, who had a supporting role in the film *Welcome to Sarajevo*.

Irrelevant facts (Macedonia) Because of Greek sensitivity over ancient Greek history and essentially Alexander the Great, the appropriation of the name 'Macedonia' has proved a sticking point between the two countries; so much so that the early post-Yugoslav republic was forced by the Greeks to change its flag in 1995. Macedonia has the lowest divorce rate in the world.

ROUTE

From **Strezimir** walk through a flattened area of razor wire and join the track which winds into the forest. Small paths cut off the bends on this initially. Stay on the track through the forest being wary of bears as they often pass this way to get to the river.

Exiting the forest follow the shepherd trail to the old abandoned **watchtower**, now used by shepherds. There is a permanent water source here; fill up as water higher on the route often runs dry.

Here the trail initially leads slightly leftwards from the shepherds' dwelling. You may find faded white and red target markers from this point on. Due to the lack of walking here the path is faint and the markers sparse. Head up the grassy hills of **Nistrovski Korab** to the ridge while walking parallel to the main Korab ridge. If you were to head direct to the summit you would have to pick your way through tumuli, so avoid this temptation.

At the head of the valley descend northwards and progress along the ridge, climbing over **Mal Korab** (**Little Korab**) on route, aiming for the knobble on the W end of the Korab ridge. The path is intermittent here.

Below the summit ridge pass a small hidden spring, faintly signed with an old 'Voda' marker on a rock. The summit hike is simple enough and winds up the grass. The summit is marked by a white trig point with a Macedonian flag on one side and an Albanian flag on the other. The rocks further along the ridge are not as high as this, although they may appear to be so.

Descent
As ascent, taking care not to veer off into Albania.

OTHER ROUTES
The mountain has a good route from the Albanian side but unfortunately, due to the possible presence of landmines planted in 2001, this should not even be considered without a metal detector and extensive specialist military knowledge. Do not be lured into a false sense of security by Albanian shepherds on the mountain.

We were awarded a certificate for scaling Mount Korab by 'the president'. The marker column has an Albanian flag on the other side ('Gilly' aka Goran)

141

MALTA: TA' DMEJREK/DINGLI CLIFFS

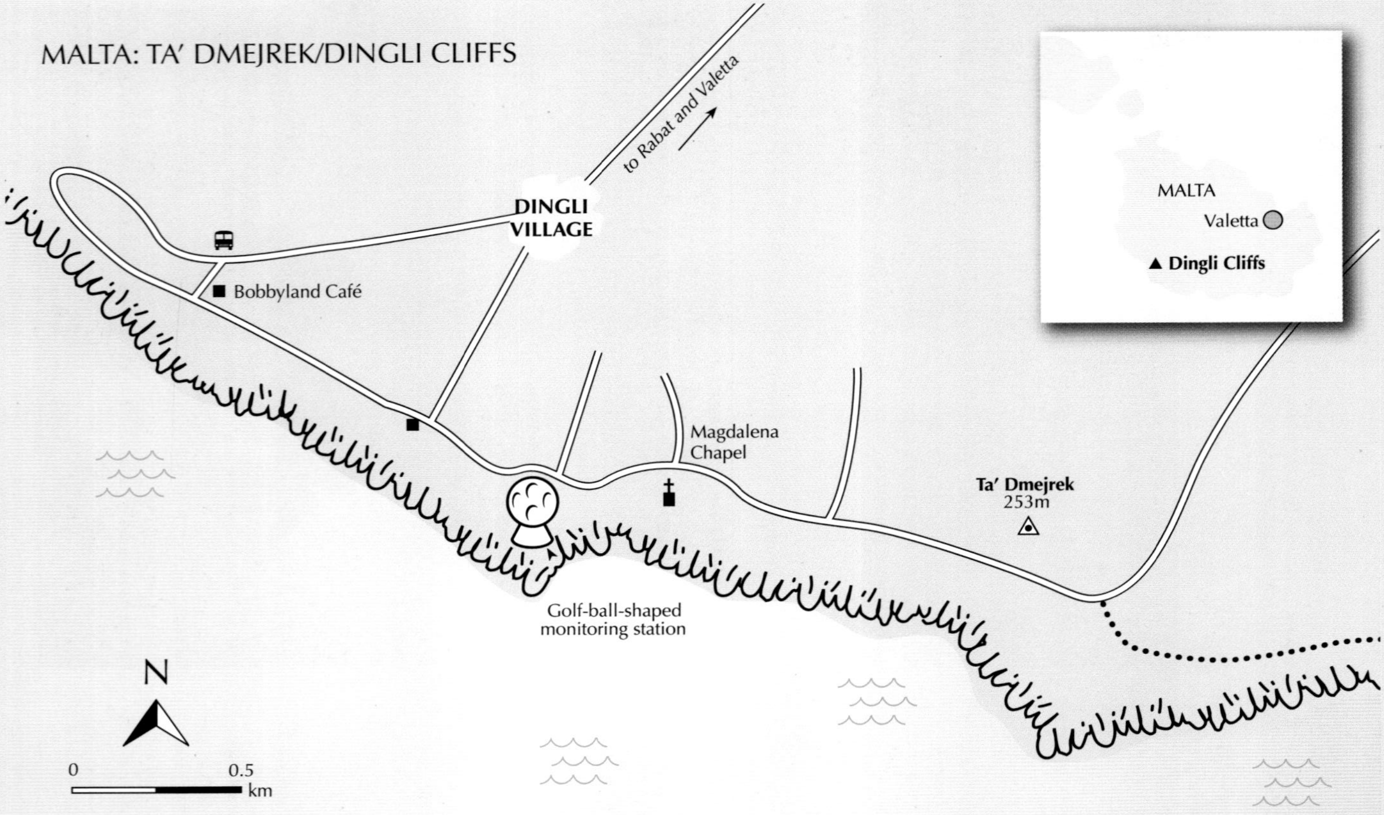
to Rabat and Valetta
DINGLI VILLAGE
Bobbyland Café
Magdalena Chapel
Ta' Dmejrek
253m
Golf-ball-shaped monitoring station
N
0
0.5
km
MALTA
Valetta
▲ Dingli Cliffs

26 MALTA

TA' DMEJREK/DINGLI CLIFFS 253M

Odd marble stone on steel rods at the 253m spot height with Valetta on the opposite side of the island in the distance

Location	Southern Malta, on main island
Start	Dingli
Map(s)	Island maps, most showing 253m spot height, readily available in Valetta; Bartholomew map also shows bus routes and walks
Equipment	None
Climbing period	Year-round
Difficulty	1
Enjoyment	***
Ascent	Minimal
Time	30mins by bus from Valetta, perhaps 1hr to walk along clifftops
Water	Café open daily in summer
Accommodation	Island small and packed with accommodation to suit all budgets
Getting there	Best way to make a day of 'climbing' to high point is to hire bicycle in Valetta and cycle to Dingli.
Public transport	No need to drive (although Dingli well signosted) as bus simple and very cheap. Most people catch no 81 bus from bus station in centre of Valetta to Dingli (every c30mins). Bus goes through Dingli and up to cliffs; get off as soon as cliffs reached.

Malta is an island with a coast characterised by rocky inlets and steep cliffs – the Dingli Cliffs are the highest – which drop straight into the sea. From the cliffs a glance one way brings views across the deep azure of the Mediterranean; turn your head in the opposite direction and you will look inland to the impressive white spread of the Maltese capital, Valetta, 24km away. The Dingli Cliffs are a good place to spend a day, and Malta is a fantastic little country in which to unwind. The pace of life is slow and languid, while the walled city of Valetta is spectacular. A former colony, the island remains popular with British holiday-makers; remnants of its colonial past are exemplified by, for example, traditional red phone boxes.

The exact high point is unfortunately a little frustrating as the Maltese have made nothing of it, and ascertaining its exact position is difficult. The Dingli Cliffs remain at roughly the same height for a stretch of 3.2km. Once there you will inevitably spend your time trying to decide which point is actually the highest, walking between the clifftop Bobbyland Café, the golf-ball-shaped 'air traffic control radar'/monitoring station, the Magdalena Chapel and then over to the scrubland marked on most maps with the highest spot height. We recommend covering your bases with a walk, or a cycle ride, along the length of the cliffs as the height differences are too small to ascertain with an altimeter or GPS. While in Malta do not miss the delicious Maltese pies: fresh tuna and spinach, and pea, are particular favourites.

ROUTE

Walk from the bus stop past the **Bobbyland Café**. You will see a steel bicycle ornament en route to the golf-ball listening post. From here head onwards to the nearby **Magdalena Chapel** (which seems to be permanently locked). From the chapel head down to the road junction. Continue to follow the

Fig trees on Dingli Cliffs with the Bobbyland café beyond

'All I want to do is ride my bicycle': unexplained metalwork on Dingli Cliffs with the monitoring station beyond

road along the cliffs to the brow of the first visible hill. Here – as far as Maltese mapping and the Maltese tourist board are concerned – is the highest point of Malta, **Ta' Dmejrek**. There is nothing to mark the spot but strange marble slabs on steel poles on an area of scrubland. The listening-post area certainly appears higher when observed from this point, but without surveying equipment it would be impossible to be certain.

Descent
With bicycles good circular routes and swimming possibilities are plentiful. It would be possible to head down to Ras Hanzir, SE of the Dingli Cliffs, for a good swim. Buses tend to stop running at around 7pm so don't get caught out.

MOLDOVA: MOUNT BALANESTI

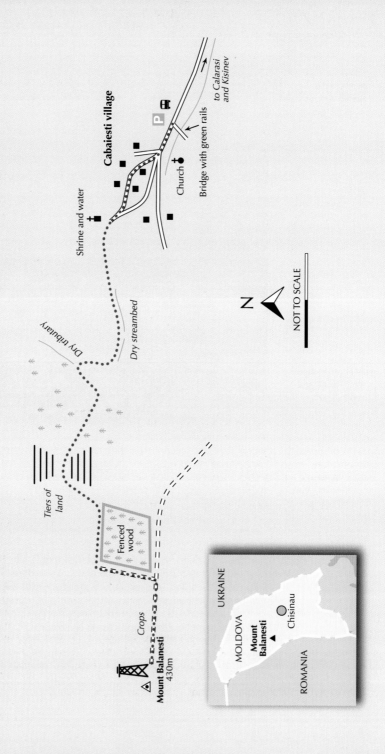

NOT TO SCALE

N

Cabaiesti village

P

Shrine and water

Church

Bridge with green rails

to Calarasi and Kisinev

Dry tributary

Dry streambed

Tiers of land

Fenced wood

Crops

Mount Balanesti
430m

UKRAINE

MOLDOVA

Mount
Balanesti

Chisinau

ROMANIA

Location	Western Moldova, 64km NW of the capital Chisinau, close to Romanian border at Ungheni
Start	Cabaiesti
Map(s)	Country map or Romanian road map available at petrol stations
Equipment	None
Climbing period	Year-round
Difficulty	2
Enjoyment	***
Ascent	100m (estimated)
Time	2hr round trip (if you do not get too lost)
Accommodation	Many motels on R1 from Chisinau
Water	Ornate drinking fountain near start of route
Getting there	Plus side: probably easier to get to start of route by public transport than by car. Down side: if going by car you will get lost! Ask everyone for directions; no one speaks English, but very friendly and helpful. Road signs virtually non-existent; roads often impassable for normal vehicles. From Chisinau take R1 (E583) to Calarasi. In Calarasi turn left to Parjolteni, signposted at other side of town from where entered; immediately cross railway line. Road becomes difficult to follow due to many road junctions, but should pass World War II war memorial; if in doubt ask. Eventually join wide rubble road running parallel to river in NW direction; follow this to Cabaiesti (marked by a sign). In village is large bridge with green railings on left; park here (also where bus would drop you).
	Note Maps mark road going much closer to Mount Balanesti, but impassable without tractor.
Public transport	Possible to go by bus from Chisinau straight to Cabaiesti; ask at central bus station; or catch bus to Calarasi and another to Cabaiesti.
Nearest high points	Goverla (Ukraine), Moldoveanu (Romania)

Moldova truly is the land that time forgot, with roadside wells and stray cows, hay carts and children running wild. There are few surfaced roads and no sprawling developments to mar the countryside. The people are generally poor, but very friendly. Visit the country in the near future to get an idea of how most of Europe used to be. Mount Balanesti is found lurking in a remote rural area but helpfully boasts a large phone mast on its summit, unfortunately completely hidden on the route from Cabaiesti. The peak is not much higher than the surrounding land, which can add to the difficulty of reaching the top. On the plus side there are tracks for most of the way. Visitors to the summit are likely to meet a local guard who lives directly beneath the communications tower in a tiny cabin: like a character fresh from the annals of Homer's *Odyssey*, you really do wonder why this solitary fellow is there.

Note As of 2007, EU citizens do not require a visa to visit Moldova.

Note A sizeable portion of eastern Moldova has declared independence, and this area is known as Transnistria. Transnistria acts as a *de facto* state, but is not recognised by the UN, nor is likely to be in the foreseeable future. Russia, however, has opened an embassy there. Visits to Transnistria can have political ramifications: up-to-date information should be sought from the Foreign and Commonwealth Office.

ROUTE

Note The peak is approximately 4.8km due W of Cabaiesti. Do not worry too much if you get lost – if in doubt simply keep going W.

Walk uphill from the bridge WNW, staying on the right side of the river, following rough tracks in this direction through the village until the buildings cease. Just after the final buildings you should reach a **painted shrine** with a water fountain.

Beyond the shrine the track forks. Take the left path, descending slightly westward.

After 200m the path splits again. This time go right and bear around a tributary valley before continuing up the main valley. In summer the riverbed will be dry.

Follow the track W, which becomes fainter until you reach a **wood**. Pass through this for 600m, still heading W and ignoring clearer paths going N–S.

Emerge onto farmed land at the head of the valley. There is a grassy slope to your right with **tiers** indicating it has previously been farmed.

The route to Mount Balanesti shortly after leaving Cabaiesti

Standing to attention: the guard at Mount Balanesti's communication tower roused himself from slumber, donned his military jacket and welcomed us to the highest point of Moldova

Turn left up the opposite slope just before a plantation of trees. If you follow the line of trees NW up the hill you will soon find yourself on another track. Follow this upwards.

At the brow of the hill you will see the **telephone mast** which marks the summit. A little further on you will intersect another track. Turn right and follow it to the mast.

The mast is manned by a security guard who will be able to confirm that you are at the right spot. Just 10m before the mast you will see on your left the earthworks that are actually the high point of the country.

DID YOU KNOW?

Famous native
King Stefan III managed to forge temporary independence for Moldova in the 15th century and now adorns Moldovan bank notes.

Irrelevant fact
Moldova was formally known as Bessarabia.

Descent
By the same route.

OTHER ROUTES
Another possible route is from Balanesti village. The mast is visible from this point about 9.6km away. Ask directions for the track to walk to Cabaiesti and you will get close enough to the mast on this to find your way.

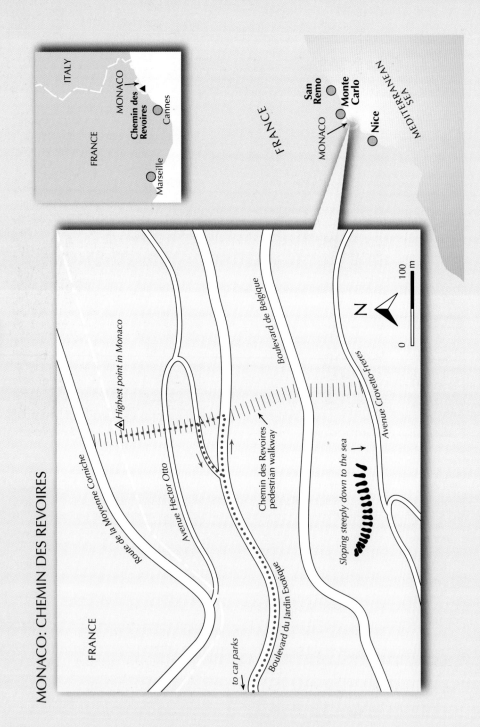

MONACO: CHEMIN DES REVOIRES

Map labels:

FRANCE

Route de la Moyenne Corniche

Avenue Hector Otto

Boulevard du Jardin Exotique

Chemin des Revoires pedestrian walkway

Boulevard de Belgique

Avenue Crovetto-Freres

△ Highest point in Monaco

Sloping steeply down to the sea

to car parks

N

0   100 m

Inset map 1:

ITALY

FRANCE

MONACO

Chemin des Revoires ▲

Cannes

Marseille

Inset map 2:

FRANCE

MONACO

San Remo

Monte Carlo

Nice

MEDITERRANEAN SEA

Monaco

Location	South of France, E of Nice.
Start	Anywhere in Monaco
Map(s)	Detailed street map
Equipment	None
Climbing period	Year-round
Difficulty	1
Enjoyment	*
Ascent	35m (162m optional)
Time	15mins
Water	Not applicable
Accommodation	Range of expensive hotels and two hostels in town
Getting there	Drive into Monaco via N7 from Nice, passing through several Cote d'Azure tolls. At 'border' of Monaco notice tall red and white national flags and parking areas right and left – park here.
Public transport	Mainline train to Monaco's only station (in harbour). Ascend the 162m either by free lift to Boulevard Jardins, or walking up steps.
Nearest high points	Pic de Coma Pedrosa (Andorra), Mont Blanc (France and Italy)

The first question about this high point is bound to be over Monaco's status as a country. While France is in its fifth republic, Monaco boasts a royal family. However, Monaco does not return an international football team, but does have a club team in the French football league. Most sources classify it as a country – so you decide. Its high point is another bone of contention, with some desperate high-pointers trying to find a peak where there is none. We can categorically assert that the highest point of Monaco is 162m on the pedestrian walkway of Chemin des Revoires, at its border with France. Any information to the contrary is inaccurate. Monaco is a bizarre place, its streets are almost stacked on top of one another, dropping vertically down to the sea and with pedestrian elevators that whisk locals up and down: it is well worth a visit.

ROUTE

From either car park walk down the Boulevard Jardins until you meet a fork in the road. There may still be a temporary cow statue here.

Either take the left fork and stay on the left-hand side of the road looking out carefully for the marble 'Chemin des Revoires' plaque and the steps going steeply N (left) next to it, or add to the ascent by continuing on Boulevard Jardins (also known as **Boulevard du Jardin Exotique**) for 100m past two apartment blocks to a lift on your left-hand side (down only). From here walk straight up the steps. At the top of these, across the road, you will see the **Chemin des Revoires** plaque.

Walk up the steps to the right of the plaque. These will eventually meet another plaque pointing Chemin des Revoires downwards. Somewhere on the steps is the invisible border with France and therefore the highest point of Monaco – well done! Now wasn't that one tough?

Note If you reach the apartment block or the road at the top of the steps you have gone too far and are now in France.

Descent

By the same route.

OTHER ROUTES

Alternatively ascend to the top of Monaco from the harbour by consulting the town map boards and heading up the stone steps which eventually lead to the Boulevard Jardins and Chemin des Revoires.

MAJA KOLATA 2534M

Also known as Maya Kolata/Kolac, Zla Kolata and Dobra Kolata
See Former Yugoslav Republics under Health and Safety in the Introduction

Location	Western Montenegro on Albanian border, S of towns Plav and Gusinje
Start	Vusanje
Map(s)	Maps not presently available. Old 1960s Belgrade maps exist, as do 1942 Soviet maps, but both outdated, have occasional inaccurate border markings and heights and nearby impossible to obtain.
Equipment	Standard hiking gear
Climbing period	April–October best; there will usually be quite a lot of snow on N faces, especially in Prokletije, until late June/early July
Difficulty	3
Enjoyment	****
Ascent	1500m
Time	5–6½hrs ascent (allowing extra time for route-finding difficulties), 3½–5hrs descent
Water	Two streams on upper part of Gralta and spring provide last water on route for up to 8hrs; take plenty of water as cool mornings can lead to sweltering afternoons
Accommodation	Plav has two hotels, and very odd unmarked campsite (toilet, fresh water) on W side of lake opposite town on main Gusinje road, by white building with green gateposts next to lake. Local police will help you find this – people in town extremely friendly and helpful. Alternatively, ask about – especially in tiny hamlet of Vusanje – and arrange to stay couple of nights with a family.
Getting there	Drive to Plav and Plav Lake S of Andrijevica (formally known as 'Ivangrad'): post office, bank, petrol station. From Plav drive round W side of lake and S to Gusinje, vibrant rural town with many sheep, goats, donkeys and cows. Go past mosque in town and take second left (after bookmakers/sports bar). After 0.5km turn right at sign for Vusanje; 3km on road forks; take left-hand route through village with white mosque and tower. Follow narrow road up out of village to reach next, Vusanje; small army barracks, speed bumps, 'no photos' sign. Route starts on track turning off left just before barracks.
Public transport	Possible to reach Plav by bus, then bus or taxi to Gusinje, from where you can easily get a taxi on to Vusanje.
Nearest high points	Djeravica (Kosovo), Maglic (Bosnia and Herzegovina), Dinara (Croatia), Korab (Macedoniä and Albania)

Dobra Kolata from Zla Kolata

MONTENEGRO: MAJA KOLATA

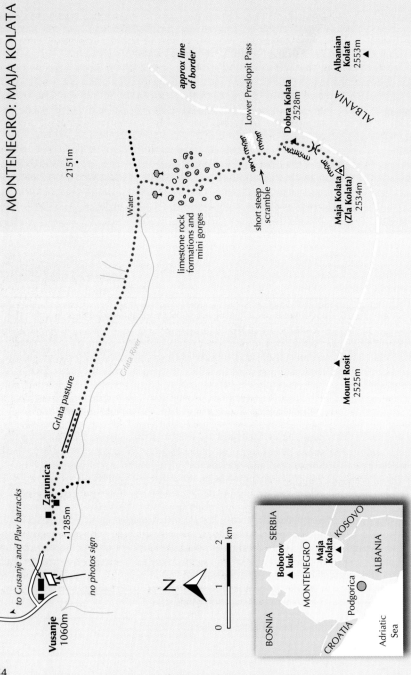

2151m

Water

Grlata River

Grlata pasture

Zarunica

.1285m

to Gusanje and Plav barracks

no photos sign

Vusanje
1060m

limestone rock
formations and
mini gorges

short steep
scramble

Lower Preslopit Pass

approx line
of border

Dobra Kolata
2528m

Albanian
Kolata
2553m

ALBANIA

Maja Kolata
(Zla Kolata)
2534m

Mount Rosit
2525m

N

0   1   2
km

BOSNIA

SERBIA

Bobotov
kuk

MONTENEGRO

Maja
Kolata

KOSOVO

CROATIA

Podgorica

ALBANIA

Adriatic
Sea

As far as the Montenegrin government is concerned, the official highest mountain in the country is Bobotov kuk on Mount Durmitor (2523m) in a UNESCO World Heritage site close to the spectacular Tara Canyon. Bobotov kuk is a wonderful mountain, complete with easy-to-follow marked trails, the amazing Ledena Pecina ice caves and even a visitors' book on top. Unfortunately the three primary experts on Montenegrin mountaineering each cite Bobotov kuk as the fourth-highest mountain, and it is to their knowledge that we have deferred.

It appears to be something of a state secret that the Maja Kolatas are the two highest peaks in the country and shows the sensitivity with which the authorities hold this particular border territory. The conceit is all the more misplaced as, when asked, most Montenegrins will proudly tell you Bobotov kuk is the highest peak. It is only in the region of Prokletije, near Lake Plav, where the population will inform you otherwise, and even then it comes in the way of a secret being passed on. Maja Kolata and Mount Rosit are marked on very few maps of the country. Nonetheless, these mountains are very impressive with tremendous limestone karst formations: we thoroughly enjoyed our time spent in the area. Montenegro is one of the most beautiful states in Europe; very much the unspoilt jewel in the crown of the former Yugoslavia. Few countries could rival a walking holiday spent here.

DISPUTE

The two highest mountains in Montenegro are believed to be the twin peaks of Maja Kolata – Dobra Kolata and Zla Kolata – 2528m and 2534m respectively. The highest peak of the Kolata massif is actually on Albanian territory and measures 2553m. The third-highest peak in Montenegro is Mount Rosit (2525m). Rosit is consistently marked on old Soviet and Yugoslav maps as a border peak and is situated near Maja Kolata. These three Montenegrin peaks are found in the remote Prokletije range in the east of Montenegro, and each shares its summit with the Albanian border. However, Maja Kolata has not been officially recognised as the highest point of Montenegro, nor the area subjected to an accurate modern survey, and so we have included a brief route description for Bobotov Kuk (the official highest mountain in the country – see below) under Other Routes.

Bobotov kuk: the traverse above Lokvice Lake

Note Another Maja Kolata in Albania is cunningly only 1200m SE of Zla Kolata.

Note At the time of going to press a permit is not required for walking in this area. Local information attests there are no landmines in the Kolata area.

Note Although there are waymarkers/paths on this mountain, there can be no question that it is particularly difficult to navigate here. Clear weather is unquestionably a distinct advantage and a compass is essential. There are no signs at the beginning of the track. You may be able to find a local who can confirm that you are heading to 'Kolata'.

The twin trapezoid peaks of Dobra and Zla Kolata from the upper Grlata pasture

ROUTE

From the **army barracks** ascend E uphill out of **Vusanje**. The tarmac on the track ceases after 150m. Continue to head E. You will probably pass donkeys laden with wood on your way.

After roughly 45mins walking, you will reach a settlement with five buildings (**Zarunica**). On your right you will pass two graves. Beyond this settlement, the track eventually turns into a path. Ignore a sharp turn off to the right (SW).

The path ascends steeply through a break in the woods, eventually passing through the trees for 150m before emerging on the **Grlata pasture**. Take the walled path up this. You will pass a shepherd's hut above you on the left.

The upper part of the pasture provides the first views of the trapezoid Dobra Kolata and eventually Zla Kolata on its right. Continue up; after crossing two small streams you reach a spring on your right, from which an old wooden pipe protrudes. This is the last permanent source of water on the route.

Once above the treeline the path soon splits. Look out for a right fork heading S where there are a few faded red waymarkers. These markers become more frequent and continue to the summit of Dobra Kolata. However, they are extremely difficult to follow and you will inevitably lose them a few times. Go through two clumps of bushes and enter a narrow rock corridor.

At the end of the corridor you will meet the first of three clearings. Follow the markers if you can, always heading for an imaginary point between Dobra Kolata and the ridge at the head of the valley (you never actually reach this ridge).

Pass a second clearing with two standing poles and a sheepfold where the markers temporarily disappear. Head round the right side and ascend to a small tree where markers reappear and lead you left up a narrow gully.

At the third clearing, turn right (SW) progressing underneath steep rock which will eventually curve you back left (SSE).

After much trial and tribulation in the gorges, you will pass under a very low arch of rock and descend into a large gully beneath the cliff face of Dobra Kolata. Here you will see permanent snow. Ascend the opposite

---

DID YOU KNOW?

Famous native
Nicola I, the last and only King of Montenegro, who reigned as Prince from 1860 to 1910 and King from 1910 to 1918.

Irrelevant fact
The capital of Montenegro, Podgorica, was renamed Titograd between 1946 and 1992 to honour Marshal Tito.

side of the gully, turning right (W), slightly back on yourself. Traverse around the crags and then descend slightly for 150m until the cliffs end and the markers lead you left (S) up grassy slopes ascending the peak.

Eventually you will swing E into a wide overgrown gully. Go straight up to the head of this where you can scramble out at the right side then continue in your original direction until reaching a grassy plateau. Here you will clearly see the summit of **Dobra Kolata**. Descend slightly to take the right-hand ridge following markers to the top. The summit is marked by names carved into the rocks.

The higher Montenegrin summit of Maja Kolata (Zla Kolata) is the nearby trapezoid form to the W, but you will have a steep descent and ascent to get over to it. Go along the ridge descending to the pass between the two peaks and ascend the ridge to the summit, where you will find only a small cairn rebuilt by the authors.

Descent
Descend the same way. In good dry weather you can avoid the climb back up over Dobra Kolata by traversing around the left side (W face) of the peak on grass that runs between sections of crag.

OTHER ROUTES

BOBOTOV KUK (CIROVA PECINA)

Start	Zabljak
Map(s)	Available at various shops in bustling Zabljak
Difficulty	3
Enjoyment	★★★★
Ascent	1200m
Time	3½hrs ascent (car park sign misleadingly states 5½hrs)
Water	Last permanent source Ivan Do near start of route
Accommodation	Campsite in Zabljak and hotels
Getting there	From Podgorica take E65/E80 or 2 N for 90km. Just before reaching Mojkovac follow road left to Bistrica, then signs to Durmitor, Tara Canyon and Zabljak. At roundabout in centre of popular mountain village of Zabljak (post office, cash machine, hotels, internet café), turn right; follow road to end, to paying car park. Park here.
Public transport	Zabljak (where route begins) can be reached direct by bus from Podgorica; alternatively train to Mojkovac, then bus

Bobotov kuk's summit crag

ROUTE
From the car park red waymarkers lead up a path away from the tarmac track and raise you above the reservoir, **Crno Jezero**, to the bridge and path junction of **Ivan Do**.

MONTENEGRO: BOBOTOV KUK

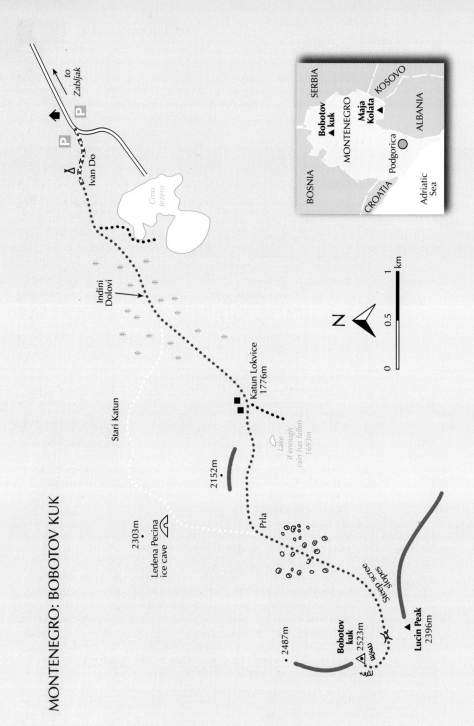

to
Žabljak

P

P

P

Ivan Do

Crno
Jezero

Indini
Dolovi

Stari Katun

Katun Lokvice
1776m

Lake
if enough
rain has fallen
1693m

2152m

2303m

Ledena Pecina
ice cave

Prla

2487m

Bobotov
kuk
2523m

Steep scree
slopes

Lucin Peak
2396m

N

0   0.5   1   km

SERBIA

KOSOVO

Bobotov
▲kuk

Maja
Kolata ▲

MONTENEGRO

ALBANIA

BOSNIA

Podgorica

CROATIA

Adriatic
Sea

Looking southwest from the summit to Samar

Cross the stream and follow a pleasant shady path through the forest. Eventually you will reach a series of limestone gullies where Bobotov Kuk is signposted.

You will soon reach a frustrating series of ups and downs in the Broijista area where, despite plenty of greenery, the limestone drains the water and there are no streams.

The route will lead you to **Katun Lokvice** mountain shelter. Two ramshackle shepherd huts here stand at the pass above the crater. 'Voda' is marked (but it, like the Lokvice Lake in the crater, had run dry when we visited the mountain).

It is possible to minimalise height loss at the Lockvize crater, though this option is not obvious in ascent and should be left for the descent. Continue to follow the main path as it sweeps you down along the inner curve of the crater before rising up fairly steeply to **Prla**.

At Prla the path splits and many hikers deviate to the very popular **Ledena Pecina ice cave**. The path now climbs up karst features out of Prla, over a shoulder and down across a short boulderfield.

The boulderfield is followed by a steep and troublesome scree slope to a pass where an alternative ascent is met. At the pass turn right and follow the path as it swings past the impressive summit crag of **Bobotuv kuk**. A decent little scramble is required to reach the well-marked summit, complete with cairns and a visitors' book.

Descent
By the same route.

THE NETHERLANDS: VAALSERBERG

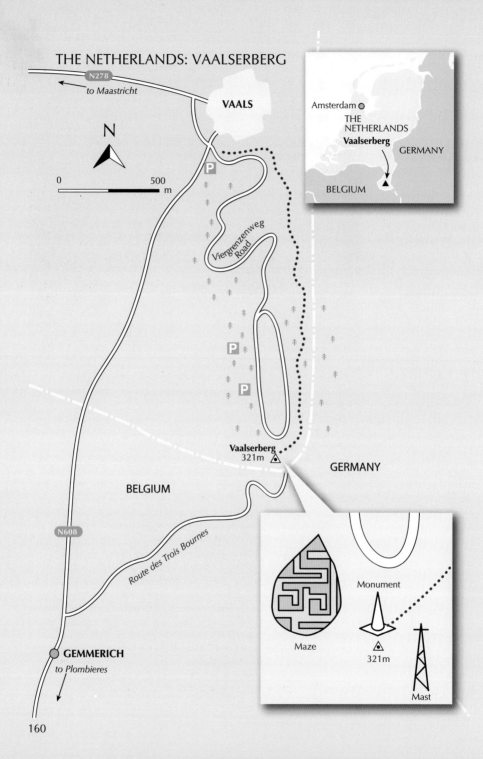

N278
to Maastricht

VAALS

N

0   500 m

Viergrenzenweg Road

Vaalserberg
321m

BELGIUM

GERMANY

N608

Route des Trois Bournes

GEMMERICH
to Plombieres

Amsterdam
THE NETHERLANDS
Vaalserberg
GERMANY
BELGIUM

Maze

Monument

321m

Mast

The steel cone marks the highest point of the Netherlands, while the giant steel tower marks the meeting of the Netherlands, Belgium and Germany

The Netherlands' highest and lowest points signed

Vaals' ascent route in autumn

Location	Dutch, German and Belgian border near Aachan, S Netherlands
Start	Vaals
Map(s)	Any good detailed road map
Equipment	None
Climbing period	Year-round
Difficulty	1
Enjoyment	*
Ascent	70m
Time	20mins
Water	Available in many cafés on Vaalserberg
Accommodation	Campsite on W side of Vaals
Getting there	From Liege take A3 (E40) W towards Aachen and Germany. Come off at junction 38 and take N67 N (signposted Henri-Chapelle). Turn right (E) on N3; follow road to Morsenet and Vaals turning (left). Winding road leads under railway viaduct. Follow signs to Gemmerich and Vaals; eventually reach full loop in road just before Vaals. Take the Drielandenpunt (Viergrenzenweg road) turning left off this. After c200m meet bend to right, brown Drielandenpunt sign and start of 'no parking' signs. Park before these are reached. (Alternatively drive to top and pay €2 to park, but walk in woods described below preferable.)
Public transport	Aachen well served by bus and train links; from here catch trans-border bus to Vaals; walk up from Vaals. Regular bus to summit in summer (why anyone would need to catch this a mystery).
Nearest high points	Signal de Botrange (Belgium), Buurgplatz/Knieff (Luxembourg)

The Netherlands is well known for being as flat as the proverbial pancake, but its high point is far loftier than those of some other European countries such as Denmark and Lithuania. Vaalserberg, a busy hill with a road up it, is not without interest as an oddity. On its summit is Drielandenpunt (Three Countries Point) where the Netherlands, Belgium and Germany's borders all touch. This was once Four Countries Point as the tiny neutral country of Moresnet (1815–1919) also used to converge here. Moresnet is now part of Belgium. The route up is described from the Dutch side. The highest maze in the Netherlands is found on the summit along with cafés, restaurants, a playground and a viewing tower.

ROUTE

At the bend you will see a green signpost marking the 'Wandelwaggen Drielandenpunt' footpath on your left. Initially the route follows a tarmac path, which passes a couple of houses.

After 50m or so, and having passed the electrical substation, a footpath branches off to the left of the tarmac path. Take this and follow it up the hill (the tarmac path leads to a restaurant).

Through the trees you will see a wooden viewing tower on your right and nearby a memorial to a 1932 plane crash; this is not the summit. Stay on the path following the occasional red/yellow and '193' waymarkers.

After passing a standing stone with an eagle carved onto it the path descends for 50m or so and passes beneath yet another restaurant with three national flags, before ascending to the plateau once more.

Follow the path and the '193' border stones until you emerge with the Dutch high point directly in front of you and the steel viewing tower to your left.

The summit of the Netherlands is marked not by the steel tower, which marks where the countries meet, but by a steel stanchion and a stone plaque close by.

Descent

By the same route.

SLIEVE DONARD 852M

The Mountains of Mourne from Slieve Donard

Location	Mourne Mountains, southern coast of Northern Ireland, SE Ulster near Newcastle
Start	Newcastle
Map(s)	Ordnance Survey of Northern Ireland Mourne Country
Equipment	Standard hiking gear
Climbing period	Year-round
Difficulty	2
Enjoyment	***
Ascent	820m
Time	1½hrs ascent, 1hr descent
Water	Plenty up to 600m
Accommodation	Number of B&Bs and youth hostel in Newcastle
Getting there	From Belfast take A24 and A2 due S to Newcastle via Carryduff, Ballinahinch and Clough. Follow A2 along seafront to 'Donard car park' at S end of town centre. Park here.
Public transport	Regular bus service from Belfast to Newcastle; walk directly up peak via Donard Wood and Glen River.
Nearest high points	Carrauntoohil (Ireland), Scafell Pike (England)

163

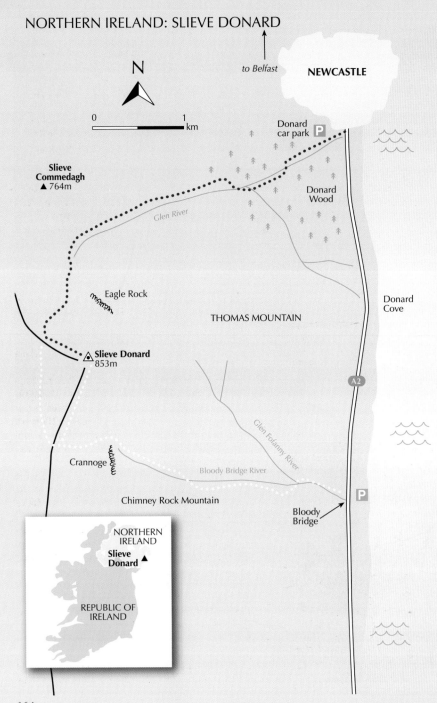

NORTHERN IRELAND: SLIEVE DONARD

N

0   1
km

to Belfast

NEWCASTLE

Donard car park
P

Slieve Commedagh
▲ 764m

Glen River

Donard Wood

Eagle Rock

THOMAS MOUNTAIN

Donard Cove

A2

△ **Slieve Donard**
853m

Glen Fofanny River

Crannoge

Bloody Bridge River

Chimney Rock Mountain

P

Bloody Bridge

NORTHERN IRELAND
Slieve Donard ▲

REPUBLIC OF IRELAND

Rising up sublimely from the Irish Sea, on clear days Slieve Donard provides hikers with magnificent summit views of Ireland, the Isle of Man, England, Wales and Scotland. Hikers will feel their hearts lift as they gaze outwards from the sweeping crags and ridges, the rolling hills and twinkling brooks of the unspoilt Mourne Mountains towards the strand of Newcastle Bay, which arcs like a bow. Myth and legend abound in this area and walkers must watch out for the ghost of the Blue Lady who is said to haunt the hills! You should also keep an eye out for the tame deer of Donard Wood. On rainy days hikers will be pleased to clamber into the tiny Hermit's Shelter on the summit. Our first ascent was during a New Year's Eve snowstorm and we were quite thrilled to find an old man in the shelter, who offered us tea.

As with any trip to Northern Ireland it is difficult to escape the national conflict which has troubled the country since its conception in 1922. The plaque at Bloody Bridge tells of the massacre of Protestants here during the Rebellion of 1641, just as many plaques elsewhere tell of the massacre of Catholics – a sad reminder of how nationalism can go too far. Thankfully modern Northern Ireland is moving on from its troubled past, and Newcastle today shows little outward sign of sectarian divide.

ROUTE

At the S end of **Donard car park** follow the tarmac track – which soon turns to gravel –past a bridge, through Donard Park and into the woods. The path now follows the Glen River to its source.

Donard Bridge is soon reached. Cross to the SE side of the river and continue to follow its course. You will see plenty of warnings to avoid the loose overhanging ground above the river.

Slieve Donard, the Hermit's Shelter

At the next bridge reached, cross back to the other side of the river. A final bridge is passed and the path soon leads the hiker out of the woods and into the glen revealing **Thomas's Mountain** – a spur of Donard. An 18th-century meat store is passed on the other side of the river, as is **Eagle Rock**.

At the head of the glen the path crosses the river and sweeps up the steep banking to the col between Donard and its sister peak **Slieve Commedagh**. Here you will meet a drystone wall, the Mourne Wall built 1904–22. Follow the wall on its northern side ESE for 0.6km up to the summit of **Slieve Donard** and the tiny Hermit's Shelter which, while grubby, can provide much-needed relief from howling wind and rain. If the weather is poor offer thanks to those souls who built it in 1910. It is quite an experience to be within its walls and hear the wind pounding the outside.

Descent

Either return the way you have come up or – to see a little more of the area – follow the Mourne

165

Wall SSW off the summit on its E side. Once the col at the Bog of Donard is reached, cross the wall by a stile and follow the path northwards past Donard's W face until the Mourne Wall is met again. Follow your ascent route back down to Newcastle.

OTHER ROUTES

From Bloody Bridge

Start	Bloody Bridge
Difficulty	2
Enjoyment	***
Ascent	850m
Time	1½hrs ascent, 1hr descent

Follow the A2 out of Newcastle for 4.8km to Bloody Bridge car park, clearly marked on the left. The car park has some public toilets. From the car park hike S along the road for 50m until a clear path is marked on the right.

The path initially follows the N side of the river, passing the tiny **Bloody Bridge** on your left. As you reach a steep banking you will see three large water pipes running perpendicular to the route. Work your way through the centre of the river and up onto the banking where you will find a stile over the fence by the water pipes. Shortly after this the hiker has the option of descending and crossing to the S side of the river and follow-ing the old quarry track, or staying on the N side on an often boggy path. Both routes head due W. We recommend opting for the firmer ground of the excellent quarry track.

Slieve Donard, just after Remembrance Day. Unfortunately a symbol such as this can have altogether different connotations in Northern Ireland

After 3km you will reach the quarry at **Crannoge**. Follow the path, which leads round to the right side of the quarry, and continue due W on a good path until the Mourne Wall is met.

Follow this on the E side, NNE to the summit. The path peters out here but the terrain is good and no difficulty will be had in reaching the Hermit's Shelter, a stone tomb on the summit.

Descent
Either as ascent, or follow the Mourne Wall W to the col at the 'The Castles', and from there cross over the wall on the stile and follow the clear path S beneath Donard's W face until your ascent route is met.

Galdhopiggen from Keilhaustopp (both images Brendan Quinn of 8th Birmingham Boys' Brigade)

Galhopiggen summit shelter (inexplicably closed in winter) with Keilhaustopp in the near distance

Location	Jotunheimen National Park, 161km NW of Lillehammer
Start	Spiterstulen
Map(s)	1:50 000 Galdhopiggen (Statens Kartverk, Norge), available from Oslo bookshops and some local petrol stations
Equipment	Standard hiking gear – upper glacier can require crampons early and late season especially; take for all climbs
Climbing period	April–October recommended
Difficulty	3
Enjoyment	***
Ascent	1400m
Time	4hrs ascent
Water	Last permanent source 1550m
Accommodation	Hotel at Spiterstulen; as all Norway wild camping permitted over 200m from habitation
Getting there	From Oslo take E06 via Lillehammer to Otta; follow RV15 to Lom; then RV55 SW for 20km and minor rubble road S to Visdalen and Spiterstulen. Park at Spiterstulen; charge about €8 in summer.
Public transport	Possible to catch train from Oslo to Otta, then bus to Spiterstulen (ask at tourist information for up-to-date times)

NORWAY: GALDHOPIGGEN

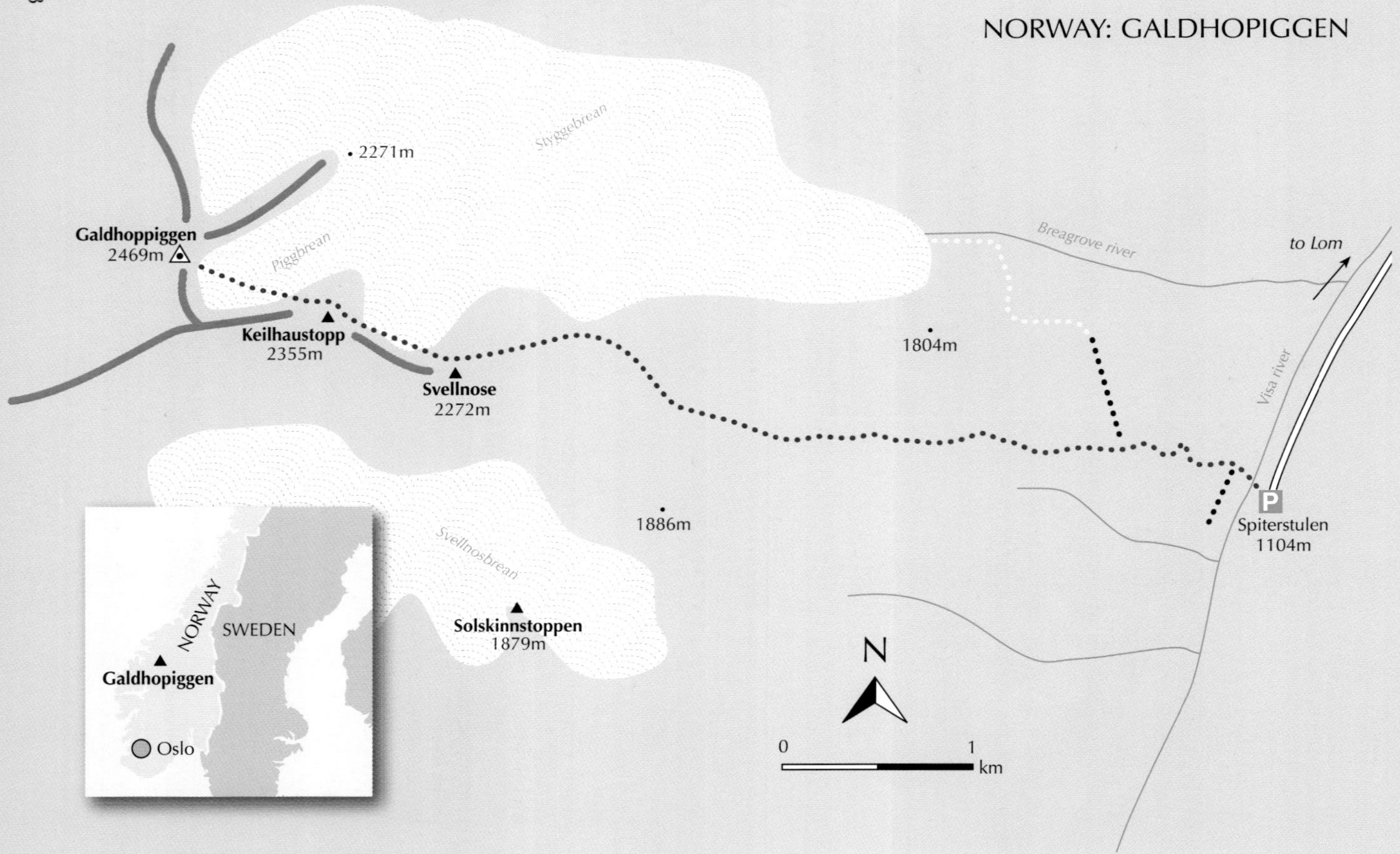

to Lom

Visa river

Breagrove river

Spiterstulen
1104m

P

•1804m

•1886m

Svellnosbrean

Solskinnstoppen
1879m

Styggebrean

•2271m

Svellnose
2272m

Keilhaustopp
2355m

Galdhopiggen
2469m

Visdalen

N

0 1 km

NORWAY

SWEDEN

Galdhopiggen

Oslo

Galdhopiggen is the highest mountain in Northern Europe. Located in the Jotunheimen National Park and Jotunheimen range, Galdhopiggen offers stunning scenery and a good solid hike. In early and late season weather conditions can deteriorate rapidly and hikers should be prepared for serious conditions. The greatest challenge might, however, prove to be overcoming the trolls which legend has it guard the slopes! This part of Norway is sparsely populated and close to the awesome meandering coastline of fjords: not to be missed on your visit. If opting to head north beyond Galdhopiggen to the high points of Finland and Sweden, we strongly recommend following the Norwegian coastal route. The country has masses to offer outdoor enthusiasts: the only possible downsides are its notorious scale and high prices.

ROUTE

From **Spiterstulen** cross the bridge over the **Visa River** due W and follow the path marked with red 'T's as it climbs steeply up from Visdalen valley.

After 100m of vertical height the path forks. Take the left-hand path marked Galdhopiggen and continue up. At 1800m or so the gradient eases.

There are the occasional snowfields here; however, they should not be prohibitive to standard hiking and crampons are rarely needed at this juncture. On the way down they may offer a good slide. The route then leads towards the ridge near the summit of **Svellnose**. While the path is hard to follow the markers and cairns are not.

From Svellnose some height is lost before making the hike up to **Keilhaustopp**. Crampons may be needed to ascend safely here. Do not chance hiking without them as the slide down onto the Styggebrean glacier is a distinct possibility.

From Keilhaustopp scramble down the rocks and follow red waymarkers until reaching the saddle beneath the **Galdhopiggen** summit climb. From the saddle the summit is WNW of you. The summit is marked by a steel theodolite post, and there is also a mountain hut – quite incredibly locked in winter! In summer it acts as a café.

Descent

As ascent. Do not try to traverse the Keilhaustopp. The Piggbrean glacier can be very icy and a slip would see climbers descending rapidly down to the Styggebrean glacier. In the dark the lower stretch of the mountain can be especially difficult to follow. Climbers in early or late season should carry head torches.

OTHER ROUTES

It is possible to ascend the mountain via the **Styggebrean glacier**. Full alpine equipment should be taken as the glacier is crevassed, albeit mildly.

Take the right-hand fork at 1200m and follow this to the **Breugrove River**. From here follow the river due W to the S lip of the glacier. The summit can be reached via the Piggbreen tongue or by simply heading to the upper ridge and traversing southwards towards the well-marked top.

DID YOU KNOW?

Famous native
Roald Admundsen, leader of the first team to reach the South Pole.

Irrelevant fact
The British author Roald Dahl, of Norwegian descent, was named after Roald Admundsen.

POLAND: RYSY

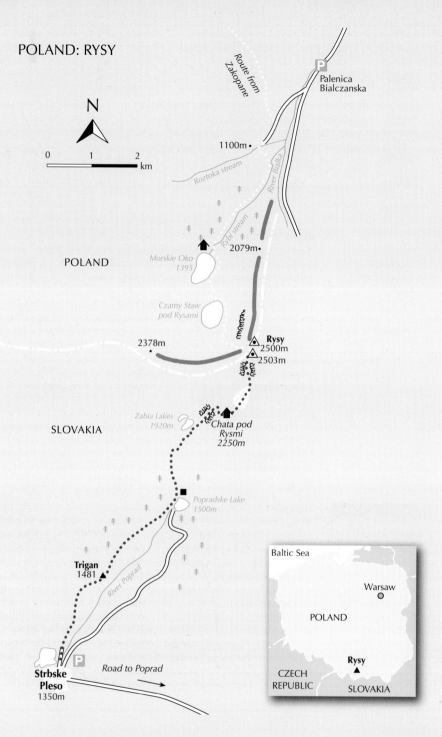

N

0   1   2
km

Route from Zakopane

P Palenica Bialczanska

1100m •

Roztoka stream

River Bialka

Rybi stream

2079m •

POLAND

Morskie Oko
1395

Czamy Staw
pod Rysami

2378m

Rysy
2500m
2503m

SLOVAKIA

Zabia Lakes
1920m

**Chata pod
Rysmi**
2250m

Popradske Lake
1500m

Trigan
1481

River Poprad

P

**Strbske
Pleso**
1350m

Road to Poprad

Baltic Sea

Warsaw ◉

POLAND

Rysy ▲

CZECH
REPUBLIC

SLOVAKIA

RYSY 2500M/2503M

Location	Tatras Mountains, S Poland, 100km S of Krakow on Slovakian border
Start	Strbske Pleso
Map(s)	Very popular hiking area; variety of 1:25,000 maps available in shops/kiosks in Strbske Pleso (eg 1:25,000 Edicia Turistickych sheet 2 Vysoke Tatry)
Equipment	Standard hiking gear; expect sudden and surprising temperature drops even in height of summer.
Climbing period	15 June–October. The route from the Slovak side is closed to normal hikers from 1 November until 15 June, due to the risk of avalanche. In high summer thunderstorms are common in the afternoon.
Difficulty	3
Enjoyment	***
Ascent	1100m
Time	4½–6hrs ascent
Water	Plenty on route; mountain refuge at 2250m serves 'Himalayan tea' and good selection of food. Best not to drink water from streams below huts.
Accommodation	Possible to stay in Chata pod Rysmi mountain refuge, but booked up in height of summer; number of campsites in area.
Getting there	From Bratislava follow D1 (E75/E50) and then 538 N to the mountain village of Strbske Pleso. From Krakow in Poland follow 7 (E77) S to Chyzne and cross border into Slovakia. At Ruzomberok take 18 W, then 537 W to Strbske Pleso. Park here.
Public transport	From Bratislava catch the mainline train to Strba (at Tatranska Strba), from where you take the rack railway to Strbske Pleso; a number of buses run along 537 to Strbske Pleso.
Nearest high points	Gerlachovsky stit (Slovakia), Kékes (Hungary)

Rysy has been for some time deservedly a very popular mountain with Central and Eastern European hikers. The wide assortment of characters attempting to get to its rocky top is bemusing: from well-equipped climbers to poorly dressed families in trainers and old men with large wooden staffs. The crowds are drawn to the mountain by the mild summer climate of its valleys, and untarnished lakes and crags which steer jaggedly upwards to the sky. The most convenient ascent is from the Slovakian side, which is described as the primary route due to its proximity to the Slovakian high point of Gerlachovsky stit. If opted for, the ascent from the Polish side is also an excellent climb. The mountain's highest point is 2503m, but this point is on Slovakian territory. As the border is crossed to the northwest, the height here is 2500m. The northwest peak is the highest point in Poland and essentially a spitting distance from the outright summit. You will not struggle to find the Polish high point, which is marked by a white border stone with a red top. There is also a border sign and a theodolite tripod. Expect mass congregations of happy hikers here in summer and, as with other Eastern Bloc mountains, do not be surprised to find people offering you a nip of their vodka. If you get a clear day, you can spy Gerlach from the summit.

Rysy in winter from Poland, with Vysoka beyond (Dariusz Bogumil)

ROUTE

From the centre of the small village of **Strbske** (1350m), head north following the many signs to Podradske Pleso along either a path on the east edge of the lake or on a short road, until a well-signed path leaves the top car park and heads due north into the woods. This is followed over Trigan (1481m) to the popular Popradske Pleso (lake). Alternatively you can follow the gated valley road from Strbske to Popradske Pleso; although this is not as pleasant.

As you reach the lake (which has a busy wasp-infested café), stay on its left side and follow the signed path which leads you in a NNW direction. After a mile you will leave the forest behind and amble through bracken and heather on a well-worn path. After a further mile you will reach a clear path which turns off to the right. Take this path and follow it up the Zabia Dolina to the Male (upper) and Velke (lower) **Zabia lakes** (1920m).

Follow the path on the E side of the lake in a NNE direction. Marmots can often be seen in this area. When the head of the valley is reached, the path snakes steeply up some crags; there are chains to aid hikers here in wet weather. In winter this area is strongly susceptible to avalanche.

The route then bears due S to cross the Dolinka pod Vahou valley. The route is well marked and leads up to the **Chata pod Rysmi refuge** (2250m). Save stopping here until you come back down.

Polish border sign near Rysy summit; there is also one for Slovakia (Urakawa Akihiko)

Beyond the refuge the route leads up over a gradual snow ramp. In early season crampons and ice axes might prove indispensable on this section. However, they should not be required for most of the summer.

The path leads over the grey rock of the spine crossed 400m lower and swings the hiker up to the summit where some mild scrambling is required. The Polish summit of **Rysy** is marked by a white border stone with a red top.

Descent

By the same route.

OTHER ROUTES

From the Polish side

Start	Palenica Bialczanska
Difficulty	3
Enjoyment	***
Ascent	1400m
Time	4½–6½hrs ascent. 3hrs descent
Getting there	From Krakow follow 7 (E77) S for 53km. After Skomielna Biala take 47 to Poronin and 960 to Lysa Polana. Do not cross border into Slovakia; follow road SW to Palenica Bialczanska car park and café. Park here.
Public transport	Connections from Krakow to Lysa Polana on Polish rail network simple; from Lysa Polana buses run to Palenica Bialczanska.

ROUTE

From Palenica Bialczanska follow the valley road S. After 200m the road splits. Take the right-hand (W) fork.

At the Dolina Roztoki River you will meet the main ascent path from **Zakopane**. Cross the river and traverse across Roztocka Czuba. The path then follows the **Rybi Potok** stream southwestwards past a campsite and a café.

Eventually you will reach the Schronisko Przy Morskie Oko mountain refuge and the **Morskie Oko lake**. Follow the E side of the lake southwards. At the bottom of the lake the path rises steeply, gaining 200m vertical height in a SSE direction to meet the impressive hanging lake of **Czarny Staw pod Rysami**.

Follow the path around the E side of the lake and then ascend Dlugi Plarg. There is occasional mild scrambling and there are Tatras chains, but no special equipment is required. The summit is marked by a white border stone with a red top.

Descent

By the same route.

Summit picnics: Rysy is very popular with Polish and Slovakian hikers

PORTUGAL

La Torre
Coimbra ▲ ○ Covilha

SPAIN

○ Lisbon

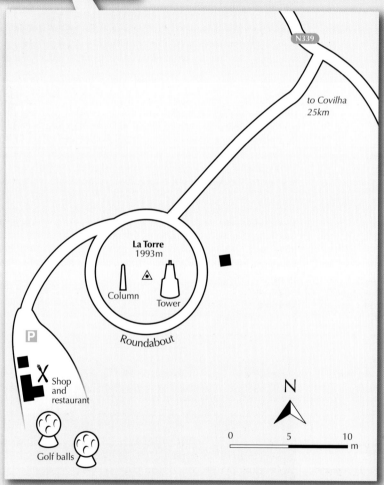

N339

to Covilha
25km

La Torre
1993m

Column

Tower

Roundabout

P

Shop
and
restaurant

Golf balls

N

0   5   10
m

LA TORRE 1993M

The top of La Torre in winter

Location	Serra de Estrela mountain range mid-Portugal 120km E of Coimbra, 100km W of Spanish border
Start	La Torre
Map(s)	Good road map
Equipment	None
Climbing period	Year-round
Difficulty	1
Enjoyment	*
Ascent	None (unless cycling from valley)
Time	None
Water	Café on top
Accommodation	In area of outstanding natural beauty, with several campsites
Getting there	From Lisbon take A1 N to junction 7; take A23 (E806) E and N to junction 30; follow signs to centre of Covilha. From Covilha take N339 via Santa Maria, Cantar Galo and Penhas de Saude to crest of mountain where short road leads off left to summit.
Public transport	Covilha on main Portuguese rail network; ask at tourist information about bus service over summit; taxi might be best option
Nearest high points	Mulhacén (Spain), Pic de Coma Pedrosa (Andorra)

La Torre is the highest point on mainland Portugal. Despite being a good height, it has a road to the summit and, being devoid of good paths, does not really encourage a good hike. Nonetheless the area around the mountain is quite beautiful and contains a number of great lava rock formations to get lost in. The summit has a number of gift shops and a café. As with Cyprus's high point, to make a challenge of the mountain it would be good – if tough – to cycle up ('Tour de France' style) the road from Covilha (650m) to the summit. The cycle ride would be roughly 25km and involve an ascent of 1350m.

As with Signal de Botrange in Belgium, the lure of whole numbers has proved just too much for the Portuguese: in the early 18th century King Joao V commissioned the construction of a 7m tower and 'La Torre' was built to raise the height of the visitor to 2000m. The little stone tower remains on the summit to this day. The old stone rampart is now, however, outsized by a pair of radar stations adjacent to it.

DISPUTE

Mount Pico (2351m) on Pico Island in the Azores is the highest point on Portuguese territory, and unlike Spain's Mount Teidi (on Tenerife) the mountain is geographically part of Europe. However, the Azores is an autonomous dominion of Portugal with its own government in much the same way as the Faeroe Islands are for Denmark. We therefore do not regard Mount Pico as Portugal's highest point.

ROUTE

No directions necessary – you're already there!

DID YOU KNOW?

Famous native
Vasco da Gama, explorer. Developed a direct sea route to India in the 15th century.

Irrelevant fact
King Pedro I of Portugal had his dead wife exhumed from her tomb so she could be by his side at his coronation in 1361; courtiers were expected to kiss her hand.

Location	Fagaras range of Transylvanian Carpathians, NW of Bucharest near city of Sibiu in centre of Romania
Start	Capra refuge
Map(s)	Muntii Fagarasului Transylvanian Alps 1:75,000, available at outdoor shop in Curtea de Arges
Equipment	Standard hiking gear, plus head torch – long route
Climbing period	May–October
Difficulty	3 (length of time on mountain)
Enjoyment	*****
Ascent	1200m
Time	4½–6½hrs ascent, 4–6 hrs descent
Water	Route tends to keep to high ground; streams not plentiful, water available from tarns
Accommodation	Camping permitted on mountain; many refuges; Podragu refuge on route most convenient
Getting there	From Bucharest take motorway to Pitesti, then N on 7C to Curtea de Arges. After Curtea head N on same road around Vidraru Lake to Capra refuge. Route starts from marked track about 1.5km after refuge to right just off sharp bend in road; marked with yellow triangle.
Public transport	Easiest to take northern route up mountain from Victoria if arriving by public transport; take train from Ucea de Jos on Sibiu–Brasov line, then bus to Victoria (see Other Routes)
Nearest high points	Mount Balanesti (Moldova), Midzor (Serbia), Goverla (Ukraine), Musala (Bulgaria)

Moldoveanu:
Buda, 2431m (left) and
Arpasu, 2461m (centre)

ROMANIA: MOLDOVEANU

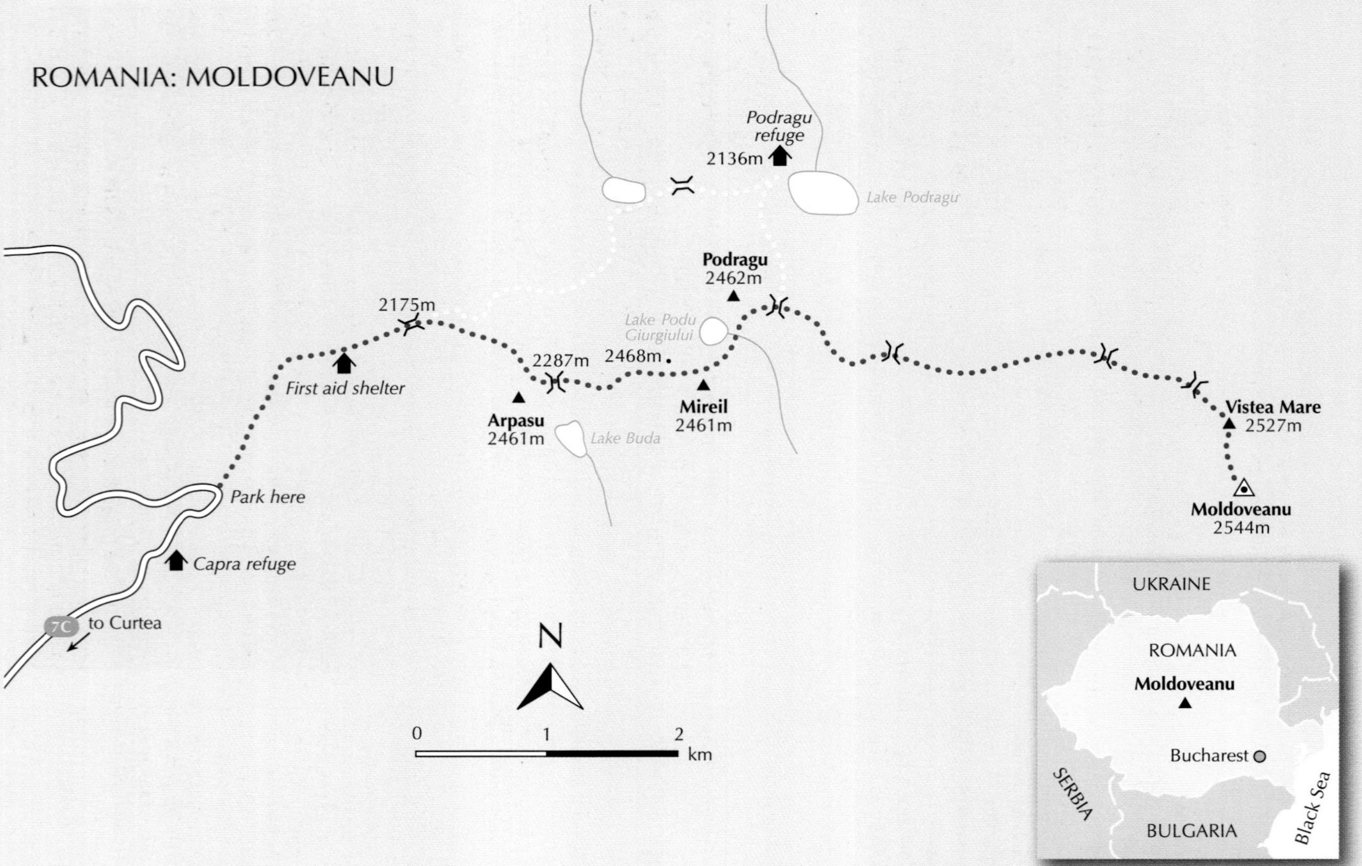

178

Map labels:

Black Sea
UKRAINE
ROMANIA
Moldoveanu
Bucharest
SERBIA
BULGARIA

Lake Podragu
Podragu refuge
2136m
Podragu 2462m
Lake Podu Giurgiului
2468m
Mireil 2461m
Lake Buda
2287m
Arpasu 2461m
2175m
First aid shelter
Park here
Capra refuge
to Curtea
7C

Vistea Mare 2527m
Moldoveanu 2544m

N
0   1   2 km

The Fagaras range (Transylvanian Alps) in Romania is one that rewards wayfarers with stunning vampire-toothed ridges, sweeping hillsides and cold ancient tarns. Moldoveanu, the highest point of the range, is justifiably popular with Romanian and Eastern European climbers but is far quieter than other national high points in the region. The mountain's massive proportions and remote setting make it a challenging hike which keeps the number of summiteers down, and trekkers will be delighted to find plenty of space to explore the wealth of different trail-marked routes available (if you can get hold of a decent map). Unless you have a 4WD vehicle there is no quick and easy way up; this is most certainly a good thing because, like a fine wine, Moldoveanu should be savoured. While much of Romania was subjected to a Stalinist-style industrialisation during the 20th century, ravaged by Ceausescu's regime and now clambering towards the unrestrained capitalism of the EU, these Transylvanian mountains are still characterised by ancient rural traditions and hallmarks such as scythe-carrying locals who stop to stare at the traffic and who could quite easily fit into 7th-century life. The area, with its occasional Gothic castle, will send chills up the spine. We found it an absolute delight.

Note A long and tiring day walk but can easily be split in two by camping or staying at one of the two refuges.

ROUTE

From the trailhead above the **Capra refuge** follow the yellow markers NNE up the track to lead you up to the head of the Capra valley. After about 45mins you will meet a **first aid hut** on your right. Go past this and keep following markers all the way up to the main ridge.

You will reach a small pass and a crossroads of paths in the ridge at 2175m. Join a red route turning E (right). Do not be tempted by the blue route which initially looks easier and gives the same time to the Podragu refuge – this is very misleading.

The route sweeps over an impressive ridge. There is some easy scrambling with fixed chains here. The path then traverses and descends slightly beneath **Arpasu** (2461m).

Ascend to another pass where there is a stone memorial. You should be able to see **Lake Buda** to the SE below you.

Keep following excellent markers along the ridge leading you close to the summit of **Mircil** (2461m). You will now see the **Podu Giurgiului Lake** below to the N. Unfortunately the ridge leads you all the way down to this; there is no alternative. Follow the red markers down the steep descent with a heart-breaking 250m vertical height loss.

The markers take you to the right of the lake and up a gradual ascent which traverses beneath **Podragu** and then leads on to the well-marked Podragu pass. From the pass you will see **Podragu refuge** to your left 20mins away; you may want to stop here for the night. A sign at the pass reads 3–3½hrs to Moldoveanu, but don't panic – this is a wild overestimate – 1½–2hrs would be more accurate.

From the pass the route traverses along the S side of the ridge where there is another fairly steep descent to make. The excellent path keeps to high ground where possible and, on fine days, provides great views of Moldoveanu's distinctive trapezoid summit ridge.

DID YOU KNOW?

Famous native Bram Stoker's infamous villain Count Dracula (Dracul means 'devil' in Romanian) lived in a palace in the Transylvanian mountains, so watch out for your neck while camping here. The real-life dictator Nicolae Ceausescu, executed in 1989, is perhaps a worse villain.

The distinctive west face of Moldoveanu in the far distance (centre)

The ridge swings N, then E to keep height gained, and leads you to a steep ascent of the **Vistea Mare** fore summit, marked by an arrow-shaped signpost. From here, the ridge goes S to **Moldoveanu**.

There is a steep 10m gap to scramble down on the ridge, but otherwise the way is not troublesome and you will soon be at the summit marked by a metal cross structure and a Romanian flag.

Descent

There is a logical circular route returning by the blue trail to the first pass mentioned. However, this is not recommended if you are attempting to get up and down Moldoveanu in one day as it is far more tiring and much longer than the red trail (it exhausted us). Return the way you came up.

If time is not important and you are making an overnight stop at the Podragu refuge the blue route is an option. **Be warned that it is less well walked and markers are far more difficult to follow than on the red route.** The blue route starts from the **Podragu refuge**. Head W uphill from the refuge and climb to a first pass. From here drop steeply into a valley and climb directly up the other side of it, still heading W. At the top of the next ridge the route traverses slightly and drops again dishearteningly, swinging SW and then climbing again. You will have one more drop and then a longer but more gradual climb to get up to the first pass of the ascent route where you will meet the route with yellow markers and descend to the **Capra refuge**.

Irrelevant fact
Ceausescu's House
of the People
(now Palace of
the Parliament)
in Bucharest
is the world's
second-largest office
building after the
Pentagon, and the
heaviest in terms of
mass. It consumes
a huge swathe of
Bucharest's centre.

OTHER ROUTES
There are too many routes to describe all of them, but most are reasonably well marked. Get a map and consider all the options because there are plenty of trails, refuges and beautiful mountains to be explored in this area.

OPTION 1
It is possible to start the main route described by leaving from the Balea Lake refuge further N along the 7C. Follow the red trail from there until meeting up with the main route at the 2175m pass.

OPTION 2
Several other routes start from the valleys on the N side of the mountain. By car it is possible to drive up several of these, for a time, from Victoria. On foot you will have to walk further and may need a three-day trip, staying at perhaps the Sambata refuge NE of Moldoveanu. The routes marked in red from the Vistea Mare valley and the Brancoveanu monastery join the main route described at **Vistea Mare** peak. The former follows a valley most of the way up the mountain and although it does not have the benefit of a spectacular ridge walk, it does not drop and regain height as does the other route.

OPTION 3
The route from the Arpas refuge SE of Victoria leads up a valley eventually to the **Podragu refuge**, where you could stay a night and again split up the epic hike.

Below left:
*Moldoveanu's
summit ridge*

Below right:
*Romanian flag on the
summit of Moldoveanu*

181

RUSSIA: ELBRUS

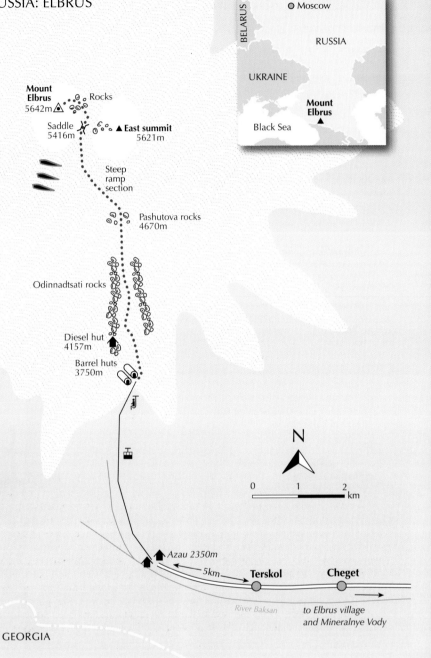

Moscow

BELARUS

RUSSIA

UKRAINE

Mount
Elbrus

Black Sea

**Mount
Elbrus**
5642m ◬   Rocks

Saddle
5416m   ▲ **East summit**
5621m

Steep
ramp
section

Pashutova rocks
4670m

Odinnadtsati rocks

Diesel hut
4157m

Barrel huts
3750m

N

0   1   2
km

Azau 2350m

5km ◀— Terskol   Cheget

River Baksan   to Elbrus village
and Mineralnye Vody

GEORGIA

36 RUSSIA

MOUNT ELBRUS 5642M

See Serious Ascents in the Introduction

Location	Caucasian Mountains, southern European Russia, 322km W of Black Sea
Start	Cheget
Map(s)	1:50,000 and 1:100,000 Russian maps available at kiosks in Cheget
Equipment	Full alpine gear: helmets unnecessary and lightweight walking rope recommended over full climbing rope (avoid heavy gear). Temperature extremes can be deadly; prepare for extreme cold (regardless of conditions) at 4000m.
Climbing period	May–September recommended (extreme winter cold)
Difficulty	4
Enjoyment	***
Ascent	1500m
Time	6–8hrs ascent, 3–5hrs descent; mainly dependent on acclimatisation and weather
Water	Last flowing water at Diesel Hut; plenty of snow. Take good supplies as may be on mountain for long time
Accommodation	Home stays (recommended) available; ask shops and taxi drivers. Large hotel in Cheget, hotels in Azau. Anywhere between Cheget, Terskol and Azau good for base due to availability of taxis and buses
Getting there	See below
Public transport	Trains run at least daily from Moscow to Mineralnye Vody and Nalchik; more practical/less tiring to fly to Mineralnye Vody airport from Moscow (train takes 24–36hrs). Bus/minibus services run between Mineralnye Vody bus station and Terskol; may need to change bus at Nalchik roundabout junction. Taxi not too expensive and easier; can be arranged (with a little haggling) from Mineralnye Vody to Terskol for c$60US.
Nearest high points	None

Europe's highest mountain – and the highest peak covered in this book – Elbrus is a colossus to be wrestled with. Standing north of the Caucasian watershed, Elbrus's broad shoulders and twin peaks cast a distinctive spell upon the viewer. It is not so much its height as its size that will make the greatest impression. As a climb Elbrus is physically but not technically taxing. The foreshortened snow ramp to the saddle pummels climbers by its sheer monotony; we were quite demoralised by the time it had been overcome. The mountain lacks technical challenges or variety. Nonetheless, the views of the Caucasian peaks to the south and southwest, especially Ushba, Dongusorun, Dych-Tau and the Bezingi Wall, are magnificent and make the climb worth the effort. Nevertheless, Elbrus lacks the magic of a great mountain like Mont Blanc. Unlike the Alps, over 90 per cent of the climbers on Elbrus are guided parties. The presence of snowploughs that chug noisily from the Barrel huts to the Pastuhova Rocks somewhat spoils the lower reaches (although they do prove handy if you are there for summer skiing).

Note Officially the Russians require you to have 'Elbrus region' on your immigration card. OVIR registration for the area and registry with the mountain rescue office in Azau are also officially required (the former is essential, the latter optional in our view). While the police are not quite as strict as you might expect, be prepared to pay a small 'fee' on the way up the Baksan valley. Travel agencies in Cheget or Terskol will, for a fee, help with OVIR registration. However, you should register in Nalchik or Mineralnye Vody before heading to the area. These regulations are on top of the mandatory visa required for EU citizens to visit Russia. Details of visa applications (which must be made well in advance of your visit) are available from www. rusemblon.org/logon_en.htm or on 0207 229 3628. These travel agencies will make the process easier for a reasonable fee: www.waytorussia.com, www.expresstorussia.com and www. russiadirect.co.uk.

Note Acclimatisation is everything on Elbrus. Its height of 5642m should not be taken lightly – every step after 4800m will feel exceedingly tough. Racing up the mountain without full acclimatisation is potentially very dangerous and hugely reduces the chances of success. Climbers are at a massive advantage if they arrive in the Baksan valley already acclimatised to 4000m+ peaks. However, this should not be relied upon, and further acclimatisation will be very helpful. Many opt for a quick climb up Cheget peak, but while this provides great views of Elbrus and has a good end scramble to the cross on its summit, it is not sufficient. We recommend (in addition to a peak like Cheget – which should be climbed from the bottom all the way to the summit cross) a hike from the Barrel huts (3750m) to the Pastuhova Rocks at 4600–4700m, then back down to 3750m. Then have a day's rest – if altitude sickness arises go back down for a couple of nights as this adjustment helps acclimatisation.

Note Lightweight skis could be very handy for strong skiers in a good weather descent.

Elbrus from Cheget Peak

Mount Elbrus's west and east summits (left and right respectively) from the Odinnadtsati Rocks (4100m)

ROUTE

Weather reports are available at the travel agency on the main road between Cheget and Terskol.

From Cheget, take the cable car and then a chairlift up the mountain to the Barrel huts at 3750m. The combined cost is around €10 return. The lifts are recommended in descent to save the knees. Awkward though they are, rucksacks are permitted on the chairlift.

Hike the 400m of vertical height directly up the snow to the Diesel hut (formerly the Priyut 11) and **Odinnadtsati Rocks** area where you should base yourself (camping or staying at the hut) for a summit attempt.

Having acclimatised properly, ascent should start from the Odinnadtsati Rocks at roughly 4100m (good camping spots are available on the rocks). An early start will make progress easier and faster on harder snow. The distinctive double band of the Odinnadtsati Rocks provides a clear catchment area. Trudge due N to the **Pastuhova Rocks** at 4600–4700m where you will need to zigzag due to the gradient change.

Here the route turns NW–NNW up a seemingly endless but direct snow ramp. Foreshortening will make this ramp appear much easier than it is: steel yourself for a tedious and time-consuming trudge. Care should be taken here in bad weather as large crevasse fields lie due S of your route.

Eventually you will be parallel with the saddle. Turn due N and hike up to the plateau between the East and West peaks. You are likely to be fatigued and demoralised, but you can do it. One tough ascent lies between you and the summit. An old mountain shelter lies ruined and almost completely buried in snow here – it is not a survival option.

Mount Elbrus: the top of Europe. Rachel feels little elation as she is cut down to size by altitude sickness and fatigue

If you are not already roped up, rope up here. At first climbing NW–NNW, hike up the ramp from the **saddle**. You will pass a band of rock and then arc due W where the gradient will ease and you will eventually meet a plateau.

You have done the hard work now; push on due W to the summit roughly 500m away. Surprisingly the summit has rock showing and is well marked with a war memorial plaque and prayer flags.

Descent

By the same route. Take great care down the tedious snow ramp, especially if visibility is lost. The most fatal error on Elbrus is to head S too early and slide off into the crevasse field. The week before we climbed the mountain seven climbers died here due to poor visibility and the fact that they were using ski poles instead of ice axes and were not roped up.

OTHER ROUTES

For the hardy, the East summit from the saddle could also be climbed. Other routes on Elbrus are reportedly heavily crevassed and no more interesting than the standard route.

Monte Titano, San Marino (Davide Orlando)

Location	Central Italy, 10km from Adriatic coast, 24km from Rimini
Start	San Marino town
Map(s)	Tourist maps showing Monte Titano's three towers available from tourist information offices
Equipment	None
Climbing period	Year-round
Difficulty	1
Enjoyment	****
Ascent	Little; depends on where you can park, or where bus drops you
Time	30mins plus extra time for negotiating narrow streets full of trinket stores
Water	Numerous cafés
Accommodation	Numerous hotels and two campsites
Getting there	San Marino signposted from A14 Bologna-Ancona autoroute. Take winding road up to San Marino town; many tourist car parks.
Public transport	Nearest station Rimini, then bus to San Marino
Nearby high point	St Peter's Dome (Vatican City)

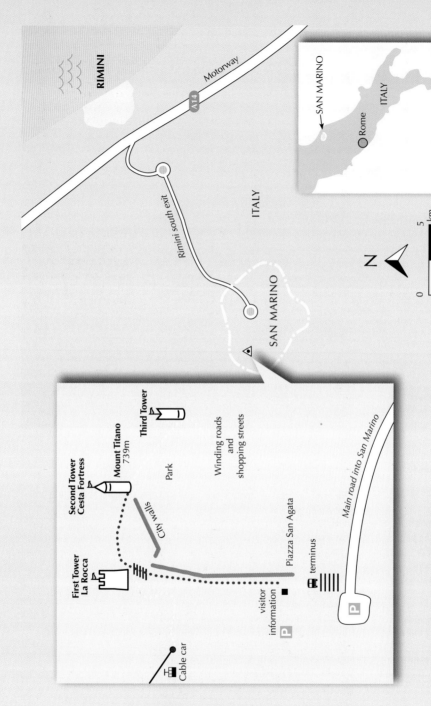

SAN MARINO: MOUNT TITANO

Tourist information leaflets for San Marino claim that this tiny republic is the most visited country in the world. I can hear some sniggers of disbelief, but this statistic is accurate if you calculate visitor numbers in ratio to native population. You will undoubtedly see plenty of holiday-makers in San Marino and are unlikely to have Monte Titano to yourself. In spite of its slightly ludicrous self-promotion, San Marino and its high point make a surprisingly interesting trip. Monte Titano is the mountain upon which the town of San Marino stands. There is something vaguely fantastical about the place, and comparisons with Jonathan Swift's Laputa are inevitable. Its highest point is the second of three spectacular fortresses which are connected by winding hilltop walkways with precipices looking down on the surrounding plains of Italy.

DID YOU KNOW?

Famous native
Davide Gualtieri, a computer salesman and scorer of the fastest-ever football World Cup goal (8 seconds). He did so in a qualifier against England in 1993.

Irrelevant facts
San Marino has a fair claim to be the world's oldest republic, founded in AD301. Napoleon in his conquest of Western Europe refused to conquer San Marino.

ROUTE

Follow signs to the '**Second Tower**', also known as Cesta Fortress (the highest point in San Marino). You must pay a small entrance fee (€3) to go into the tower and the bizarre museum of weaponry inside (opening hours are 9am–5pm all year, except between Christmas and New Year). Go through the museum until you find a set of wooden steps leading upwards and take these. Go through two trapdoors and out onto a viewing platform at the top of the tower. You will have great views of the other two lower towers, the plains below and the coastline.

Cesta Fortress (the second tower), the highest point of Monte Titano

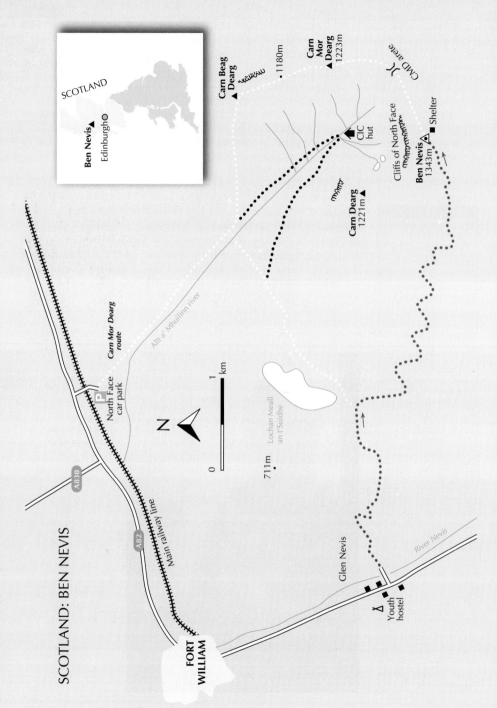

SCOTLAND: BEN NEVIS

SCOTLAND

Ben Nevis ▲
Edinburgh ○

Carn Beag
▲ Dearg

• 1180m

Carn
Mor
▲ Dearg
1223m

CMD arête

CIC
hut

Cliffs of North Face

Carn Dearg
1221m ▲

Ben Nevis △
1343m ■ Shelter

Carn Mor Dearg
route

Allt a' Mhuilinn river

P
North Face
car park

A830

A82

Main railway line

N

1 km

0

Lochan Meall
an t'Suidhe

711m •

Glen Nevis

River Nevis

Youth
hostel ⌂

FORT
WILLIAM

38 SCOTLAND

BEN NEVIS 1343M

United Kingdom of Great Britain and Northern Ireland high point

Ben Nevis: remains of the observatory/hotel

Location	Grampian Mountains, NW Scotland near Fort William
Start	Glen Nevis
Map(s)	Ordnance Survey 1:25,000 Ben Nevis and Fort William Explorer 392, Ordnance Survey Landranger 41 1:50,000, available in most bookshops
Equipment	Standard hiking gear. In winter temperature can drop to -20°C; compass indispensable.
Climbing period	Year-round. In height of winter (December–March) crampons advisable as black ice forms on lower stretches of tourist path, although not prohibitive.
Difficulty	2
Enjoyment	***
Ascent	1300m
Time	2½–4hrs ascent. 2hrs descent
Water	Last flowing water at 700m
Accommodation	Glen Nevis campsite; Fort William and Glencoe area brimming with B&Bs and hostels
Getting there	To avoid traffic jams in Glasgow follow A80 and M80 to Stirling, then A84 to Lochearnhead. Take A85 to Crianlarich, then A82 through Glencoe to Fort William. Bypass Fort William; at roundabout on NW end of town follow signs to Glen Nevis. After 3.2km reach Glen Nevis youth hostel just past Glen Nevis campsite; start of route is to E. Alternatively take more direct, slower A82 from Glasgow around Loch Lomond (and likewise through Glencoe).
Public transport	Trains and National Express buses run daily to Fort William from Glasgow; short walk to start of route.
Nearest high points	Scafell Pike (England), Snowdon (Wales)

'The Ben', as it is locally known, is not to be scoffed at. This grand old man of the Scottish Highlands has been a popular mountain ascent for over 200 years; the first recorded ascent was by James Robertson in 1771. There was even a very small hotel attached to the observatory on the summit before World War I. Despite its low altitude the mountain is well pronounced with ascents starting just above sea level. The north face offers a number of exceptional winter climbing routes ranging from easy to some of the toughest climbs in the world. In summer these provide good technical rock-climbing routes, but due to the number of rainy days here (Fort William tends to be one of the wettest towns in Britain) these cannot be relied upon. In winter especially the broad shoulder of Nevis can be difficult to navigate due to bad weather and has, over the years, proved fatal. There will be few climbers who have topped-out of a winter ice route and not come across ill-equipped hikers lost in a white-out and needing help on the summit plateau.

Note The primary tourist route is perfectly fine, if a little dull. The circular and exciting route via Carn Mor Dearg is strongly recommended (see Other Routes).

North face of Ben Nevis
in April from
Aonach Mor

DID YOU KNOW?

Famous native
Alexander Graham Bell, inventor of the telephone.

Irrelevant fact
Ben Nevis was climbed by the poet John Keats in 1818.

ROUTE

Cross the river and go through the gate opposite the Glen Nevis campsite. The path climbs steeply to join the gradual path up from Achintee/Fort William (another possible route).

From here ascend gradually on the clear tourist path trending SE.

Eventually the path arcs NE towards **Lochan Meall an t'Suidhe**. Make sure the main path off right (E) is taken and follow the zigzags up the W face of the Ben.

The path leads to the broad backbone of the mountain. Follow the route due E to the summit, taking care to avoid the edges of the steep N-facing cliffs. In winter these can be heavily and dangerously corniced. The summit is well marked with the famous ruined observatory and a large war memorial cairn.

Descent

By the same route.

WARNING – FIVE FINGERS GULLY

In good visibility the descent from Ben Nevis is straightforward. However in poor visibilty hikers need to be careful to remain on the left (south) of the very steep north face, especially if it is still snow covered. Care is also needed to avoid Five Fingers Gully, a known accident blackspot in poor conditions and especially in a winter whiteout. If in any doubt or in low visibility, walk 150m SW from the summit triangulation point. Then follow a compass bearing of 282 degrees (roughly WNW) until the well-marked zig-zag paths can be folllowed down to Lochan Meall an t-Suidhe.

OTHER ROUTES

ASCENT VIA CARN MOR DEARG

Start	North Face car park
Difficulty	3
Enjoyment	***
Ascent	1280m
Time	4–5hrs ascent, 2hrs descent
Getting there	Take A82 out of Fort Wiliam. Shortly after junction with A830 turn right, signposted Torlundy/North Face car park. Narrow road leads over small steep railway bridge with traffic light. Turn right after bridge down rubble track to free car park. If not driving start route from Glen Nevis; hike across Lochan Meall an t'Suidhe (lake) to access Carn Beag Dearg (see descent below).

A far better and more rewarding ascent – if slightly awkward to access – is the route up Ben Nevis via Carn Mor Dearg northwest of the mountain. It is more thrilling and far more challenging than the standard hike. In mid-winter this route can be very tricky and may require a rope and crampons.

ROUTE

From the car park follow the gated track for 200m. On the bend there is a stile off to the right. Take this.

A brand new path has been constructed here. Having ascended by the horrendously boggy original path on numerous occasions, we can recommend this new route (which will not be marked on older editions of OS maps). Follow this clear path up through the woods until an upper parking area is met near a small dam.

Climb over the stile here and pass through the electronic counter gate before following the distinct path up the valley on the NW side of the **All a' Mhuilinn River**. While the main body of Ben Nevis lies to your SSE, take a minor and ill-defined path away from the main path to ascend **Carn Bearg Dearg** to your left (E). Once you have reached the top of this peak the climbing is fun.

Follow the spine SE–S to reach the summit of **Carn Mor Dearg** (1223m). From here descend to the arête and follow the knife-edge as it curves SW towards Ben Nevis. Much care is required in bad weather.

Scramble up the rocks over awkward boulders, steeply ascending to the summit of **Ben Nevis**.

Descent

Follow the tourist route W down to **Lochan Meall an t-Suidhe** (see primary route). Follow the newly laid path to the head of the lake. Unfortunately the path inexplicably peters out here and a sludgy hike through boggy ground is required in order to rejoin the ascent path on the NW side of the **Allt a' Mhuilinn River**. Occasional wooden posts help with direction. If you have an especial aversion to wet feet this route is probably not for you. This descent does, however, make for a rewarding circular route.

Most winter climbs on Ben Nevis start from the CIC mountain rescue hut on the north face (unmanned, permission required for residence). These climbs require two ice axes and a full winter climbing rack. Ice screws and deadmen will prove essential. Avalanche risks can be high, with the potential of being knocked off a route or hit by rockfall. Weather and avalanche risks are provided online at www.metoffice.gov.uk/weather Climbing here is very popular in winter, especially on weekends. *Winter Climbs: Ben Nevis and Glen Coe* by Alan Kimber is recommended (see Appendix 5, Further Reading).

39 SERBIA

MIDZOR 2169M

See Former Yugoslav Republics under Health and Safety in the Introduction

Border stone 400m from the summit of Midzor

Location	70km E of Nis in eastern Serbia on Bulgarian border
Start	Babin Zub
Map(s)	1:50,000 maps of Stara Planina exist but very hard to come by
Equipment	Standard hiking gear
Climbing period	Year-round; skiing possible in winter
Difficulty	2
Enjoyment	***
Ascent	400m from Babin Zub
Time	1½hr ascent from Babin Zub
Water	No streams crossed from Babin Zub
Accommodation	Rooms available at Hotel Babin Zub; do not enquire until summit has been reached.
Getting there	From Nis take 25 (E771) NE to Knjazevac, then road SW to Kalna via Donja Kamenica. At Kalna take mountain road NE following signs to Hotel Babin Zub. Road in terrible state – landslides, potholes, tree felling (2007) – and winds up mountain for long time. As mountain head reached turns into rubble track.
Public transport	Midzor not easy to reach by public transport; best to catch train to Pirot (on Serbian mainline). From Pirot buses go to Temske (possibly some to Topli Do – taxi better), but services sporadic. An achievement (possibly quite expensive) to taxi up to Babin Zub.
Nearest high points	Djeravica (Kosovo), Musala (Bulgaria), Moldoveanu (Romania), Maja Kolata/Bobotov Kuk (Montenegro)

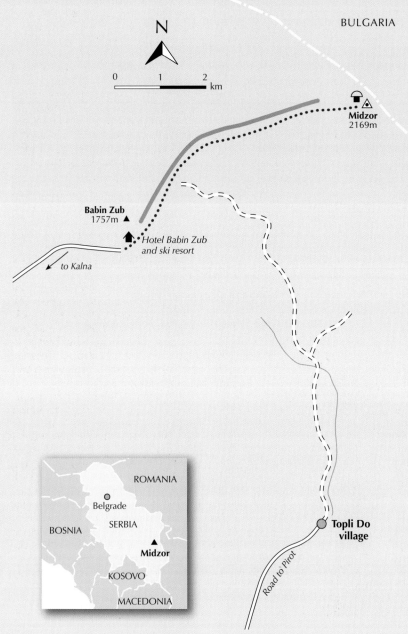

SERBIA: MIDZOR

N

0   1   2 km

BULGARIA

Midzor
2169m

Babin Zub
1757m ▲

*Hotel Babin Zub
and ski resort*

to Kalna

ROMANIA

Belgrade

BOSNIA   SERBIA

▲ **Midzor**

KOSOVO

MACEDONIA

**Topli Do
village**

Road to Pirot

As Kosovo now has an independence of sorts, Serbia can no longer realistically regard Djeravica in Kosovo as its highest mountain; that honour now goes to Midzor in the Stara Planina. Midzor is a pleasant enough grassy peak, but it lacks the sylvan mysteries, mountain lakes and steep slopes of Djeravica and one can understand the Serbs mourning the loss of their former high point. Nonetheless, Midzor does offer good hiking, varied wildlife and top ornithological opportunities (an eagle launched itself from beneath our feet during our visit to the mountain). The border with Bulgaria is consistently marked by white pillars along the Midzor ridge, while the summit has a large concrete pillar bespeckled with Cyrillic 'Midzors'.

Note We were forced to ascend the peak from Topli Do after we were refused permission to climb it from Babin Zub by border police who claimed a border permit was required. While this seemed mere phantom red tape, possibly designed to encourage us to stay at the hotel, the situation remains unclear. If you are refused permission to ascend from Babin Zub, see Other Routes below. We recommend that you set off confidently as soon as you arrive at Babin Zub before the border police have an opportunity to bother you. Save visits to the hotel and its café until you have returned from the summit.

ROUTE

From the **Hotel Babin Zub** follow the track NE in the opposite direction from which you have come. This will lead you up to a distinct ridge.

Follow the ridge, which swings eventually E to ESE. Midzor is the very large grassy hill which dominates the skyline.

Midzor

You will pass round a knobble on the ridge by the N side. Stay with the track. On a clear day you will see two large white border pillars on Midzor. These are not on the summit but they are close by.

Either ascend directly onto the ridge of **Midzor** where you will meet the white border stones and a path, or continue along the track until you meet a clear path off to the left which will lead you directly to the summit. Do not branch off to the white pillar.

The summit is marked by a grey concrete triangulation point covered in yellow-sprayed Cyrillic 'Midzors'.

Descent

By the same route.

OTHER ROUTES

FROM TOPLI DO

Ascent	c1400m
Time	4–6hrs ascent
Water	Streams crossed in forest
Getting there	From Kalna take the pitted road S to Temska. Take the 1–12 (E80) from Nis towards Pirot; 17km after Bela Palanka note turn-off left to Temska, take this. At Temska road makes sharp bend to Kalna, where road to Topli Do begins in northerly direction. Check right directon with people in village. Road to Topli Do surprisingly good; Topli Do is like the village that time forgot and looks like fantasy film set. Follow main tarmac up through village until it runs out; track continues but only really passable for 4x4s. Also strong risk that shaky wooden bridges N of village could collapse under weight of vehicle. Park here, but remove all valuables from vehicle.

The route up from Topli Do is very much a second choice. The ascent is great and the distance covered sizeable. Expect to take an absolute minimum of 4hrs for the ascent, and more likely 6hrs because the forest track goes on and on and on...

ROUTE

On leaving **Topli Do** follow the red dirt track beside the river. You will cross a wooden bridge. Occasionally you will see red waymarkers, but do not place much stock in these as they tend to be intermittent.

Eventually you will reach a T-junction at a stream. The right-hand track might prove to be a shorter route up the mountain via a shepherd hut, but we feel it is best to stick with the forest track. Take the left track over the stream.

The track climbs up away from the stream for a while but eventually swings back over its upper tributaries and brings you out finally on the ridge a galling 30mins from the **Hotel Babin Zub**. Midzor is roughly 1hr's hike E of here; follow the main route description.

Descent

By the same route.

FROM GORNI LOM, BULGARIA

The peak can be climbed from the Bulgarian side. A new eco-trail has been marked out to the peak as part of an eco-tourism project in the region. The 15km trail starts from the village of Gorni Lom and takes about 4hrs. **Note** This route has not been checked by the authors but recommended by a locally-based mountain guide.

> ### DID YOU KNOW?
>
> **Famous native** Gavirlo Princip, the man who lit the touch paper of World War I.
>
> **Irrelevant fact** The Serbian inventor extraordinaire Nikola Tesla was portrayed by David Bowie in the 2006 Christopher Nolan film *The Prestige*.

GERLACHOVSKY STIT 2654M

Also known as Gerlach

See Serious Ascents in the Introduction

Gerlachovsky stit (left), Rysy (centre), Vysoka (right) and Vel'ky Mengusovsky (far right) (Dariusz Bogumil)

Location	Tatras Mountains, near Strbske and Poprad, northern Slovakia, 150km NE of Bratislava
Start	Vysny Hagy
Map(s)	1:25,000 maps of area easy to come by in Strbske Pleso (eg 1:25,000 Edicia Turistickych sheet 2 Vysoke Tatry); usually show both Gerlach and Polish high point Rysy.
Equipment	Helmet essential. Harnesses and walking rope, couple of cams and wires strongly recommended as route-finding very difficult; easy to climb into difficulty. In early season snow in gully can be very hazardous; crampons or at very least belay should be used. Do not underestimate Gerlach.
Climbing period	June–September. Serious winter mountain requiring full rack and two ice axes; treat as winter alpine ascent. In high summer, afternoon thunderstorms are common.
Difficulty	4 UIAA Grade II
Enjoyment	****
Ascent	1500m
Time	4–7hrs ascent; take your time, allow for route-finding.
Water	Last supplies at 1880m, Batizovske pleso
Accommodation	Plenty of hotels in Strbske Pleso; good number of campsites in area, nearest one on main road to Poprad
Getting there	From Bratislava follow D1 (E75/E50) and then take 538 N to the mountain village of Strbske Pleso, then 5km along 537 to Vysny Hagy.
Public transport	From Bratislava mainline train to Pleso or Poprad. From these several buses run along 537 connecting Strbske Pleso, Stary Smokovec and Podbanske. Ask to be dropped at Vysny Hagy.
Nearest high points	Rysy (Poland), Kékes (Hungary)

SLOVAKIA: GERLACHOVSKY STIT

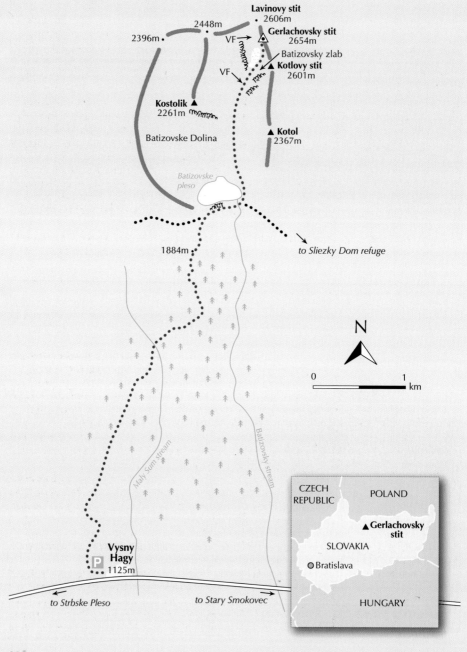

Lavinovy stit
2606m

Gerlachovsky stit
2654m

2448m

2396m

VF

Batizovsky zlab

▲ **Kotlovy stit**
2601m

VF

Kostolik ▲
2261m

Batizovske Dolina

▲ **Kotol**
2367m

Batizovske pleso

to Sliezky Dom refuge

1884m

Maly Sum stream

Batizovsky stream

N

0   1
km

Vysny Hagy
1125m

to Strbske Pleso

to Stary Smokovec

CZECH REPUBLIC

POLAND

▲ **Gerlachovsky stit**

SLOVAKIA

◉ Bratislava

HUNGARY

The highest point of the Tatras, Gerlach's steep craggy faces cast imposing shadows over climbers wishing to ascend it. It is not an easy mountain by any means. While it is possible to climb the mountain without anything more than standard hiking equipment, it is neither safe nor wise to do so. Gerlach presents a sound challenge to the climber. Tricky route-finding, the possibility of rockfall, and the steep exposed nature of the ascent combine with weather systems which change rapidly from brilliant sunshine to zero visibility and blizzard. As such the Slovakian government are very protective of their national high point and those who climb it and a number of rules make independent walking difficult. Officially, guides are required for standard ascents of the mountain. If you are a member of any mountaineering club (carry some form of ID with you), then you are permitted to ascend the mountain by way of its more challenging routes and are permitted to descend the mountain via the easier ascent routes. However, there are no TANAP rangers up here and hikers should not be too worried about the red tape. The worst you are likely to face is a few questions from local guides who are, for the most part, more concerned with their clients than your presence on the peak. We recommend ascending the mountain in one day and avoiding the Sliezky Dom refuge where the guides and their parties congregate. The suggested route minimalises contact with guides and uses the standard descent route for both ascent and descent.

Note In wet conditions Gerlach is extremely dangerous and parties should be roped together and have basic climbing gear. Rockfall is a major hazard due to large loose boulders and the gradient of ascent. Helmets are indispensable.

Note There are some climbers and members of the local population in this region who take an instinctive dislike to the mountain's 'Russified' name.

Gerlachovsky stit from the north (Tomasz Swist)

ROUTE
From the W side of Vysny Hagy follow the path marked with yellow waymarkers N through the woods. You will find yourself hiking over an endless run of tree roots until eventually exiting the woods where the path is made of stone and well maintained.

Eventually you will intersect the path from **Sliezky Dom** to Podradske Pleso. Follow this eastwards for 300m.

Here a minor path leads up into the **Batizovske Dolina**. Follow the E side of the **Batizovske Pleso** (lake) over large boulders. Marmots can be spotted here.

The next part of the route is the most difficult; it is neither marked nor obvious. From the NE corner of the lake head 5° W of N for 500m to the waterfall/smooth rock at the E end of the **Kostolik** wall. Do not walk up the scree on the W side. Find a way up the waterfall to a very small cirque halfway up the embankment. This may, especially in early season, be full of snow. Do not descend into the cirque but head due E towards the face up **Batizovske Zlab**.

Above the snow the rock appears too smooth to climb. It is not and a ramp will lead you up over the slabs and past the old rusty spokes which once held a chain here. To the right as you head up you will find a poorly worn path. Follow this, scrambling for the most part, and looking out for the occasional mark or cairn.

After a short distance you will meet some chains, roughly 200m in length. In the middle of the chain section you will reach a metal ladder which overcomes a tricky overhang. Even the ladder is not particularly easy to ascend. The ladder is followed by another short section of chains.

Remembering the location of the chains on the right of the gully for your descent, follow the gritty and worn rock. There should be a small stream on your left (depending on the weather and climbing period). Eventually you will cross this stream and move to the left of the gully. When the mountain shows two distinct gullies take the one on the left (the right one leads you to **Kotol**, which is extremely difficult to get across from).

If you can get onto the rocks on the left side of the snow gully this will save having to traverse the steep snow much higher up. If you do ascend on the right, ensure you are belayed across the snow.

Passing a steep lip at the top of the first snow section, ascend on either the left or right side. However, while the climbing on the right side will initially prove more difficult this will eventually lead you directly to the peak without a tricky traverse. The climbing here is not difficult, though it may prove wise to place the odd runner. Continue on steeper ground straight up, trending slightly northwards.

At the top of this upper snow gully do not allow yourself to be led off to the right. You should trend northwards along the ridge to the final summit climb. Near the summit you will find the aid of 25m of steel cables. The summit is quite exposed and marked with an ornate steel cross. You will have to climb to the summit either with or without the aid of the chains. If you have not found the cross you are not on the summit. If this happens take great care locating the summit as the ridge has many sheer cliff faces which are often hidden and make progress along it impossible without the use of an abseil. If in doubt, descend to re-ascend.

Descent
By the same route.

OTHER ROUTES
The most popular guided ascent goes up the E face from Sliezky Dom, but due to the risk of being caught and fined by mountain rangers this route is not recommended. Route-finding will not prove any easier on the east face.

Gerlachovsky stit summit cross, with celebratory vodka – of course (Tomas Kristofory)

Location	Julian Alps within the Triglav National Park, near the village of Mojstrana in NW Slovenia not far from Italian border
Start	Alijazev
Map(s)	Triglav 1:25,000 Planinska zveza Slovenije available at Kranjska Gora tourist information centre
Equipment	Standard hiking gear plus via ferrata gear recommended for primary ascent; essential if descending via Luknja route
Climbing period	June–September
Difficulty	3+ (4 if Luknja route chosen)
Enjoyment	****
Ascent	1850m
Time	5–6½hrs ascent, 4hrs descent
Water	No permanent water after leaving Vrata valley, but available at Triglavski Dom and Dom Valentina Stanica (refuges)
Accommodation	These is b&b-type accommodation in Dovje and Mojstrana, a convenient campsite at Dovje close to Mojstrana and a small info centre at Mojstrana; plenty of hotels in Kranjska Gora (small winter ski resort). Many refuges on mountain, one very close to car park at Alijazev Dom.
Getting there	From Ljubljana take main road NW towards Bled and Jesenice. Go through Jesenice following signs for Kranjska Gora. About 10km before Kranjska turn left to Mojstrana; go through small village with 'Mount Triglav' museum, taking road SW to Aljazev Dom. Continue along decent unsurfaced road for 10km up Vrata valley to Aljazev (paying car park for hikers, €2 per day); route starts here.
Public transport	Mainline railway station at Jesenice; bus to Dovje and Mojstrana; then hiking, hitching or taxi
Nearest high points	Dinara (Croatia), Grossglockner (Austria)

The summit of Triglav, with its three separate peaks, (Triglav, like Tryfan, means triple-headed) holds a special place in the hearts of Slovenes and is an object of immense national pride, even appearing on the Slovenian national flag. The mountain has its own museum and was revered by ancient Slavic people who believed it to house a three-headed god who ruled the sky. Triglav is extremely popular with Slovenes and visitors alike, and especially well known because it was the highest point in Yugoslavia before the break-up of the country into its constituent parts. Triglav justifies its hype with fantastic cliff faces and an exciting route to its peak. This is perhaps the most morbid of the high points of Europe; we came across an exceptional number of plaques dedicated to dead climbers. It has been a very popular mountain for climbers since the mid-19th century.

SLOVENIA: TRIGLAV

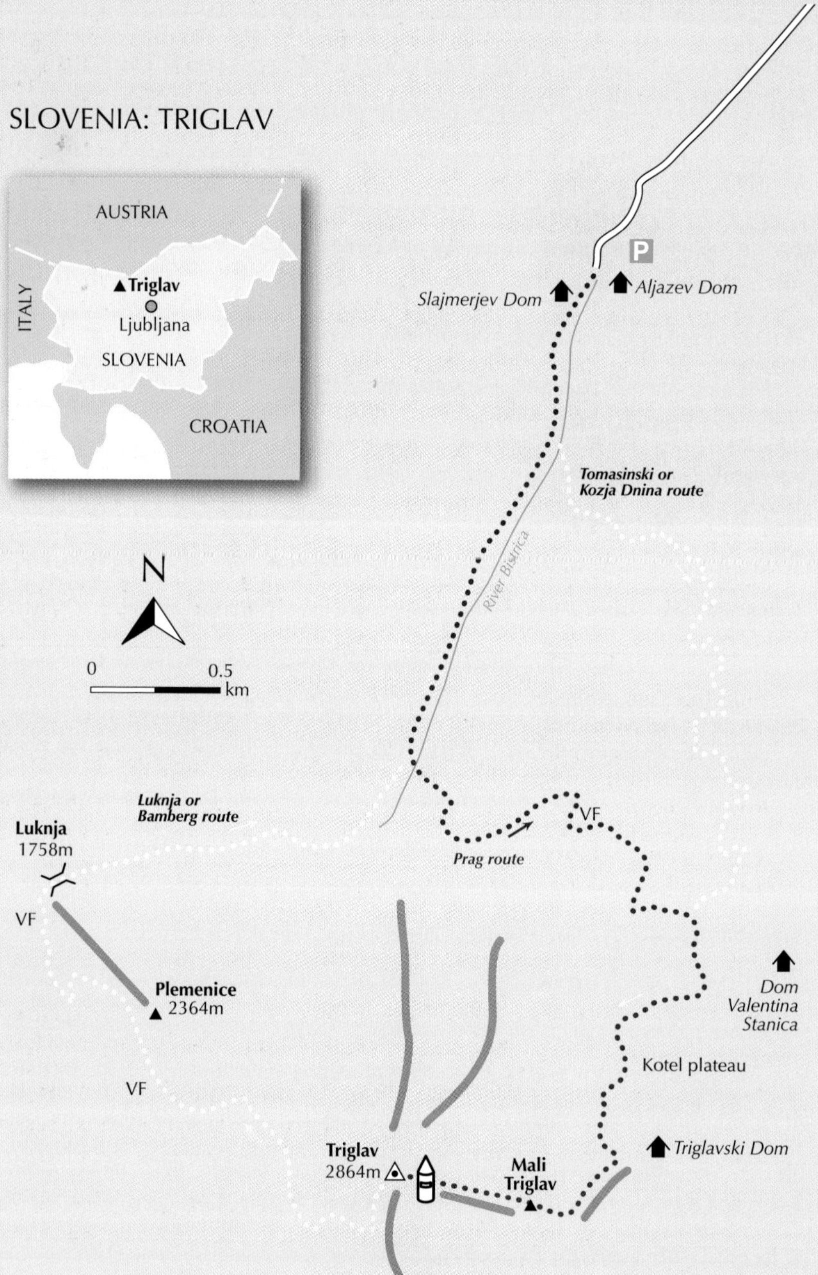

AUSTRIA

▲ **Triglav**

○ Ljubljana

ITALY

SLOVENIA

CROATIA

N

0   0.5
km

Slajmerjev Dom   **P** *Aljazev Dom*

*Tomasinski or
Kozja Dnina route*

River Bistrica

**Luknja or
Bamberg route**

VF

Prag route

Luknja
1758m

VF

Plemenice
▲ 2364m

*Dom
Valentina
Stanica*

Kotel plateau

VF

Triglav
2864m △

**Mali
Triglav**
▲

Triglavski Dom

View north from Triglavski Dom (Tomaz Amon)

Note There are two main routes up the impressive north face of the mountain, and the Prag route (in red on the map) is described here. It can be done in one day with an early start or could be broken into a two-day trip staying at the Triglavski Dom refuge on the shoulder of the summit at 2515m.

Note Timings on signs in the area can be over-optimistic, especially on the Luknja route. You will be slowed down by via ferrata climbing, difficult scree terrain and route-finding.

Note The top section of the Prag route can have snow and ice on it year-round so check the weather reports and conditions at the tourist office in Kranjska before setting out.

Bombproof!

ROUTE

The track begins from the back of the car park. After 100m or so you pass a refuge, from where you will continue up a well-marked path to **Prag**. You will pass a giant karabiner monument to WW2 partisans on route.

Follow the path keeping on the right-hand side of the **Vrata Bistrica** (river) heading up the valley towards the N face of Triglav. Pass a signpost pointing to the **Kozja Dnina/Tomasinski** route (a more technical option for those wanting a round trip).

At a later sign marking the **Prag/Luknja** routes, cross the river then bear left on the track, eventually traversing over to the face by going S and starting to ascend.

You will find steel pitons in the rock on the route, marking the start of much scrambling (there are no via ferrata cables here yet). Much of the ferrata and pitons date back to as early as 1909.

After a long climb through breaks in the face, the path brings you to a rather demoralising sign telling you that you are at 1700m – there is still a long way to go.

Shortly after this is a brief section of more technical via ferrata. Put on your kit, as this can be tricky in wet weather (and in descent).

Continue scrambling until at 2050m your path meets the Tomasinski route (which split off much earlier). After another 15mins you will come out onto the large **Kotel plateau** with karst limestone paving reminiscent of Yorkshire's Malham Cove.

Take care not to lose the red markers as you pick your way across this; steel posts help orientation. You should see **Dom Valentina Stanica** to the W.

The route heads up to near the **Triglavski Dom** refuge at 2515m (originally built in 1896). This is the beginning of the summit ridge.

Traverse right (W) just beneath the refuge and join the ridge (do not be misled by the refuge's water pipes). It should take around 1hr to the summit from here.

Ascend steeply using via ferrata placements up the ridge until reaching the summit of **Mali Triglav** or 'little Triglav'.

Head over this and follow the ridge, descending slightly before ascending steeply to the main summit with a fixed cable to guide you. The summit is marked by a little conical white cabin (the Aljazev Stolp, placed there in 1895 by Jakob Aljazu, the father of Slovenian climbing). Inside is a wonderful 360° painting of the surrounding mountains which should be visible on a clear day (including Grossglockner).

Descent

The easiest option is to descend by the same route, perhaps popping in at either of the nearby refuges for refreshments.

For those who ascended by the Kozja Dnina route, descent via Prag would provide an alternative (and vice versa).

Alternative circular descent

Descent via the Luknja route is physically very demanding, with exposed difficult technical via ferrata, and frustrating sections of ascent (descent time 5½–6hrs; ascent 6½–8hrs). Do not go this way if pushed for time or if the weather conditions are poor. This route gives spectacular views of the Vrata valley.

Following markers head off the summit in the opposite direction (SW) to that in which you ascended. If you lose sight of the red and white markers you have gone wrong and should retrace your steps to pick up the route again.

The route should lead you down from the summit southwards before turning NW and leading into a flattish area (Zaplanja) where cairns supplement the waymarkers.

The route may seem interminable. Trust the red waymarkers, and take care not to be misled by other routes.

DID YOU KNOW?

Famous natives
Iztok Cop and Luka Spik who won the first-ever Olympic gold medals for an independent Slovenia.

Irrelevant fact
Slovenia was the first of the Yugoslav countries to break away. It did so without causing many problems, no mean feat when considering Yugoslavia's subsequent break-up.

'We're off to button moon' – the Aljazev Stolp summit shelter

Triglav: via ferrata just after the demoralising '1700m' sign

Make your way down past Sfinga (2384m) before ascending up a ferrata chimney to **Plemenice** (2364m) on the Plemenice ridge.

From here a series of challenging via ferrata routes lead you down the ridge where the path makes a sudden switchback off the ridge and zigzags its way down the W side, before turning N down more ferrata to the **Luknja Pass**.

Note Slovenian maps inaccurately mark the route as following the top of the ridge all the way to the Luknja Pass. This is not the case, so trust the red dots. Do not, under any circumstances, attempt to descend the scree slopes N–NE off the Plemenice ridge, as these lead to precipices.

There are clear signposts at the Luknja Pass, giving impossible ascent times to Triglav. If you have descended this way you can amuse yourself by considering how inaccurate these would have been if this had been your chosen ascent. If you are ascending from here – good luck. From the pass head straight down the scree slopes to the valley. Ignore the longer route via the Bivak pod Luknjo, and continue down through the woods to the **Bistrica River**, where you will join your original route.

OTHER ROUTES

Triglav is a fantastic mountain and has ample routes (too many to list here) via which to explore its beauty. There are approaches up four different valleys – the Vrata, Kot, Krma and Triglav Lakes Valley. There is no way of avoiding the exposed cliffs of the summit. However, the route from the south via Dom Planika, Noga and Triglavska Skrbina is less daunting for unconfident climbers. There are 26 Doms and Kocas (mountain huts) on or around the Triglav massif, so extended routes are well catered for. Expert rock climbers will find Triglav a veritable paradise, with the dramatic north face providing a great number of long multi-pitch ascents.

OPTION 1
For the **Luknja** route from the Vrata valley see 'Alternative circular descent' above and reverse the directions.

OPTION 2
For the **Kozja Dnina** (or **Tomasinski**) route head SSE from **Aljazev Dom** for 500m. Here you will see the route signposted over a bridge across the **Vrata Bistrica** (river). The route is well marked and should not be difficult to follow. Via ferrata kit is essential.

SPAIN: MULHACÉN

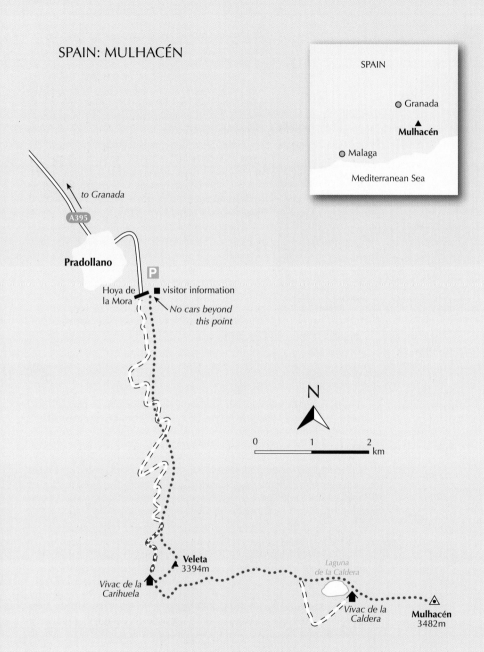

SPAIN

◎ Granada

▲ **Mulhacén**

◎ Malaga

Mediterranean Sea

to Granada

A395

Pradollano

P

Hoya de
la Mora

■ visitor information

No cars beyond
this point

N

0   1   2
km

Veleta
3394m

*Laguna
de la Caldera*

Vivac de la
Carihuela

*Vivac de la
Caldera*

▲ **Mulhacén**
3482m

42 SPAIN

MULHACÉN 3478M

Mulhacén from the shoulder of Veleta

Location	Sierra Nevada, near Granada, Andalusia, southern Spain
Start	Hoya de la Mora
Map(s)	Perfunctory and adequate free maps available at information hut at start
Equipment	Standard hiking gear. Sturdy trainers (not sandals) would suffice as terrain not overly rugged, but prepare for sudden and unexpected temperature drops. Sun cream essential.
Climbing period	May–October. Winter climbing more serious undertaking, but could be aided by ski season and lifts up to Veleta.
Difficulty	3
Enjoyment	***
Ascent	1300m
Time	3½–5½hrs ascent, 3–5hrs descent (Spanish information estimates 6hrs for ascent, but generous)
Water	Mineral-rich tarn below summit climb, but no flowing water; due to potential intense heat and time carry 1½ litres per person from outset
Accommodation	Two unmanned refuges on Mulhacén (no blankets/mattresses). Veleta refuge small; Mulhacén refuge a 'Tardis' and useful stop for acclimatisation/relaxation. Tourist hotspot of Granada has bountiful accommodation.
Getting there	From Granada bypass follow signs to Sierra Nevada (should show skier emblem) and A395 to Veleta. On route pass tourist information centre. Just before entering ski resort of Pradollano take sharp hairpin bend left; winds above town to two hotels and car park. Here road gated, but guided tour groups occasionally allowed through. Park here. Wooden information hut on left as pass gate; start route here. Mountain suitable for mountain biking as long track between Veleta and refuge Vivac de la Caldera offers excellent cycling.
Public transport	Granada well linked by road and rail; at least two buses a day from bus station to Hoya de la Mora (Veleta)
Nearest high points	Portugal (La Torre), Andorra (Pic de Coma Pedrosa)

Despite its aridity, Mulhacén is a beautiful mountain. Along with its sister peak Veleta, Mulhacén offers stunning panoramic views and entry into an almost Martian landscape. On clear summer days (as most tend to be in this region) a climb to the top takes the hiker into the world of aeroplanes. The air is thin enough to incur altitude sickness, especially in conjunction with the rapid ascent by road to 2450m. Add to this the stronger southern sun unhindered by moisture particles which tend to settle in the valley above Granada, and climbers can find themselves roasted on route: do not skimp on sun cream. The free maps claim that a distance of 19km is covered from Veleta (Hoya de la Mora) to the summit of Mulhacén, but we think this is a slight exaggeration. It is nonetheless a long way and climbers should be prepared for a fair hike.

DISPUTE

Often regarded as Spain's highest mountain, Mount Teide on the Canary Islands at 3718m is higher than Mulhacén. However, while the Canary Islands return members to the Spanish senate, the islands are principally self-governing and therefore act as a dominion of Spain in much the same way as the Azores for Portugal and the Faeroe Islands for Denmark. Ultimately, in addition to the political situation, the Canary Islands are very much an archipelago of Africa and therefore do not fall within the parameters of Europe's high points.

Note Three British mountaineers (Colin Riddiough, Paul Dick and John Pews) died of suspected hypothermia on Mulhacén in March 2006. They were caught out by a severe cold front, and there is a commemorative plaque on the summit. This event should remind climbers that ascending even the most apparently straightforward peak can prove fatal.

Note Most people who go walking here only ascend Veleta, so do not follow the crowds.

ROUTE

Follow the road until a clear track to the left appears. Follow the good well-defined path SSE-S in the direction of Veleta. There are occasional alternative paths but all lead to roughly the same place below the summit climb of Veleta. You will have good views of the observatory to the W and, looking back, you may see the high-altitude athletics track in Pradollano.

Mulhacén shrine and pillar

As you reach the last stretch of road below **Veleta** avoid the temptation to ascend the peak (it is time-consuming and does not allow a direct descent to Mulhacén). Traverse S on the road until you reach a fork. A tarmac road leads uphill towards the ridge. Take the rubble road which curves slightly downhill and joins the ridge at the refuge **Vivac de la Carihuela**.

From here follow the main track as it winds downhill. Avoid the temptation to follow a false trail which leaves the main track to the left (this does not actually cut off any distance as it is virtually impossible to descend from). The track eventually

View north from the summit of Mulhacén

levels out and swings above the very small tarn of Laguna de Aguas Verdes (Lake of Green Waters). Follow the clear track due E in the direction of Mulhacén. You will pass through a sheered rock gateway.

Eventually the track will bank due S to navigate a promontory (Loma Pela). This long cut can be avoided by maintaining a due E direction and following a clear path which leaves the track uphill to the left – take this.

From the brow of the promontory descend steeply (some care required here) and pass the mineral-rich tarn of **Laguna de la Caldera** on its northern side. The refuge **Vivac de la Caldera** is just beyond the lake.

Due E of the refuge is the steep W face of **Mulhacén**. While there are no false summits (the highest ground you can see is the summit of Mulhacén) the path is deceptively long. Expect the ascent to take at least 45mins to 1hr from here. Three paths converge into one well-defined trail up the peak.

As you reach the ridge swing northwards to the nearby summit which is marked by a concrete pillar and a small shrine (a large wrought-iron cross disappeared from the summit sometime between 1998 and 2007).

Descent

By the same route. Take care not to follow paths off to Pradollano if you have parked at Veleta (Hoya de la Mora).

OTHER ROUTES

It is possible – but quite impractical – to ascend the mountain from the south via the track that leads from Bubion via Pardo Llano, Alto Del Chorrillo and eventually meets the main route at the Vivac de la Caldera refuge. This involves 1400m of ascent from Control Hoya del Portillo and an extra 10km distance; the route does however permit a good long-distance cycle ride over the Sierra Nevada. The traditional way up is from Trevelez in the Alpujarras, a route which has been in use since before the Sierra Nevada road was built.

SWEDEN: KEBNEKAISE

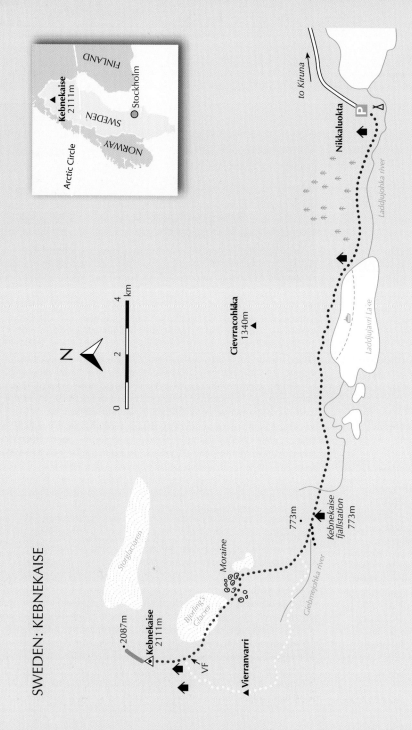

N

0   2   4
km

Kebnekaise
2111m

Arctic Circle

NORWAY

SWEDEN

FINLAND

Stockholm

Cievrracohkka
1340m

·2087m

Kebnekaise
2111m

Storglaciaren

Bjorling's
Glacier

Moraine

VF

▲ **Vierranvarri**

773m

*Kebnekaise
fjallstation*
773m

Giebmejohka river

Laddjujavri Lake

Laddjujohka river

Nikkaluokta

P

to Kiruna

43 SWEDEN

KEBNEKAISE 2111M

See Serious Ascents in the Introduction

Location	Northern Sweden, 161km N of the Arctic Circle, 64km W of Kiruna
Start	Nikkaluokta
Map(s)	BD6 1:100,000 Lantmaterietes; 1:20,000 map of Kebnekaise exists but does not mark route to fjallstation. Maps available in petrol stations and tourist information in Kiruna.
Equipment	Full alpine gear – walking rope will suffice. Two slings per person, with two standard clipgates for via ferrata section.
Climbing period	June–September ideally. Volume of snow and short dark days in winter months would mean severe undertaking.
Difficulty	4
Enjoyment	**** on summit day
Ascent	1400m
Time	3 days: summit day 4½–6hrs ascent, 3–4hrs descent
Water	Plenty on route to fjallstation; last guaranteed water 1150m when crossing Darfalijohka River
Accommodation	Kebnekaise fjallstation more hotel complex than mountain refuge with smart restaurant. Climbers' accommodation c€30 per night (includes use of kitchen). Food overpriced (evening meal €40 euros) and shop expensive. Take food. Camping at ample spots on route and around fjallstation: no restrictions. Refuge at E end of Laddjujavri (lake).
Getting there	From Kiruna ring road follow 64km road to Nikkaluokta
Public transport	Trains from Stockholm to Narvik (Norway) run through Kiruna; probably best and cheaper to fly in. Buses run from Kiruna to Nikkaluokta daily; for up-to-date times check at tourist information.
Nearby high point	Halti (Finland)

'Start here for Kebnekaise,' Nikkaluokta

Kebnekaise is a tremendous peak 161km north of the Arctic Circle. Climbers may have the opportunity to experience the midnight sun in the summer months and the aurora borealis in autumn and spring. There may also be some pretty severe temperatures to deal with. The popularity of the interminable 19km hike to the Kebnekaise fjallstation with school groups and large parties will give climbers the initial impression that the mountain will be very busy, but this is not the case; only a small percentage of people heading to the fjallstation ascend the mountain. As long as the east route is chosen then climbers are likely to have a wonderful and enjoyable day on the mountain, passing waterfalls, a glacier and via ferrata until ultimately climbing the dramatic snow pyramid of the summit to stand above all of Sweden. If the west route (for some unknown reason the standard route) is chosen, then expect a frustrating and miserable day. The mountain is best attempted over three days. While it is possible to climb it in two, this is not recommended as the 19km hike back to Nikkaluokta on an awkward boulder-strewn path will ask too much of weary limbs.

Note Crampons and an ice axe are essential for the summit. In strong winds it may be necessary to set up a belay as the summit itself is extremely exposed. Ignore large parties which may opt for the more popular, but awful, west route.

ROUTE

TO THE TRAILHEAD

From **Nikkaluokta** the 19km trail to the fjallstation begins at a wooden gateway. The trail leads to the Ladtjoluspekatan refuge at the E end of the **Laddjujavri lake**. During the day in summer a small café is open here that sells reindeer burgers. Many people opt for a boat trip across the lake, but this is expensive and only cuts 4km from the total distance. The trail eventually becomes increasingly difficult to walk as boulders embedded in its course prove awkward. The endless runs of wooden planks do, however, make life easier. Eventually, after 4½–6hrs, you will reach the circus of the fjallstation.

The tiny summit space of Kebnekaise

EAST ROUTE

From the **fjallstation** follow the track due W, S of the trapezoid form. You will reach a fork in the path after a few hundred metres. Take the upper fork. After another 500m you will reach a second fork where the W and E routes are signposted.

Follow the *ost/oster* (E) route which strikes up the hill in a NNE direction on the right-hand (E) side of the river. Follow the path until it fades out.

Cross the river only 100m S of the convergence of two large waterfalls (one will be hidden until you have crossed the river). There is a clear path on the W bank although this may be difficult to spot at first. Follow the path as it snakes up the steep hillside in an easterly direction.

Nothing better to do? The cairnfield on top of Vierranvarri

Eventually cairns will help guide your way northeastwards to the edge of a small steep glacier which you will not have to walk on. Once past this, follow the cairns across the plateau.

At the W end of the plateau you will meet a tough band of **moraine** with very large boulders. Cross this in an ENE direction. Here you will descend slightly to the **Bjorling's glacier** (named after the first Swede to climb the mountain).

The glacier tends to be in very good condition, but the climber should be prepared for crevasses. This mountain would be excellent practice for first-time glacier crossing as the risks are low, but use a rope. Head ENE across the glacier to a spine of snow coming off the Kebnekaise E face. At the top of the spine you will meet the first of the fixed ropes. These lead you steeply up a short 50m stretch of shingle/ice/snow terrain to the beginning of the via ferrata.

Experienced climbers in dry conditions are likely to find this via ferrata very easy going. While the rocks appear steep, progress is generally pleasant enough. Nonetheless, the bronze plaque commemorating the death of the unfortunately named 'Marcus Severed' at the top should act as a warning to all climbers not to be complacent. Follow the cables up, using your slings and clipgates when necessary – these will be essential in descent.

After passing the plaque you will come out on the ridge near a small area cleared for helicopter landing. Less than 100m to the N you will see the Fangstarm wooden shelter. There is another shelter parallel to this, but out of view 200m to the W.

From the wooden shelter ignore the metal poles which merely guide you between the shelters and follow red-painted rocks due N. Eventually the gradient will ease and you will meet a plateau with a cairnfield.

At the northern end of the cairnfield the dramatic and unlikely snow pyramid of **Kebnekaise**'s Nordkapp is visible. Put on your crampons; the snow looks easier than it is. The summit is tiny, unmarked and two-thirds bordered by vertical drops. Take great care here, even if you see others not doing so. The snow tends to be very firm.

Descent
By the same route, taking extra-special care down the via ferrata. Avoid the temptation to make it a circular route if you value your knees, ankles and state of mind.

OTHER ROUTES

WEST ROUTE
This should be avoided. Having wearily walked its course (albeit in descent) it is very difficult to understand why the Swedes regard it as the primary route up the mountain. While the via ferrata section is circumvented, crampons are still essential because of the tremendous exposure of the summit. The route does not give a distant view of the summit as might be expected when looking at the map.

From the **fjallstation** head due W, S of the trapezoid. Take the upper fork when the path forks. After 500m the second fork is reached. Take the lower fork following the *vaster* (W) route sign.

Follow the path up the Kittelbacken valley. The outstanding conical peak of Duolbagorni will be passed to your left. Eventually you will have to pick your way across the fast-flowing **Giebmejohka** river.

Once across the river, red waymarkers lead you up ankle-breaking boulders to a flat saddle between Duolbagorni and **Vierranvarri**. From here work your way northwards up to the plateau marked with a number of cairns.

Following red waymarkers descend northwards, losing 170m vertical height, into the narrow col between Vierranvarri and Kebnekaise. Again follow red waymarkers northwards to the Fangstarm hut. Traverse E to the second hut and follow directions as for the east route.

DUFOURSPITZE 4634M

Also known as Monte Rosa

See Serious Ascents in the Introduction

Monte Rosa/Dufourspitze (4634m) from the Matterhorn (4478m)

Location	Alps, SW Switzerland, near ski resort of Zermatt
Start	Rotenboden
Map(s)	Swisstopo1348 1:25,000 Zermatt (available in Tasche and Zermatt)
Equipment	Full alpine gear. One or two middle-sized cams/wires very handy to protect final move up to summit via Sattel route
Climbing period	June–August
Difficulty	5 (via Sattel route), PD+ with climbing to II+, snow/ice to 40°
Enjoyment	*****
Ascent	2150m in total; summit day from Ob Plattje 1450m (recommended) or 1850m from Roshutte (not recommended)
Time	2 days: Rotenboden station to Monte Rosahutte 1½–2¼hrs; Monte Rosahutte to summit 6½–9hrs (depending on route and glacier conditions)
Water	Permanent water until Ob Plattje (3200m), unless very early season when last water at Monte Rosahutte. Very long hot day possible – essential to carry extra water.

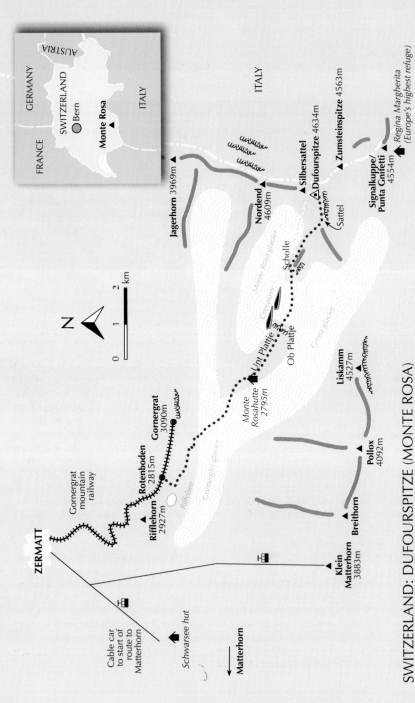

SWITZERLAND: DUFOURSPITZE (MONTE ROSA)

FRANCE

GERMANY

SWITZERLAND
● Bern

▲ Monte Rosa

ITALY

AUSTRIA

ITALY

Jägerhorn 3969m

Nordend 4609m

Silbersattel

Dufourspitze 4634m

Zumsteinspitze 4563m

Signalkuppe/ Punta Gnifetti 4554m

Regina Margherita (Europe's highest refuge)

Sattel

Scholle

Monte Rosa glacier

Crevasses

Grenz glacier

Liskamm 4527m

Unt Plattje

Ob Plattje

Monte Rosahütte 2795m

Pollux 4092m

Gornergrat 3090m

Rotenboden 2815m

Riffelhorn 2927m

Riffelsee

Gornergrat mountain railway

Gornergletscher glacier

ZERMATT

Breithorn

Klein Matterhorn 3883m

Schwarsee hut

Cable car to start of route to Matterhorn

◄ Matterhorn

N

0   1   2 km

218

Accommodation	Tasche has two campsites: one 2km N of town, other by railway station; campsite in Zermatt. Both towns have many expensive hotels. Monte Rosahutte (more expensive than French huts) should have space on weekdays; phone from tourist offices in Tasche and Zermatt. Bivouacking not prohibited on remote Monte Rosa.
Getting there	From Geneva take A9 and R9 (E62) W to Visp, then Tallestrasse road in direction of Zermatt. Park at Tasche (€4 for 24hrs); vehicles prohibited in tourist mecca of Zermatt. From Tasche take mainline train to Zermatt – pricey 15SF (£8) return for a 5km ride. From Zermatt expensive electric Gornergrat railway to Rotenboden (not to Gornergrat – would make descent more difficult) for 65SF (£32) open return. If planning to climb a few peaks check price of area pass (not much more expensive). Route starts at Rotenboden. Could hike up over Riffelberg to Rotenboden from Zermatt, but route not recommended due to endless crevasse fields of Gornerglet glacier
Public transport	Possible to travel by train to start of route (see above)
Nearby high point	Mont Blanc (France/Italy)

The Monte Rosa massif places you firmly in the land of Toblerone and muesli, surrounded by breathtaking mountains that resemble great gods vying for position in some metaphysical game. The pounding avalanches of Liskamm's north face roar across glacier-filled valleys, drumming the sides of the Matterhorn and Monte Rosa. This is serious mountain country. As the greatest of these mountain 'gods' Monte Rosa's highest peak, Dufourspitze, should not be underestimated and qualifies as the most difficult high point in this book. While it does not present the psychological barrier of Mont Blanc, there is no question that this mountain provides a far tougher physical and technical challenge. The introduction of a fixed rope leading up from the col between Nordend and Dufourspitze does provide a far easier ascent to the summit than following the classic ridge from Sattel, but nonetheless the worsening condition of the crevasse field above Ob Plattje makes for a dangerous outing. Incredibly, despite its height, we found Dufourspitze uncrowded. In comparison to the dramatic Matterhorn (which is swamped by climbers) Dufourspitze is a peaceful – if more than a little scary – climb; and a greater experience for it. The ascent from the Rosahutte to the summit in one day is brutal. To increase the likelihood of a successful ascent, we therefore assume readers will shun the hut and follow our advice and camp at 3200m on the Ob Plattje rock table.

Note The classic ridge ascent over Sattel is described. However, those climbers doubting their physical or technical capacities should consider the far easier alternative fixed-roped route from the col between Nordend and Dufourspitze (see Other Routes). If staying in the Monte Rosahutte use the alternative route as you will struggle, even with the hut's 2am start, to return in time to cross the Ob Plattje crevasse field before 1pm (regardless of fitness). Unless this crevasse field has improved, this would be an extremely dangerous position. If you have any doubts regarding weather conditions, do not use the Sattel route as escape from the ridge will prove extremely difficult. The Sattel route requires good fitness and acclimatisation as quite a lot of time is spent over 4000m. It does, however, reward the climber with a spectacular breathtaking ascent which is well worth the effort.

Looking back from the summit at the exposed and challenging Dufourspitze ridge

ROUTE

Day 1
From **Rotenboden** station follow the long gradual path E down towards the **Gornerglet glacier**. This is easy going and should take no real time. You will eventually meet a right (S) turn in the path where a signpost directs you to the refuge. Here the route zigzags steeply to the glacier. **Note** A lot of ill-equipped day-trippers and people hiking to the refuge pass this way. The Monte Rosahutte is very difficult to make out against the cliffs of Unt Plattje.

Once down at the glacier you will find a small preliminary glacier with a silt-filled stream running off it. Follow the waymarkers over this and a bank of lateral moraine before reaching the main glacier. Here you will find a crystal-clear stream. The main glacier is dry and extremely beautiful, giving exceptional views of the Matterhorn due W. You should not need to rope up on this glacier, but crampons should be worn. The crevasses are all visible, some of them very deep. Ice axes should definitely be in hand. Many day-trippers attempt to cross this in nothing more than trainers: this seems extremely foolhardy.

After crossing the dirty edges of the glacier, you will follow markers steeply up over the lateral moraine and then follow fixed cables to the Rosahutte (which for most of the way is not visible).

At the **Monte Rosahutte** stock up with water (do not economise on fluid). From the hut a clear path follows the ridge SSE. While this is well walked, it leads to a horrendous debris field, which is very poorly marked and extremely slow and troublesome to cross; in the dark it is excruciating. Avoid the temptation to take this path; instead, head due E from the refuge for 400m, before bearing ESE/SE up the **Unt Plattje**, over the more forgiving lava-flow rock terrain. This is much quicker to negotiate than trying to cross the debris field on the ridge proper, or to the right (S) of the ridge, and should take at least 1hr less.

You will eventually reach the **Ob Plattje** cliffs. There are a number of ways up them and all are fine. An excellent route on the left (N) edge of the cliffs exists, but this may be more effort to find than it is worth. At the top of Ob Plattje cliffs (3200m) you may look for a good spot to camp; you will find the occasional bivouac circle. This is an excellent place to camp as you can then start the route on snow in the morning. **Note** Do not attempt to gain any further advantage than the top of the Ob Plattje cliffs as the hazardous crevasse field soon follows.

Day 2

Note Often the ludicrously early alpine starts are just too early, but this is not the case with Dufourspitze. However, darkness will make crossing the Ob Plattje crevasse field (3400–3500m) even more troublesome. Hopefully this crevasse field will not be in the same state as in 2005. You must be roped up at all times; solo crossing is not an option. **If there are strong winds on the mountain do not consider the Sattel ridge ascent.**

From the cliffs of the Ob Plattje head ESE up the snow until you reach the jagged ruptured snow of the crevasse field. There is simply no easy way across this; you cannot go around it, and many climbers turn back here. Aim to head ESE-E across it, taking special care over areas of soft snow and snow bridges. Take your time.

Once across the crevasse field head E–ESE up the glacier to the **Scholle** (3900–4000m). Here the route continues 200m to the left of the 4031m Scholle peak. In this area you will see a series of large broken seracs. Likely enough a snow path will head due E descending into a col SW of the **Nordend** ridge (Nordend will appear higher than Dufourspitze at this point – it is only 25m lower).

The Dufourspitze summit cross with Signalkuppe and the Regina Margherita refuge – the highest in Europe (top left)

To reach Sattel you must pick a way through or around the seracs heading SSE. If you descend at all, you are going the wrong way for the Sattel route.

Ascend the ever-steepening snow of the Sattehole to the **Sattel** ridge (4359m). Here you will begin the ascent of the very steep ice/snow route to 4499m on the Dufourspitze ridge. From this summit you will descend for roughly 30m vertical height before completing another gruelling, yet shorter, steep icy hike up to the fore summit of the **Dufourspitze** ridge.

From this point on the actual summit is no more than 400m away. However, as the climbing here is extremely exposed and fairly technical, you will need to belay almost everything. Continue along the ridge to the summit – leave your crampons on as there will be exposed snow bridges and ice to negotiate. There are plenty of good natural belay points, use them.

Close to the summit you will ascend over a tricky large square column. Having negotiated this you are very close to the summit. To reach it, however, you must overcome a short but challenging climb – really just one tough move. A runner would be wise here. Use your ice axe for leverage. The satisfaction of getting up this to the summit cross and plaque is immense. You will have excellent views of Nordend, the terrifying N face of Liskamm (4527m), the Signalkuppe (with the refuge Regina Margherita – the highest in Europe) and the Matterhorn over in the W.

Descent

From the summit head due E for roughly 60m. Before the climb up to Grenxgipfel on the E end of the Dufourspitze ridge, you will see a large fixed rope that leads down a steep snowy gully. Be careful of loose rock and icefall and give absolute care and attention to those ascending. The ropes should allow you a safe descent into the cirque at the head of the **Monte Rosa glacier**. From here follow the 'Other Routes' ascent in reverse.

OTHER ROUTES

Option 1 Via the Nordend/Dufourspitze col

An easier ascent, safer in strong winds.

Follow the normal ascent until you reach the col SW of the Nordend ridge.

Descend into the cirque due E in the direction of Nordend. The snow route will lead you up onto the base of the Nordend ridge, before zigzagging on the upper **Monte Rosa glacier** over bergschrund and crevasses and into the Dufourspitze col. About 100m W of the Silbersattel (head of the glacier) on the N face of the Dufourspitze ridge you should see a fixed rope.

Using slings to ensure safe support, ascend steeply for just over 200m vertical height to the top of the **Dufourspitze** ridge. Once on the narrow ridge turn right (W). The summit is marked by a cross and a plaque and is only 50m away.

Option 2 UIAA grade AD- from refuge Regina Margherita

A fantastic ascent of Dufourspitze can be made from the refuge **Regina Margherita**, on the Italian border 1km SE of the summit of Dufourspitze.

From the refuge descend in a NW direction into the Colle Gnifetti before ascending **Zumsteinspitze** (4563m). Follow the knife-edge snow ridge to Grenzsattel (N). Stay with the ridge heading NW to the summit of Grenzgipfel. The climbing here is technical and exposed, of a level slightly harder than that of the Dufourspitze–Sattel ridge. A good selection of cams and wires should be taken. From the summit of Grenzgipfel descend steeply for 5m vertical height before ascending to the summit of **Dufourspitze** 50m away. Rock gear needed.

45 TURKEY

MAHYA DAGI 1030M

Summit of European Turkey/Thrace. Also known as Maya Dagi, Maja Dagy

Location	Istranca Daglari, near Kirklareli, Turkey
Start	Yenice
Map(s)	Good road map
Equipment	None
Climbing period	Year-round (or not at all depending on whether or not you choose to ignore army warnings)
Difficulty	1
Enjoyment	*
Ascent	None
Time	None
Water	Many water fountains on road up to mountain and on track following ridge to summit
Accommodation	Seaside town of Igneada good place to stay and for swimming
Getting there	See Route below
Public transport	Kirklareli on main Turkish rail network. From here catch bus to Yenice via Uskupdere; if on bus to Igneada will run directly past start of Mahya Dagi ridge
Nearest high points	Musala (Bulgaria), Mount Olympus (Greece)

While the magnificent stand-alone mountain of Ararat (Agri Dagi) by the Iranian border is the highest mountain in Turkey at 5137m, it is 2000km east of Turkey's 'Welcome to Asia' sign on the east side of the Bosporus and firmly beyond the geographical borders of Europe. Therefore, with no stretch of the imagination could we regard Ararat as a European mountain. However, western Turkey – often referred to as European Turkey or Eastern Thrace – is part of Europe and therefore we have included the highest point of this area. As this is not a national high point we can completely understand high pointers omitting it from their pursuit.

Is it worth crossing the Turkish border to visit Mahya Dagi? Not really. Firstly, the mountain lacks any real character and secondly, there is a road to the top. Thirdly (rather significantly), it is not permitted to go to the summit of the mountain due to the military installation there.

The summit is visible from over 48km away due to its poorly camouflaged golf-ball listening post and TV towers. Do not expect quite the same relaxed atmosphere as you might find on Cyprus's Mount Olympus. The Turks do not take kindly to random visitors taking pictures on Mahya Dagi and you may end up in a Turkish prison for doing so – you have been warned! The warning signs are in Turkish, so playing dumb is a very good plan (it worked for us).

Note At the time of writing Turkey still requires that EU citizens purhase a visa on entering the country. This is available with little fuss at all borders and costs about £10.

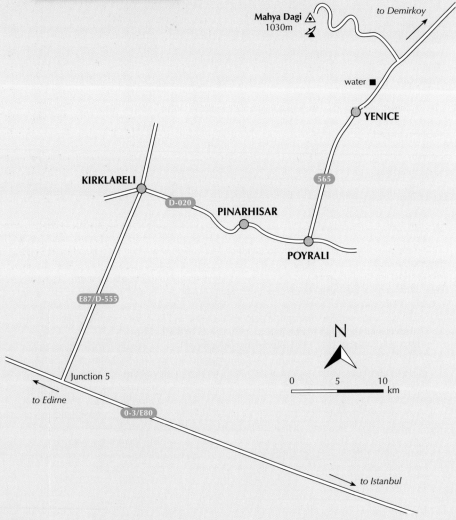

*No photos!
Mahya Dagi, the highest
point of European Turkey*

Famous native
Mustafa Kemal
Ataturk, founder of
the modern republic
of Turkey. He
appears on all the
bank notes.

Irrelevant fact
In the CS Lewis
novel *The Lion,
the Witch and the
Wardrobe*, Edmund
joins the side of
the evil queen after
being bribed with
copious amounts of
Turkish delight.

ROUTE

From Edirne take O-3 (E80) E to junction 5. Take D-555 (E87) N to **Kirklareli**, then D-020 for 40km in the direction of **Pinarhisar** and Vize. At **Poyrali** turn left (N) on 565 to **Yenice**, Erciler and Demirkoy.

After passing through Yenice the road heads uphill. Watch out for a water sign; shortly after this you will pass a water fountain and café. Follow the road up until a sharp bend left where you will see a good rubble road heading W into woods (ruined bus shelter here). The summit is roughly 6.4km away.

Follow the track as it traverses the forest and leads you directly to the listening post. The summit is consumed by the golf ball itself and, as with Mount Olympus in Cyprus, standing on the highest ground is not possible. Turn around and go down before someone puts you in prison. **Whatever you do, do not be seen taking any photos!** (That said, the soldiers were very friendly towards us.)

Descent

By the same route.

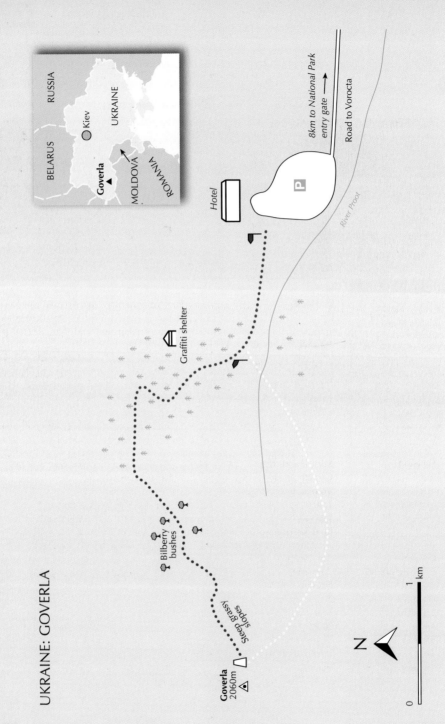

UKRAINE: GOVERLA

RUSSIA

BELARUS

UKRAINE

Kiev

MOLDOVA

Goverla

ROMANIA

Hotel

8km to National Park
entry gate →

Road to Vorocta

River Proot

Graffiti shelter

Bilberry
bushes

Steep grassy
slope

Goverla
2060m

N

0   1
km

226

46 UKRAINE

GOVERLA 2061M

Also known as Hoverla (УКРАЇНА – Говерла)

The summit of Goverla with its many markers

Location	SW Ukraine halfway between Chernivtsi and Uzhorod in northern Carpathians, near small town of BOPOXTA 'Vorocta'
Start	Vorocta
Map(s)	1:50,000 maps of area exist but very hard to come by; cheap (30p) 1:100,000 Ukrainian topographical maps easier to obtain, available in Chernivtsi (Sheet 165/184). Mountain very well marked, with no technical difficulty. Unless planning extended stay in area map not essential.
Equipment	Standard hiking gear
Climbing period	Year-round; April–October best, September especially recommended as less rain than height of summer
Difficulty	2
Enjoyment	***
Ascent	900m
Time	1½–2¼hrs ascent, 1hr descent
Water	Early part of route follows stream –no water past this
Accommodation	Homestays in Vorocta. Camping permitted on W side on Goverla. Many cheap hotels on main roads and in towns.

Getting there	From E drive to Yremcha (RPEMYA) then continue S on P–03 to Tatarov (TATAPOB). Take turning S marked KOCIB and BOPOXTA, continue on through BOPOXTA. **Note** Vorocta has very severe speed bumps. After crossing wide railway lines continue on road S of BOPOXTA for 8–9km. Meet fork in road with Goverla signposted right; take this. After few kilometres of tarmac reach toll-booth charging under €2 entry to National Park. From here road unsurfaced but still reasonable. Continue for 8km, passing forestry works, until road end with small parking area, chapel, and large hotel.
Public transport	Possible to get to BOPOXTA by train and bus. From there buses run occasionally but taxi simplest way to trailhead. May be possible to join Ukrainian coach tour to mountain as popular national outing.
Nearest high points	Mount Balanesti (Moldova), Kékes (Hungary), Gerlachovsky stit (Slovakia), Rysy (Poland)

Goverla is a mellow green humpback mountain which rises from a bed of forests to arc into the clouds. There are no dramatic cliff faces here, but the steep gradient of Goverla's grassy hills makes for a rewarding and pleasant hike. The mountain's upper reaches will remind British hikers of many a Yorkshire Dales' fell, and those ascending might be forgiven for feeling they are spending an agreeable afternoon ambling about on Buckden Pike or Great Whernside while readying themselves for a wholesome pint of ale and some Yorkshire puddings on their return. Instead, hikers on Goverla might well prepare themselves for a nip of vodka and a good bowl of bortsch.

While Ukraine's torrid history has been characterised by famine, war, disease, genocide and cultural annihilation, the country is on the move. The national anthem which declares 'Ukraine is not yet dead' has long symbolised the will and determination of the nation to overcome its troubles. Success at the Eurovision song contest in 2004 and the subsequent hosting of the competition in 2005 seems to have given the country a kind of 'fun factor'. On entering Ukraine from Moldova we were confronted by a foot soldier at the border who was surprised to meet two Brits. 'I must get my commander,' he said. That the commander was a buxom 6ft-tall brunette wearing full army uniform, a pair of stilettos and a healthy application of blue eye shadow and bright red lipstick certainly suggested that the Soviet era had been left long behind. The fact that we were then waved through, with smiles and goodwill and no demands for visas or fees, only helped confirm that Ukraine was not going to be the miserable sour-faced affair one might expect. In short, Ukraine is quite a different kettle of fish from Russia.

The Soviet era has not left Ukraine unscarred as the residual radiation left over from the 1986 Chernobyl disaster most notably reminds us. Despite this, Goverla finds itself in a veritable Eden. Ornate wooden houses with polished tin facades line much of the surrounding countryside, and while not everyone has electricity the simple way of life appears idyllic and one is left with memories of scenes that could easily be picked out of David Lean's 1965 epic *Dr Zhivago*. A visit to both Goverla and this part of Ukraine might well prove to be a surprising highlight of an extended trip.

Note In late 2007 the summit monuments of Goverla were shamefully vandalised by pro-Russian separatists.

Goverla in late autumn

ROUTE

At the top of the car park a signpost indicates Goverla peak to be 4.1km away, but this is an underestimate.

From here follow the red and white flag-shaped markers through the forest for about 1.5km. At another sign telling you that the peak is 3km away the path splits, but not obviously so. Stay right on the path leading uphill away from the stream.

About 150m after passing the '**graffiti shelter**' the route takes a sharp turn right (NE), before swinging back W and following small stone pillars.

The path will then bring you out of the forest and leads steeply up through bilberry-shrub covered land.

After 600m the shrubs cease and the path continues up open grass slopes to the visible summit.

The summit is marked with several monuments and a time capsule placed by Prime Minister Viktor Yushchenko to be opened in 2015.

Descent

An alternative descent is possible. Head off the summit the way you came up but quickly take a right fork in the path and follow a clear route ENE down to the forest and eventually the parking area.

VATICAN: ST PETER'S DOME

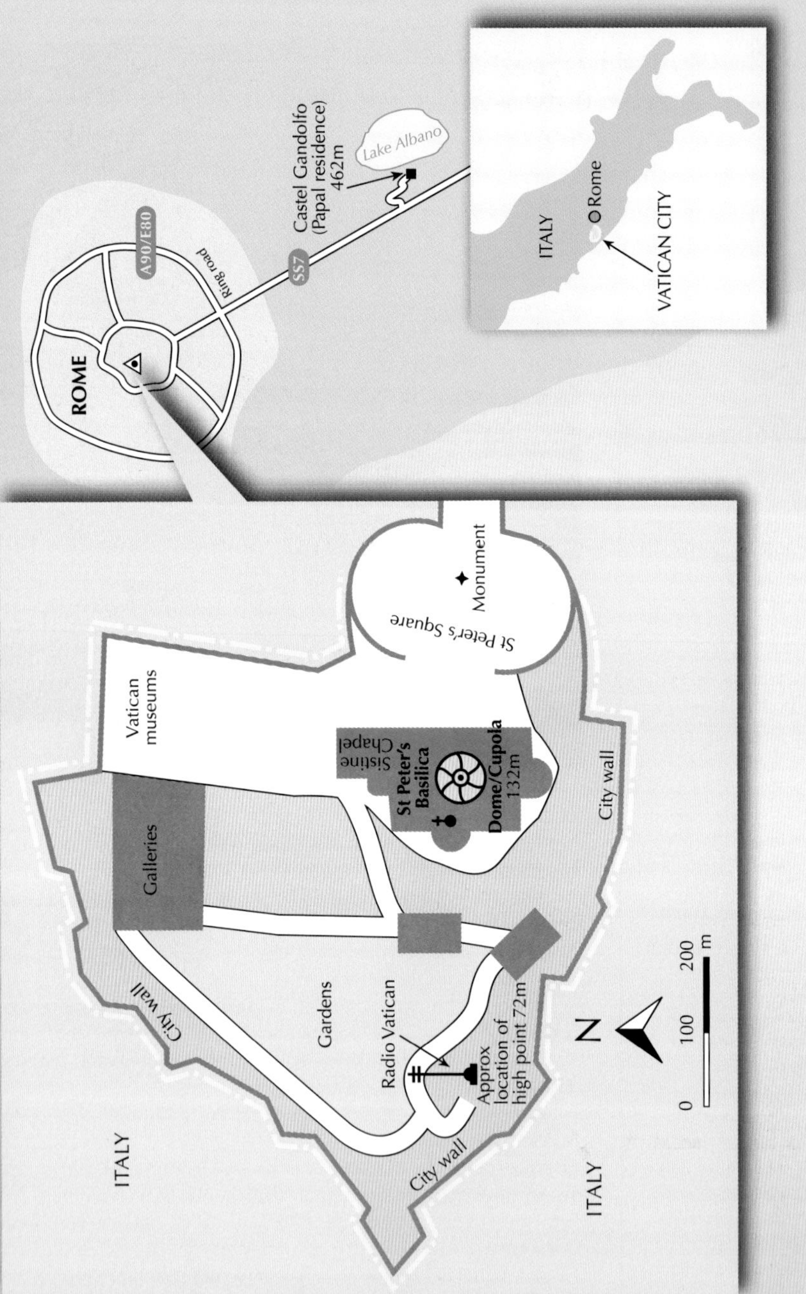

ITALY

Rome

VATICAN CITY

A90/E80

ROME

Ring road

SS7

Castel Gandolfo
(Papal residence)
462m

Lake Albano

Vatican museums

Galleries

City wall

Gardens

Radio Vatican

Approx location of
high point 72m

City wall

Sistine Chapel

St Peter's Basilica

Dome/Cupola
132m

St Peter's Square

Monument

City wall

ITALY

ITALY

N

0   100   200
                    m

47 VATICAN CITY

ST PETER'S DOME 132M

Lorenzo Bernini's tremendous dome from the roof of St Peter's Cathedral

Location	St Peter's Cathedral, centre of the Vatican City in Rome
Start	Vatican City
Map(s)	All maps of Rome mark the Vatican
Equipment	None
Climbing period	Year-round; open 8am to sunset every day
Difficulty	1
Enjoyment	****
Ascent	60m
Time	15mins plus queuing time (can be very long if the Pope has made an appearance)
Water	Free water fountains in St Peter's Square and at first viewing platform of St Peter's Dome
Accommodation	Plentiful in Rome
Getting there	Go to centre of Rome to find walled Vatican City; enter at Bellini's imposing St Peter's Square. At the head is St Peter's Cathedral – burial place of Jesus' right-hand man, world headquarters of Catholic Church and home to the Pope (if you're lucky you might see him).
Nearby high point	Monte Titano (San Marino)

The Vatican: the Eternal City from the Cupola

Although a visit to the very top of the Vatican City does not sound too daunting a prospect, there are two key difficulties. The first is in convincing yourself that somewhere which calls itself a city and is not much bigger than a football pitch is really a country. The second is deciding exactly where its highest point is. We have given the Vatican City the benefit of the doubt and decided it just about counts as a country. Nonetheless, some people might reasonably decide to omit it from their list of European high points. We also believe that the most logical high point of the Vatican is the top of St Peter's Dome (132m). It is the highest point you can reach in the Vatican City and is a dazzling architectural experience, having been designed by Lorenzo Bernini. From the top you can see all of Vatican City and enjoy sensational views of the eternal city beyond. Of course, you may not want to count man-made high points and might settle for an unmarked point just below the radio mast in the Vatican Gardens at 72m (tours of the garden need to be booked in advance). However, as the entire area has been fully landscaped it would be difficult to view even this point as 'natural'. A third debatable highest point is outside Rome at a subsidiary Papal residence called Castel Gandolfo (426m), 32km away from the Vatican proper. We have omitted Gandolfo by the same logic that we would exclude a Dutch embassy high up in Kathmandu: on the grounds that it is a diplomatic residence rather than true territory. Again, use your own judgement.

   Note You will not be allowed into the cathedral if you are wearing revealing clothing such as vests, shorts or the like.

ROUTE

The queue to enter the cathedral starts on the right-hand side of the square. Follow signs directing you to the cathedral entrance through metal detectors. Once past these turn right to join another queue to ascend to the dome, marked 'Cupola'. Although entry to the cathedral is free, access to St Peter's Dome costs €4 if you walk up to the top or €7 to take the lift up to the halfway point. The dome is open until 6pm. There are 559 steps, so be warned – you may have to put in more effort than you thought. Following the wide spiral stone steps upwards, you will first reach a viewing gallery within the cathedral at the point where the dome begins. Continue up much steeper steps to a corridor which slopes so much that it is impossible to stand up straight. A spiral staircase with a rope rail then leads you further up – there are often traffic jams of exhausted pedestrians at this point. You will eventually emerge onto the open-air viewing platform at the top of the cathedral's cupola. From here you will get 360° views of the Vatican City and Rome, including the Colosseum.

Descent

Due to the narrowness of the staircases, there is a one-way system in operation for visitors to the dome. The descending staircase will bring you out onto the cathedral's roof, where there is a rooftop souvenir shop and a drinking fountain. Continue down a wider staircase which takes you into the cathedral itself. There is therefore no point in queuing to go into the cathedral before ascending to the dome.

OTHER ROUTES

OPTION 1

The highest point on the ground in the Vatican City (72m) is in the Vatican Gardens, which are not ordinarily open to the public. You will have to pre-book an appointment for an official tour of the gardens. Then you will have difficulty in finding the unmarked high point as the ground all seems relatively level. From the top of St Peter's Dome you will be able to see the point at the back of the Vatican on the left-hand side. It is not far from the mast for Radio Vatican and the wall separating the city from the rest of Rome.

OPTION 2

Castel Gandolfo is the highest point owned by the Vatican. To get there, follow the road to Appia (ring road exit 23) until about 32km outside Rome and then follow signs. The papal residence at Castel Gandolfo is in the centre of town but is not open to the public. There may be higher points than the residence in the town but the castle building is the only structure owned by the Vatican.

DID YOU KNOW?

Famous native
Pope Joan (John Anglicus): possibly the only female Pope, who held the post for two years in the 850s or the 11th century depending on which source is referred to. The scandal of the female who disguised herself as a man remains a distinct possibility. It is even rumoured she was driven from office after giving birth.

Irrelevant facts
Lucretia Borgia, infamous *femme fatale* and daughter of Pope Alexander VI, was a resident of the Vatican. For more irrelevant 'facts' read *Angels and Demons* by Dan Brown.

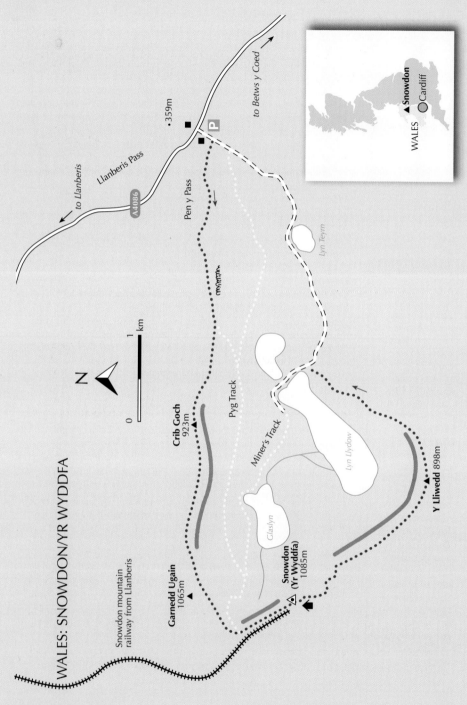

WALES: SNOWDON/YR WYDDFA

Snowdon mountain railway from Llanberis

Carnedd Ugain 1065m

Crib Goch 923m

Snowdon (Yr Wyddfa) 1085m

Y Lliwedd 898m

Pyg Track

Miner's Track

Glaslyn

Lyn Llydaw

Lyn Teyrn

Pen y Pass

Llanberis Pass

to Llanberis

A4086

•359m

P

to Betws y Coed

N

0 1 km

WALES

Snowdon ▲ ○Cardiff

SNOWDON/YR WYDDFA 1085M

Location	Snowdonia National Park, North Wales, 32km S of Bangor
Start	Llanberis Pass
Map(s)	Ordnance Survey Explorer OL17 1:25,000 Snowdon, available in most British bookshops
Equipment	Standard hiking gear. **Note** Route via Crib Goch can be serious winter ascent; rope may be needed.
Climbing period	Year-round. March–November best for Crib Goch and Pyg Track routes. Path from Llanberis (if a little monotonous) always fine to climb.
Difficulty	3
Enjoyment	****
Ascent	700m
Time	2–2½hrs ascent via Crib Goch
Water	Last permanent water at 500m on recommended route. Summit café open March to October.
Accommodation	Pen-y-Pass youth hostel; many campsites in the area
Getting there	From M6 Junction 20 take M56 westbound to A55 signposted Conwy and Holyhead. Take A470 S before Conwy. At Betws-y-Coed take A5 NW signposted Bangor. Just after Capil Curig take A4086 (signposted Llanberis). Pen-y-Pass youth hostel and car park at Llanberis Pass (£4 to park all day at time of writing). Alternatively park in Llanberis and catch bus to Pen-y-Pass.
Public transport	Bangor well served by train; regular buses to Llanberis. From Llanberis gradual, dull path leads up mountain, or catch bus to Pen-y-Pass: every 30mins spring, summer and autumn, every hour in winter (waiting room at Pen-y-Pass; £3.50 return at time of writing).
Nearest high points	Scafell Pike (England), Ben Nevis (Scotland)

It is rather an extraordinary sight to behold after traversing the exposed Crib Goch–Garnedd Ugain ridge to near the summit of Snowdon: a steam train 'choo-chooing' up the mountain. While purists might balk at this bizarre aberration of nature, it is rather a marvellous and rare thing to see which somehow enhances the wonder of the peak.

Snowdon is a fine and dramatic mountain when ascended from the east side. The ascent via the ridge between Crib Goch and Garnedd Ugain (1065m) offers a dramatic knife-edge which, although well within the capabilities of the average hiker, will delight even the most seasoned mountaineer. A new summit café was unveiled in June 2009 and will surely be packed with crowds clamouring for cups of tea and slices of cake as the old one used to be. By descending via the Bwlchysaethau ridge the summit crowds and train station can soon be left behind for the delights of a breathtaking circular route – the Snowdon Horseshoe.

Note A number of pure rock climbs on the east face are possible. For descriptions of these *Rock Climbing in Snowdonia* by Paul Williams is recommended (see Appendix 5, Further Reading).

ROUTE

Start from the N end of the **Pen-y-pass** car park on the S side of the road. Two paths exit the car park. Follow the most northerly path westwards, signposted as the **Pyg Track**.

Sheep in the pass of Llanberis, Snowdon

At a stile on the saddle at 650m you will see a track leaving the main route to your right along the ridge, and a small signpost. Follow the Crib Goch direction (unless the weather is truly horrible, in which case follow the Pyg Track to Snowdon). After another stile you will soon be required to scramble up some rocks. While the dramatic ridge is the most exposed part of the route, these rocks can be the most awkward obstacle, especially in wet weather, and care should be taken here. The odd cairn helps mark the way. Avoid leaving the centre of the ridge.

Snowdon: go via Crib Goch – it's more fun!

DID YOU KNOW?

Famous native
Richard Burton, actor, who married Elizabeth Taylor – twice. He was nominated for an Academy Award six times without winning.

Irrelevant fact
The Welsh town of 'Llanfairpwllg-wyngyllgogerych-wyrndrobwllllan-tysiliogogogoch' is the longest place name in the world. It translates as 'St Mary's Church in the hollow of the white hazel near a rapid whirlpool and the Church of St Tysilio of the red cave'.

Eventually you will reach the summit cairn of **Crib Goch** (923m). In wet weather or strong winds make sure you keep all four points in contact with the ridge, and make your way carefully along the majestic spine. The early section is the most exposed and dangerous.

The ridge is fairly time-consuming, but very pleasing. Eventually two large impassable buttresses will be reached. Descend for 20m vertical height into a narrow gully on the S side of the ridge, before climbing to rejoin the spine. A series of knobbles must then be clambered over. After a brief descent onto a grassy saddle with a fence on its left, a further series of scrambles eventually leads up to the triangulation pillar of **Garnedd Ugain** (1065m).

The route down from Garnedd is obvious and soon joins the Llanberis and Pyg tracks at a large standing stone. Follow the pleasant path parallel with the railway to the summit. The summit has a café open year-round, a train station and an ornate triangulation pillar.

Descent
To complete the Snowdon Horsehoe follow the path southwards from the summit for a short while before descending eastwards to follow the Bwlchysaethau ridge. The path is rough with occasional scrambling but easily followed.

Hike over the crest of **Y Lliwedd** (898m) and descend gradually until the path leads you northwards to meet the old **Miner's Track** at **Llyn Llydaw** (lake). Follow the track northeastwards back to the car park.

OTHER ROUTES
If there are extremely strong winds ascend the mountain by the following standard route.

Follow the **Pyg Track** from **Pen-y-Pass** to the saddle as for the Snowdon Horseshoe.

Ignore the turning to Crib Goch and follow the excellent path as it descends slightly and swings around the S face of **Crib Goch** and **Garnedd Ugain**, emerging on the saddle just below Snowdon's summit. Turn southwards to reach the summit.

Descent
As for the Snowdon Horseshoe or, if short of time, by your ascent route. A split in the **Pyg Track** allows descent to the lakes and the **Miner's Track**.

Above: *The magnificent Mount Teide on Tenerife, Canary Islands*
Below: *Where is Noah's Ark? Mount Ararat after the storm clouds finally shifted*

SOME DISPUTED HIGH POINTS

PORTUGAL – AZORES – MOUNT PICO 2351M

Mount Pico is the highest point on Portuguese territory, and is situated on Pico Island in the Azores, a Portuguese dominion in the mid-Atlantic. To reach the high point requires nothing more than a pleasurable 2½hr hike.

From Santa Luzia drive to Madalena. Take the main road east out of Madalena for roughly 14km to the northwest side of the mountain. Turn right at Cerrado de Sonicas, and follow the road around the west side of the mountain until it curves back on itself. At the end of the road is a parking area at 1200m.

The path to the summit is well marked and signed with little pillars. The ascent is sometimes steep but not difficult, and both the crater and top should be reached in 2–2½hrs. In winter months crampons may be necessary.

SPAIN – CANARY ISLANDS – MOUNT TEIDE 3718M

Mount Teide, a dormant volcano, is the highest point on Spanish territory, situated on the Canary Island of Tenerife off the West African coast. A convenient road and subsequent cable car make the mountain a popular destination for tourists. However, after a suicide pact on the mountain in 1996 and a foiled suicide pact there in 1998, the authorities have introduced a permit system for access to the summit. Permits are free and can be obtained from the park office at 5 Calle Emilio Calzadilla in Santa Cruz. Public buses run once a day up the mountain, although many private coach tours also aid access. A road leads up to the cable car station at 2350m. The cable car can be taken to 3500m and a clear well-signposted track can be followed to the top.

Money can be saved and a proper ascent made if the cable car station is ignored in favour of a short hike. Free maps are available at the information centres at Canada Blanca or El Portillo. Teide can be ascended on a decent path direct from El Portillo or from a subsidiary path which leaves the road 3km east of the lower cable car station. Both routes swing past the north side of Montana Blanca and pass the unmanned Refugio de Altavista on route to the summit of Teide proper. They are not more than 8km in length.

DENMARK – FAEROE ISLANDS – SLAETTARATINDUR 882M

Slaettaratindur is the highest point on the Danish dominion of the Faeroe Islands and thus the highest point of European territory belonging to the Danes. It is situated on the northern end of Eysturoy or East Island between the villages of Eioi and Gjogv. You can get close to the peak by following the road between these villages and stopping when it reaches its highest point at roughly 300m. There are some cairns to get you started on the route. From here the top can be reached by following the mountain's eastern ridge. There is some minor scrambling involved and the occasional bit of descent before the top is reached.

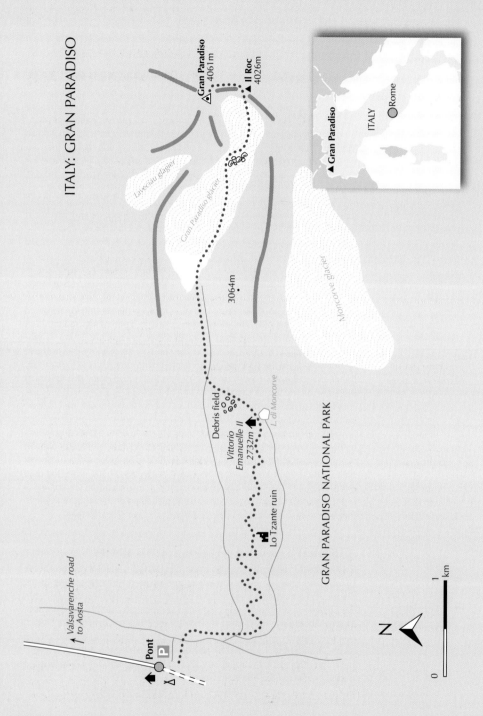

ITALY: GRAN PARADISO

Gran Paradiso
4061m

Il Roc
4026m

Laveciau glacier

Gran Paradiso glacier

Moncorve glacier

3064m

Debris field

Vittorio
Emanuelle II
2732m

L. di Moncorve

Lo Tzante ruin

GRAN PARADISO NATIONAL PARK

Valsavarenche road
to Aosta

Pont
P

ITALY

Rome

▲ Gran Paradiso

N

0   1
km

ITALY – GRAN PARADISO 4061M

See Serious Ascents in the Introduction

Location	Graian Alps. Northwestern Italy 80km N of Turin, 40km S of Aosta in Gran Paradiso National Park near French border.
Start	Pont
Map(s)	101 Gran Paradiso 1:25,000 (Istituto Geografico Centrale); topographical maps available from local shops and campsite shop in Pont
Equipment	Full alpine climbing gear
Climbing period	June–September
Difficulty	4. French alpine rating F+ snow to 35° with UIAA climbing I and II.
Enjoyment	****
Ascent	2100m: Day 1 850m, Day 2 1350m
Time	2 days: 3hrs to Vittorio Emanuelle II refuge, 4–6hrs summit climb
Water	Water trough at Vittorio Emanuelle II refuge, stream to 3000m (just beneath Gran Paradiso glacier)
Accommodation	Campsite at Pont; refuges on mountain
Getting there	From Aosta take SS26 W to St Pierre. Continue past St Pierre to roundabout and take turning signposted Pont. Follow road to head of Seiva/Savara valley to campsite after Pont; park (huge car park). Supplies can be purchased in campsite shop.
Public transport	Bus to Pont from Aosta via Villeneuve
Nearby high point	Dufourspitze (Switzerland)

Gran Paradiso is the highest mountain with its summit entirely in Italy. It is a very pleasant peak in excellent surroundings and has the added attraction of a Madonna statue on top. Its ease and its height make it a very popular destination and an excellent practice peak for newcomers to alpine ascents. A 4000er, Gran Paradiso is an excellent acclimatisation peak.

Note Snow conditions become exceptionally hazardous as the morning wears on and climbers should be back at the Vittorio Emanuelle II refuge no later than 1pm. For this reason the ascent should be split over two days so that an early start can be made on the second.

ROUTE

From the car park at **Pont** go through the wooden gateway and cross the river. Follow the wide path '1' S (upstream). Many hikers walk up to the refuge for lunch and an overnight stay with little intention of climbing the peak. Tourist signs often overestimate ascent times; this is not the case here as the Pont sign claims 2hrs 15mins to the refuge. Expect to be closer to 3hrs.

The route turns left (E) after the best part of 1km. It snakes back and forth up the mountain through shampoo-advert scenery. On route you will pass the **Lo Tzante ruin**. If staying at the **Vittorio Emanuelle II refuge** (2732m), it is recommended that you book in advance due to the mountain's popularity. Ample good bivouacking areas exist below the refuge or, if you continue on the route and head beyond the debris field around the refuge, there is an excellent flat grass area. Expect to be visited by herds of ibex complete with bells. Spend the night here.

Pass between the refuge and the lake and turn left (N) across a tricky debris field marked with cairns. Once across the debris field a distinct path leads you E towards the **Gran Paradiso glacier**. Try to follow the cairns as the route criss-crosses over the long flat rocks and stay on the left (N) side of the stream (maps wrongly mark the route on the S side). Always remain between both ridges.

Once at the steep glacial lip at the head of the valley, stop, rope up and put on your crampons. Wind up the steep glacier whichever way seems simplest. The route will inevitably be well trodden and icy.

Continue up the more gradual snow slope. If clear, you will be afforded views of the summit ridge and the Madonna (appearing like a needle from the ridge). The route will pass through a short rock section and eventually swing you right (S) beneath huge seracs, before switching back N to lead upwards beneath the pillars of **Il Roc** (4026m/4015m).

Ascend to the main summit ridge. You will have to cross a wide bergschund – in fresh snow great care should be taken here. Scramble along the ridge in the direction of the Madonna; the final few metres are incredibly exposed and dramatic. There is no fixed rope here, although two handy belay points should make life simpler. This section can naturally become very congested and patience is essential.

To most climbers – ourselves included – this Madonna, placed early last century by a group of boy scouts, is the spiritual summit. However, with a further 15mins climbing along the ridge you can reach an unmarked point on the snow which is marginally higher. To achieve this, descend and follow a fixed rope beneath the Madonna to the left (W) and climb up to the knife-edge snow ridge past the Madonna summit. This should not be attempted in bad weather as the Madonna summit is fulfilling enough.

Descent
Descend by the same route, making sure to sample the excellent food at the refuge (served 12–3pm).

OTHER ROUTES
An alternative ascent via the Chabod refuge (2750m) up Costa Savolera is possible. This route requires two days and leaves from the campsite at Plan de la Passe 2km N of Pont.

From the refuge the route follows a boulder-strewn ridge on the N side of Laveciau glacier, before traversing the said glacier and joining the normal ascent at Schiena d'Asimo (3600m).

Mont Blanc de Courmayeur from Mont Blanc

ITALY – MONT BLANC DE COURMAYEUR 4748M

Note If on the summit of Mont Blanc and the weather is severe or coming in, do not attempt Courmayeur as the 400m to its summit could be as much as 1hr round trip, too long to be hanging around on the roof of Europe in poor conditions. In some years the snow will form more promisingly than others. Always use your own judgment. Deadmen and ice-screw belays could prove indispensable here. This has a difficulty rating of 5.

ROUTE
Follow directions to the summit of Mont Blanc (Route 14 – France and Italy).

From the small plateau summit descend for 40m vertical height to the W before curving SSE onto a snow ridge to La Torette snow hump (4741m).

Climb over the snow hump and descend into the Col Major. This is a seriously exposed hazardous knife-edged snow bridge. Belay across this. Ascend to the snow-covered peak by staying on the right (SW) side of the ridge next to the rocks, which provide some belay protection. Do not hang about here. Get straight back to Mont Blanc and then down to relative safety as quickly as possible.

ITALY – NORDEND 4609M (MONTE ROSA)
Not to be considered in poor weather.
Follow the route description for Dufourspitze (Route 44 – Switzerland), avoiding the Sattel–Dufourspitze. This has a difficulty rating of 5 UIAA PD+.

From the head of the Monte Rosa glacier turn left (N) up the extremely exposed uber-knife-edge of Nordend, until you reach the rock section.

The fairytale Nordend from the Dufourspitze ridge

Here the climbing is difficult and exposed, similar to the Dufourspitze ridge. Use sling runners, deadmen and ice screws as ice-axe arrest would prove near impossible. The summit is marked by a small stone turret.

Note The Nordend ridge is covered with large cornices that are often overhanging. Where possible you should stay as far to the left as is safe.

TURKEY – MOUNT ARARAT 5137M

Also known as Agri Dagi

See Serious Ascents in the Introduction

Start	Dogubayazit
Difficulty	4
Enjoyment	***
Ascent	3000m
Time	2–3 days
Water	Running water source at camp
Accommodation	Set camping areas on mountain, range of accommodation in Dogubayazit

The national high point of Turkey is 2000km inside Asia and is not a European mountain. Nonetheless, some climbers may wish to ascend it – if only to search for the remains of Noah's Ark. Ararat casts an impressive figure. Rising alone from the Turkish plains, this dormant volcano by the Armenian and Iranian borders can be seen from every direction many miles away.

The standard route up the mountain is not remotely technical, but its altitude makes it a severe enough challenge. The biggest problem with Ararat is the attitude of the Turkish government, guides and local population. Because of its location close to Iran – and in an area which once belonged to Armenia – the Turkish government is very sensitive about the mountain. A government permit and an official guide are required. We found that these two hurdles are inextricably linked. The mountain is also under the *de facto* control of a cartel of summer guides aiming to make money out of wealthy and not-so-wealthy would-be ascenders. Likewise, the permit situation is not one to be reckoned with lightly and ignoring it can lead to expulsion from the country. A military base between the nearby town of Dogubayazit (hotels and cash machines) and the standard route on the mountain means that guides and locals who do not find their services paid for will report you (and indeed are required to do so by law). Do not leave an unattended vehicle in this region. If you like being part of a guided party then Ararat is for you. If you do not, you will find the mountain atmosphere spoilt and the red tape tedious.

The actual ascent is roughly 3000m. This will be reduced slightly if you manage to get a lift to Elikoy – marked as a village but really a collection of huts at 2500m on the south side of the mountain. The standard route is very popular with guided parties, and avoiding these will prove extremely troublesome.

To get there take the main Turkey–Iran road (E80) E out of Dogubayazit. After several kilometres take a signed turning left to Topcatan. Despite a proliferation of satellite dishes, this village looks as if a plague has passed through. From here a very rough road, only suitable for high-clearance vehicles, makes its way up to the small settlement of Elikoy. A variety of tracks then lead to the first camp at 3100m (guided groups will have permanent tents here during the summer months). It should not take more than 2hrs to get from Elikoy to the first camp. A clear and well-walked path leads up from the first camp to the second at 4200m, and while the going is tough it should not take more than 3hrs. The second camp has a running water source on the glacier. From here under 1000m of ascent separates you from the summit. The route winds up steeply through the rocks and a number of cairns mark the way. Once the rocks have been left behind the snow gradient continues fairly steeply before easing to the summit ridge. This is wide and the route to the summit is straightforward, but conditions can be especially vicious and cold here. It would be wise to have plenty of water on the lower stretches of the mountain as 'good' water sources are not passed.

Country	Time Zone	Dialling Code	Population	Capital	Currency	Visa Needed	Language
Albania	GMT+1	355	3.5M	Tirana	Lek	No	Albanian
Andorra	GMT+1	376	67,800	Andorra la Vella	Euro	No	Catalan
Austria	GMT+1	43	8M	Vienna	Euro	No	German
Belarus	GMT+2	375	9.7M	Minsk	Belarusian Ruble	Yes	Belarusian and Russian
Belgium	GMT+1	32	10.4M	Brussels	Euro	No	Dutch/French/German
Bosnia and Herzegovina	GMT+1	387	4.4M	Sarajevo	Convertible Mark	No	Bosnian/Serbian/Croat
Bulgaria	GMT+2	359	7.4M	Sofia	Lev	No	Bulgarian
Croatia	GMT+1	385	4.5M	Zagreb	Kuna	No	Croat
Cyprus	GMT+2	357	788,000	Nicosia	Cyprus Pound	No	Greek
Czech Republic	GMT+1	420	10.2M	Prague	Czech Koruna	No	Czech
Denmark	GMT+1	45	5.4M	Copenhagen	Krone	No	Danish
England	GMT	44	51M	London	Pound Sterling	No	English
Estonia	GMT+2	372	1.4M	Tallinn	Kroon	No	Estonian
Finland	GMT+2	358	5.1M	Helsinki	Euro	No	Finnish and Swedish
France	GMT+1	33	60M	Paris	Euro	No	French
Germany	GMT+1	49	82.4M	Berlin	Euro	No	German
Greece	GMT+2	30	10.7M	Athens	Euro	No	Greek
Hungary	GMT+1	36	10M	Budapest	Forint	No	Magyar
Iceland	GMT	354	299,000	Reykjavik	Icelandic Krona	No	Icelandic
Ireland	GMT	353	4M	Dublin	Euro	No	English and Gaelic
Italy	GMT+1	39	57.3M	Rome	Euro	No	Italian
Kosovo	GMT+1	381	2.1M	Pristina	Euro	No	Gheg/Albanian/Serbian
Latvia	GMT+2	371	2.3M	Riga	Lat	No	Latvian
Liechtenstein	GMT+1	423	34,900	Vaduz	Swiss Franc	No	German
Lithuania	GMT+2	370	3.4M	Vilnius	Lita	No	Lithuanian
Luxembourg	GMT+1	352	454,000	Luxembourg	Euro	No	Luxemburgish French, German

COUNTRY	TIME ZONE	DIALING CODE	POPULATION	CAPITAL	CURRENCY	VISA NEEDED	LANGUAGE
MACEDONIA	GMT+1	389	2M	SKOPJE	DENAR	NO	MACEDONIAN
MALTA	GMT+1	356	404,000	VALLETTA	MALTESE LIRA	NO	MALTESE
MOLDOVA	GMT+2	373	4.4M	CHISINAU	LEI	NO	MOLDAVIAN
MONACO	GMT+1	377	32,100	MONACO	EURO	NO	FRENCH
MONTENEGRO	GMT+1	382	620,000	PODGORICA	EURO	NO	MONTENEGRIN
THE NETHERLANDS	GMT+1	31	16.2M	THE HAGUE	EURO	NO	DUTCH AND FRISIAN
NORTHERN IRELAND	GMT	44	1.7M	BELFAST	POUND STERLING	NO	ENGLISH
NORWAY	GMT+1	47	4.5M	OSLO	KRONE	NO	NORWEGIAN
POLAND	GMT+1	48	38.6M	WARSAW	ZLOTY	NO	POLISH
PORTUGAL	GMT	351	10.4M	LISBON	EURO	NO	PORTUGUESE
ROMANIA	GMT+2	40	22.2M	BUCHAREST	LEI	NO	ROMANIAN
RUSSIA	GMT+2 TO +12	7	144.5M	MOSCOW	RUBLE	YES	RUSSIAN
SAN MARINO	GMT+1	378	28,100	SAN MARINO	EURO	NO	ITALIAN
SCOTLAND	GMT	44	5M	EDINBURGH	POUND STERLING	NO	ENGLISH
SERBIA	GMT+1	381	8M	BELGRADE	DINAR	NO	SERBIAN
SLOVAKIA	GMT+1	421	5.4M	BRATISLAVA	EURO	NO	SLOVAK
SLOVENIA	GMT+1	386	1.9M	LJUBLJANA	EURO	NO	SLOVENIAN
SPAIN	GMT+1	34	42.7M	MADRID	EURO	NO	SPANISH
SWEDEN	GMT+1	46	9M	STOCKHOLM	KRONA	NO	SWEDISH
SWITZERLAND	GMT+1	41	7.5M	BERN	SWISS FRANC	NO	GERMAN, FRENCH, ITALIAN
TURKEY	GMT+2	90	68.1M	ANKARA	LIRA	YES	TURKISH
UKRAINE	GMT+2	380	48M	KIEV	HRYVNIA	NO	UKRAINIAN
VATICAN CITY	GMT+1	39	911		EURO	NO	ITALIAN
WALES	GMT	44	3M	CARDIFF	POUND STERLING	NO	ENGLISH AND WELSH

APPENDIX 2

MOUNTAIN ROUTES GRADED BY DIFFICULTY

Including disputed peaks

GRADE 5

Full alpine kit required. Will involve prolonged exposure to high altitude, steep terrain, narrow ridges, climbing, crevasses, avalanche and rockfall risk. Likely to involve very low temperatures. If severe weather encountered retreat may prove extremely difficult.

- Dufourspitze/Monte Rosa 4634m, Switzerland
- Mont Blanc 4808m, France
- Mont Blanc 4808m, Mont Blanc de Courmayeur 4748m, Nordend 4609m, Italy

GRADE 4

Will certainly require protection of a rope or via ferrata kit. Likely to involve exposure to steep terrain and may involve climbing, crevasses, avalanche risk, rockfall risk, very low temperatures and high altitude in addition to the difficulties of a grade 3 hike.

- Mount Elbrus 5642m, Russia
- Gerlachovsky stit 2654m, Slovakia
- Grossglockner 3798m, Austria
- Hvannadalshnukur 2111m, Iceland
- Kebnekaise 2111m, Sweden
- Triglav 2864m, Slovenia
- Zugspitze 2962m, Germany

GRADE 3

A hike complicated by difficulties in any of the following areas: route-finding, time, altitude, ascent, scrambling.

- Djeravica 2656m, Kosovo
- Galdhoppigen 2469m, Norway
- Grauspitz 2599m, Liechtenstein
- Halti 1328m, Finland
- Maglic 2387m, Bosnia and Herzegovina
- Maja Kolata 2534m, Bobotov Kuk 2523m, Montenegro
- Moldoveanu 2544m, Romania
- Mulhacén 3478m, Spain

- Mount Olympus 2917m, Greece
- Pic de Coma Pedrosa 2942m, Andorra
- Rysy 2500/2503m, Poland
- Mount Snowdon 1064m, Wales

GRADE 2

A standard hike.

- Ben Nevis 1343m, Scotland/United Kingdom of Great Britain and Northern Ireland
- Carrauntuohil 1041m, Ireland
- Dinara 1831m, Croatia
- Goverla 2061m, Ukraine
- Midzor 2169m, Serbia
- Mount Balanesti 430m, Moldova
- Mount Korab 2764m, Macedonia and Albania
- Musala 2925m, Bulgaria
- Scafell Pike 978m, England
- Slieve Donard 852m, Northern Ireland
- Snezka 1602m, Czech Republic

GRADE 1

Easy tourist amble.

- Buurgplatz 559m/Kneiff 560m, Luxembourg
- Chemin des Revoires 162m, Monaco
- Dzarzhynskaya 345m, Belarus
- Gaizinkalns 312m, Latvia
- Aukstojas/Juozapine Kalnas 294m, Lithuania
- Kékes 1014m, Hungary
- La Torre 1993m, Portugal
- Mahya Dagi 1030m, Turkey (European Turkey/Thrace)
- Møllehøj 170m/Yding Skovhoj 170m, Denmark
- Mount Olympus 1951m, Cyprus
- Signal de Botrange 694m, Belgium
- Suur Munamagi 318m, Estonia
- St Peter's Dome 132m/Vatican Hill 73m, Vatican City
- Ta' Dmejrek/Dingli Cliffs 253m, Malta
- Monte Titano 739m, San Marino
- Vaalserberg 321m, The Netherlands

APPENDIX 3

TABLE OF MOUNTAIN HEIGHTS

Mount Elbrus
Russia 5642m

Mont Blanc/Monte Bianco
France and Italy 4808m

Dufourspitze/Monte Rosa
Switzerland 4634m

Grossglockner
Austria 3798m

Mulhacén
Spain 3478m

Zugspitze
Germany 2962m

Pic de Coma Pedrosa
Andorra 2942m

Musala
Bulgaria 2925m

Mount Olympus
Greece 2917m

Triglav
Slovenia 2864m

Mount Korab
Macedonia and Albania 2764m

Djeravica
Kosovo 2656m

Gerlachovsky stit
Slovakia 2654m

Grauspitz
Liechtenstein 2599m

Moldoveanu
Romania 2544m

Maja Kolata
Montenegro 2534m

Rysy
Poland 2500m

Galdhopiggen
Norway 2469m

Maglic
Bosnia and Herzegovina 2387m

Midzor
Serbia 2169m

Hvannadalshnukur
Iceland 2111m

Kebnekaise
Sweden 2111m

Goverla
Ukraine 2061m

La Torre
Portugal 1993m

Mount Olympus
Cyprus 1951m

Dinara
Croatia 1831m

Snezka
Czech Republic 1602m

Ben Nevis
Scotland 1343m

Halti
Finland 1328m

Snowdon
Wales 1085m

Carrauntuohil
Ireland 1041m

Mahya Dagi
Turkey 1030m

Kékes
Hungary 1014m

Scafell Pike
England 978m

Slieve Donard
Northern Ireland 852m

Monte Titano
San Marino 739m

Signal de Botrange
Belgium 694m

Buurgplatz
Luxembourg 559m

Swiss skyline at dawn from Weissmies (4023m),
with Monte Rosa/Dufourspitze (4634m) far left and Dom (4545m) far right

Mount Balanesti			**Aukstojas/Juozapine Kalnas**	
Moldova	430m		Lithuania	294m
Dyarzhynskaya			**Ta' Dmejrek/Dingli Cliffs**	
Belarus	345m		Malta	253m
Vaalserberg			**Møllehøj**	
The Netherlands	321m		Denmark	170m
Suur Munamagi			**Chemin des Revoires**	
Estonia	318m		Monaco	162m
Gaizinkalns			**St Peter's Dome**	
Latvia	312m		Vatican City	132m

APPENDIX 4

Abseil Descending on a rope safely, usually by using an abseil device such as a belay plate.

Acclimatisation Getting the body accustomed to functioning at high altitude in rarefied air.

Arête A narrow ridge of snow, ice or rock.

Belay The means by which a climber is protected from falling by the rope, anchor and belayer.

Bergschrund A big crevasse situated at the top of a glacier.

Bivouac Spending the night in a rudimentary shelter on a mountain when a route is too long to complete in one day.

Buttress A rocky protrusion which stands out from the main mass of the mountain.

Cams/camming devices Anchors which expand and jam to fit in cracks, often referred to as 'friends'.

Cirque/corrie A curved bowl area often found in the upper reaches of mountains.

Col A saddle or pass in a mountain ridge

Cornice A snowy overhang often formed along the edge of a ridge at the top of a gully.

Couloir A large gully.

Crampons Metal spikes attached to the soles of boots for walking on snow and ice.

Crevasse A crack, often very deep, in the surface of a glacier.

Deadman A metal plate with a wire cable used for an anchor in snow.

Face A wall of rock or side of a mountain.

Fixed rope A rope which is left *in situ* on the mountain. Climbers can clip onto this for protection.

Glacier A river of ice usually found in a mountain valley.

Gully A break or large fissure in a face.

Harness Reinforced item of equipment worn by climbers to attach the rope to and comfortably hold a fall.

Helmet Headgear worn by climbers to protect them from falling rocks and ice.

Ice axe Hand-held tool for climbing and balance on snow and ice.

Ice screw A metal screw which can be placed as an anchor in ice in order to hold a fall.

Karabiner Metal loop with a locking mechanism which allows the climber to fasten onto a rope or anchor.

Karst Eroded limestone or dolomite rock formation.

Moraine Debris carried by ice found deposited in wall-like lengths at the bottom or edges of a glacier.

Moving together The process where two climbers are roped together and move at the same time.

Névé Permanent or compressed snow.

Nut Chocks or wedges of metal designed to be placed in cracks as anchors.

Overhang A slope so steep as to be more than vertical.

Pegs/pitons Metal spikes often found *in situ* on alpine and via ferrata routes to anchor a fixed rope or chain.

Prusik A sliding friction knot that can be used to ascend a rope.

Ridge The thin crest of a mountain.

Rimaye see Bergschrund.

Scramble Climbing at an easy standard needing use of hands but not usually requiring the use of a rope.

Scree Loose rocks usually covering a slope beneath a cliff.

Serac A particularly unstable massive block or wall of ice and snow which has broken away from its surrounding snow or glacier.

Slings Band of rope or specially sewn tape.

Snow bridge A bridge of snow going across a crevasse or narrow area of a ridge.

Snow field An expanse of permanent snow.

Talus see Scree.

Traverse To travel laterally rather than vertically.

UIAA Union Internationale des Associations d'Alpinisme; the governing body of mountaineering.

Via ferrata Paths following iron or steel chains and ladders up cliffs for protection.

White-out Lack of visibility due to snow.

Wires A metal nut on a wire used to protect a climber.

MOUNTAIN SAFETY

The Handbook of Climbing (BMC) Alan Fyffe and Iain Peter (Pelham Books, 1997)

The Hillwalker's Guide to Mountaineering Terry Adby and Stuart Johnston (Cicerone, 2007)

Map and Compass: The Art of Navigation Pete Hawkins (Cicerone, 2008)

EUROPEAN HIGH POINTS

A Coast to Coast Walk Alfred J Wainwright (Frances Lincoln, 2007)

A Pictorial Guide to the Lakeland Fells, Book 4: The Southern Fells Alfred J Wainwright (Michael Joseph, 1992)

Ben Nevis Simon Richardson (Scottish Mountaineering Club, 2002)

Classic Climbs in the Caucasus Friedrich Bender (Diadem Books, 1991)

Eastern Alps: The Classic Routes on the Highest Peaks Dieter Siebert (Diadem Books, 1992)

Eastern Europe 1939–2000 Mark Pittaway (Hodder Arnold, 2004)

Easy Ascents in the Mont Blanc Range Francois Burnier and Dominique Potard (Vamos, 2002)

Lake District Rock: Selected Rock Climbs in the Lake District (Fell and Rock Climbing Club, 2003)

Lake District Winter Climbs Brian Davison (Fell and Rock Climbing Club and Cicerone, 2006)

Mont Blanc Massif Volume 1 Lindsey Griffin (Alpine Club, 1996)

Mont Blanc Massif Volume 2 Lindsey Griffin (Alpine Club, 1991)

Rock Climbing in Snowdonia Paul Williams (Constable, 2004)

Scafell, Wasdale and Eskdale A. Phizacklea (Fell and Rock Climbing Club, 1996)

The Alpine 4000m Peaks Richard Goedeke (Baton Wicks, 2006)

The Collapse of Yugoslavia 1991–1999 Alastair Finlan (Osprey, 2004)

The High Tatras Colin Saunders and Renata Narozna (Cicerone, 2006)

The Mountains of Montenegro – A Mountaineering Guide Daniel Vincek, Ratko Popovic and Mijo Kovacevic (Podgorica Books, 2004)

Walking in Norway Connie Roos (Cicerone, 2006)

Winter Climbing: Ben Nevis and Glencoe Alan Kimber (Cicerone, 2003)

NATURAL HISTORY

Birds of Britain and Europe Jurgen Nicolai, Singer, and K Wothe (Harper Collins, 1994)

Wild Animals of Britain and Europe Helga Hoffman (Harper Collins, 1995)

Wild Flowers of Britain and Europe Bob Gibbons and Peter Brough (Bounty Books, 1998)

NOTE FROM AUTHORS

Anyone successfully ascending all of Europe's high points should email europeshighpoints@hotmail.co.uk.

Andorra – Pic de Coma Pedrosa
The Mountains of Andorra,
Walks and Climbs in the Pyrenees

Austria – Grossglockner *
Walking in Austria

Croatia
Walking in Croatia

England – Scafell Pike
Fellranger: The Mid-Western Fells,
Ridges of England, Wales and Ireland,
Great Mountain Days in the Lake District

France and Italy – Mont Blanc/Monte Bianco
Alpine Ski Mountaineering
Vol 1 Western Alps

Germany – Zugspitze *
Walking in the Bavarian Alps,
Klettersteig – Scrambles in the Northern
Limestone Alps

Greece – Mount Olympus
The Mountains of Greece

Hungary – Kékes
Walking in Hungary

Ireland – Carrauntoohil
Ridges of England, Wales and Ireland,
The Mountains of Ireland

Malta – Ta' Dmejrek/Dingli Cliffs
Walking in Malta

Montenegro – Maja Kolata
The Mountains of Montenegro

Northern Ireland – Slieve Donard
The Mountains of Ireland

Norway – Galdhopiggen
Walking in Norway

Poland – Rysy
The High Tatras

Romania – Moldoveanu
The Mountains of Romania

Scotland – Ben Nevis
Backpacker's Britain: Central
and Southern Scottish Highlands,
Ben Nevis and Glen Coe, Scotland's
Mountain Ridges, The Munros Vol 1 –
Southern, Central and Western Highlands,
Winter Climbs Ben Nevis and Glencoe,
Scrambles in Lochaber

Slovakia – Gerlachovsky stit
The High Tatras

Slovenia – Triglav
Trekking in Slovenia,
The Julian Alps of Slovenia

Spain – Mulhacén
Walking in the Sierra Nevada

Wales – Snowdon/Yr Wyddfa
The Mountains of England and Wales:
Vol 1 Wales, Ridges of England, Wales
and Ireland, Hillwalking in Wales Vol 2,
Backpacker's Britain: Wales,
Ridges of Snowdonia, Hillwalking in
Snowdonia, Scrambles in Snowdonia,
Welsh Winter Climbs

* Covers walking in the region but not the summit ascent.

LISTING OF CICERONE GUIDES

For full and up-to-date information
on our ever-expanding list of guides,
please visit our website:
www.cicerone.co.uk.

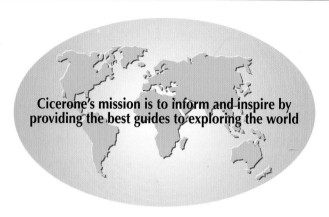

Cicerone's mission is to inform and inspire by
providing the best guides to exploring the world

Since its foundation 40 years ago, Cicerone has specialised in
publishing guidebooks and has built a reputation for quality and
reliability. It now publishes nearly 300 guides to the major destinations for outdoor enthusiasts, including Europe, UK and the rest of
the world.

Written by leading and committed specialists, Cicerone guides are
recognised as the most authoritative. They are full of information,
maps and illustrations so that the user can plan and complete a
successful and safe trip or expedition – be it a long face climb, a
walk over Lakeland fells, an alpine cycling tour, a Himalayan trek
or a ramble in the countryside.

With a thorough introduction to assist planning, clear diagrams,
maps and colour photographs to illustrate the terrain and route,
and accurate and detailed text, Cicerone guides are designed for
ease of use and access to the information.

If the facts on the ground change, or there is any aspect of a guide
that you think we can improve, we are always delighted to hear
from you.

Cicerone Press
2 Police Square Milnthorpe Cumbria LA7 7PY
Tel: 015395 62069 Fax: 015395 63417
info@cicerone.co.uk www.cicerone.co.uk

CICERONE